THE BLUEBOOK UNCOVERED

A PRACTICAL GUIDE TO MASTERING LEGAL CITATION

(Twentieth Edition of The Bluebook)

■ ■ ■

by

Dionne E. Anthon
Florida International University College of Law

AMERICAN CASEBOOK SERIES®

WEST
ACADEMIC
PUBLISHING

American Casebook Series is a trademark registered in the U.S. Patent and Trademark Office.

© 2015 LEG, Inc. d/b/a West Academic
    444 Cedar Street, Suite 700
    St. Paul, MN 55101
    1-877-888-1330

West, West Academic Publishing, and West Academic are trademarks of West Publishing Corporation, used under license.

Printed in the United States of America

ISBN: 978-1-63459-537-7

For

Mom, Dad, Dean, Aaron, Maria, Vivian, Isabella, & Ava

Thank you for your constant
love, inspiration, and guidance.

About the Author

Dionne E. Anthon joined the Legal Skills and Values Program at Florida International University College of Law in 2015, where she teaches legal research and writing to first-year law students. Prior to joining FIU Law, she was an Associate Professor of Legal Methods at Widener University Commonwealth Law School and taught legal research and writing there for seven years. Professor Anthon has presented on citation, teaching, assessment, and technology topics at numerous regional and national conferences.

Professor Anthon graduated from the University of Pennsylvania Law School, where she was an Arthur Littleton and H. Clayton Louderback Legal Writing Instructor and a Production Editor of the Journal of Constitutional Law. After graduating from law school, Professor Anthon clerked for United States District Judge Christopher C. Conner of the Middle District of Pennsylvania. She earned a Master of Business Administration degree from the McDonough School of Business at Georgetown University and a Bachelor of Science in Economics degree from the Wharton School of Business at the University of Pennsylvania. Before law school, Professor Anthon worked for six years in information technology consulting, primarily developing training materials and teaching consultants and clients the programming language for a business management software package.

Summary of Contents

Contents

Preface

This book is designed to help first-year law students master the fundamental Bluebook citation rules that will be needed in legal research and writing courses (LRW) and in legal practice. It can also act as a Bluebook refresher for other law students, clerks, attorneys, judges, and paralegals.

This book presents the detailed citation rules that are scattered throughout numerous sections of the Bluebook in an organized and easily accessible manner. In addition, this book includes exercises to aid in understanding and mastering the rules.

Part I of this book provides an introduction to legal citations. Part II covers basic citations to the most commonly cited primary authority (cases, statutes, constitutions, rules, administrative regulations, rules, court and litigation documents) and secondary authority (books and periodicals). Part III addresses additional information that may be included on basic citations — case history, parallel citations, parenthetical information, and information regarding nonprint sources. Part IV presents Bluebook topics that are not specific to just one citation or one type of authority — quotations, string citations, introductory signals, pinpoint information, and capitalization.

Part V of this book contains a comprehensive exercise that incorporates concepts from many of the chapters in the previous parts. The comprehensive exercise puts citations in the context of a legal document, requiring the type of review and editing necessary in LRW courses and in practice.

Students and practitioners are often frustrated when trying to apply Bluebook rules in their writing. My goal with this book is to provide an easy to understand guide to the rules that alleviates those frustrations and allows students and practitioners to spend more time on other aspects of their writing and on research and analysis.

Dionne E. Anthon
July 2015

Acknowledgments

I need to thank many people who contributed to this book. Professors Anna Hemingway and Amanda Smith encouraged me to transform my course materials into this book. They, along with Professor Jennifer Lear, provided invaluable feedback on early drafts.

Other legal research and writing professors—those at Widener University Commonwealth Law School and Florida International University College of Law—also provided feedback. In addition, I received student perspectives and feedback from the first-year students at Widener Law in 2013-2014 and 2014-2015 and at FIU Law in 2014-2015.

I also thank Mac Soto, Carol Logue, Louis Higgins, and Christopher Hart at West Academic for their help and guidance in the publishing process. In addition, I would like to thank the countless others there who worked behind the scenes to help publish this book.

Last, but certainly not least, I must thank Alexander Sharpe. Without his meticulous review, edits, and suggestions involving all drafts and the release of a new edition of The Bluebook, this book and corresponding Teacher's Manual would not be possible. Thank you, Alex.

The Bluebook Uncovered

Part I

Introduction

Chapter 1
Legal Citations

A. When & Why You Must Cite

In legal writing, like all writing, you must provide citations for your authorities (or sources) of information, regardless of whether you directly quote or paraphrase an authority, so that you do not plagiarize someone else's work or ideas. According to the Legal Writing Institute, you should provide citations in the following five scenarios:

1. Acknowledge direct use of someone else's words.

2. Acknowledge any paraphrase of someone else's words.

3. Acknowledge direct use of someone else's idea.

4. Acknowledge a source when your own analysis or conclusion builds on that source.

5. Acknowledge a source when your idea about a legal opinion came from a source other than the opinion itself.[1]

Notice that only the first rule involves direct quotations. Therefore, you still need to cite in many other instances to avoid plagiarism, even if you are not directly quoting from an authority.

In legal writing, not only does citing help you avoid plagiarism, but it also adds credibility to your analysis of the legal issues you are addressing. To be able to trust your analysis, your reader (e.g., a supervising

---

[1] Legal Writing Inst., *Law School Plagiarism v. Proper Attribution* 4 (2003), http://www.lwionline.org/publications/plagiarism/policy.pdf. In a CALI Lesson, Rebecca Trammell and Ashley Chase add a sixth rule: "Common knowledge does not require a citation. However, in legal writing, all statements of the law should be supported by correctly cited authority, preferably primary legal authority or, if none is available, persuasive secondary legal authority." Rebecca S. Trammell & Ashley Krenelka Chase, *Plagiarism – Keeping Out of Trouble*, http://www.cali.org/lesson/1119 (last visited Nov. 6, 2014) (note: you must have an active CALI account to access this lesson).

attorney or judge) will want to know that it is based on valid law. Your citations provide that assurance to the reader.

B. The Bluebook

There are two main sources of rules for citing to legal authority: (1) <u>The Bluebook: A Uniform System of Citation</u> (20th ed. 2015) and (2) <u>ALWD Citation Manual: A Professional System of Citation</u> (5th ed. 2014).

TAKE NOTE

This book covers <u>The Bluebook</u> (20th edition). Specifically, it covers the first version of the 20th edition of <u>The Bluebook</u>, which was released in May 2015. At times, the editors of <u>The Bluebook</u> make slight changes and updates before publishing a new edition. You can view such changes and updates on <u>The Bluebook</u>'s website (http://www.legalbluebook.com).

TIP

To master the fundamental Bluebook citation rules, your goal should not be to memorize all of the rules. Your goal should be to become familiar with the different types of citations and rules so that you can easily look up and apply the applicable rules.

The Bluebook consists of three main parts (in this order):

1. The Bluepages
2. The Rules (i.e., the "Whitepages")
3. The Tables

Look through your Bluebook as you read the descriptions below of these three main parts.

The Bluepages: The Bluepages contain the citation rules and tables applicable to the types of documents that one would write in practice (e.g., a brief, a memo, or an opinion), which are the subject of this book. The Bluebook sometimes refers to these types of documents as "non-academic legal documents" (see the Bluepages Introduction). Do not be confused by this term. It is referring to the types of documents that you will write in your legal research and writing (LRW) courses and in practice, so you will follow the Bluepages rules.

TAKE NOTE

In the Bluebook, "academic legal documents" refers to the scholarly writing you find in law reviews and journals. In law school, you will write and edit such documents if you join one of your school's journals or law review. You will also typically write such a document to fulfill your school's writing requirement, which is often accomplished in a seminar course. When writing such academic legal documents, you will use only the rules in the Whitepages, not the Bluepages.

Even when writing non-academic legal documents that follow the Bluepages rules, you will still need to consult the Whitepages rules because those rules are the basis for the Bluepages rules, and they provide more details. In fact, a Bluepages rule will often refer you to related Whitepages rule(s).

NAVIGATE

The Appendix covers the main ways that citations in academic legal documents (i.e., scholarly writing) differ from citations in non-academic legal documents. If you are participating in a competition to join the law review or a journal at your law school or you are writing a seminar paper, this Appendix will help you understand how the citations differ from those you used in your LRW courses.

Bluepages Rules B1 through B9 are general rules, and Bluepages Rules B10 through B21 are rules that are specific to particular types of authority. For example, Bluepages Rule B5 involves quotations, and Bluepages Rule B10 involves cases.

The Whitepages: The Whitepages contain 21 rules, the topics of which mirror those in the Bluepages. For example, both Bluepages Rule B10 and Whitepages Rule 10 involve (or pertain to) citations of cases. The Whitepages rules contain more details than the Bluepages rules.

TIP

Although the Whitepages rules contain more details, you should generally begin your search for answers in the Bluepages because they contain the most common rules needed for the types of documents that you will write in your LRW course and in practice, and they refer you to additional details in the Whitepages.

The Tables: Supplementing the citation rules in the Bluepages and Whitepages are tables that provide additional information for the rules. For example, Table T6 contains a list of words that you should abbreviate in case names in citations. The rules will refer you to the applicable table(s). Most tables come after the Whitepages, but the Bluepages have two tables at the end of the Bluepages.

TAKE NOTE

This book refers to a rule in the Bluepages as "BP Rule Bx" and a rule in the Whitepages as "Rule x" (where "x" is the rule number). Likewise, this book refers to a table in the Bluepages as "BP Table BTx" and a table after the Whitepages as "Table Tx" (where "x" is the table number).

To help you find the rules relevant to a particular authority you wish to cite, you can use the <u>Contents</u> pages that appear before the Bluepages or the <u>Index</u> that appears after the tables. In addition, you can use the <u>Quick Reference Guide</u> on the inside *back* cover of the Bluebook to view some common citation forms and their applicable rules (note: the inside *front* cover contains examples for citations in law reviews and journals).

TIP

When you consult the rules in the Whitepages and the tables after the Whitepages, be aware that the examples conform to the standards for law reviews and journals, not the "non-academic legal documents" that you will be writing. You always need to check the Bluepages rules to determine what, if any, changes are appropriate for your writing.

For example, a case name in the Whitepages and tables may not be underlined or italicized, but, according to BP Rule B2, the Bluepages require a case name to be underlined or italicized.

WARNING

When citing to authority, do not rely on the citations that you see in other sources (e.g., citations that you see in cases). Likewise, do not rely on any citation help features of electronic databases such as Lexis Advance, WestlawNext, and Bloomberg Law.

Although such citations may appear to be, or are supposed to be, in Bluebook format, often they are not. You will have to use your Bluebook to ensure proper citation format.

C. Jurisdiction- or Court-Specific Citation Rules

Some jurisdictions or courts have their own specific citation rules that take precedence over Bluebook rules. These citation rules may be found in a jurisdiction's court rules, style guide, or other jurisdiction- or court-specific documents. When preparing a legal document in practice, be sure to follow any of these specific citation rules.

TAKE NOTE

Your professor may require you to follow any jurisdiction- or court-specific citation rules. Generally, such rules do not differ significantly from Bluebook rules, and often they do not encompass everything covered in Bluebook rules. Therefore, you will normally also need to learn Bluebook rules.

You can use BP Table BT2 to determine whether a jurisdiction or court has any specific citation rules or style guides. For example, the Florida state court listing in this table has the following entry:

▶ Fla. R. App. P. 9.800 (citation of various types of legal authority)

Given this entry, you would need to review Rule 9.800 of the Florida Rules of Appellate Procedure, which gives some specific citation rules and indicates that citations not covered by this rule should follow Bluebook rules or, if no appropriate Bluebook rule exists, the Florida Style Manual.

BP Table BT2 comprises two subparts—BT2.1 involves federal courts and BT2.2 involves state courts.

TAKE NOTE

This book does not cover any jurisdiction- or court-specific citation rules; it covers only Bluebook rules.

D. Where to Put Citations

For the types of documents that you will write in your LRW course (i.e., non-academic legal documents), your citations should appear directly within the main text of your document, not in footnotes as Rule 1.1 requires for academic legal documents, unless jurisdiction- or court-specific citation rules permit or require citations to be in footnotes (see BP Rule B1.1).

Because you will generally put your citations directly with your text, you should understand three phrases you will encounter throughout the Bluebook:

- <u>Textual sentence</u> – This phrase refers to *your* sentence. In other words, it is essentially any of your writing that is not a citation.

- <u>Citation sentence</u> – This phrase refers to a citation that is contained in a separate sentence after a textual sentence (i.e., your textual sentence should end with a period and then your citation sentence should begin with a capital letter and end with a period). A citation sentence should be used to cite to a particular authority or authorities that relate to the entire preceding textual sentence. To illustrate, imagine that you write a sentence (a textual sentence) that gives part of a rule, and you got that part from one case. After your sentence, you would need to cite to that case, and you would do so in a citation sentence after your textual sentence.

- <u>Citation clause</u> – This phrase refers to a citation that is contained *within* your textual sentence. Unlike a citation sentence, it does not automatically begin with a capital letter (unless the first letter would otherwise be capitalized according to the rules), nor does it automatically end with a period (unless the citation clause is at the end of the textual sentence). Citation clauses should be used to cite to a particular authority or authorities that relate to only part of a textual sentence, and they should immediately follow that part of the sentence and be set off by commas (unless the citation clause is at the end of the textual sentence, in which case a period should be used at the end of the clause to represent the end of the textual sentence).

WARNING

You should use citation sentences, not clauses, whenever possible because citation clauses break up the flow of your textual sentence and make reading it more difficult.

TAKE NOTE

This book uses one space between sentences—textual and citation sentences. If you use two spaces between sentences, you do so between all sentences, whether textual or citation sentences.

BP Rule B1.1 discusses the distinction between citation sentences and clauses. The following example illustrates all three phrases:

> Under Pennsylvania's right-of-publicity statute, a person's "name or likeness" cannot be "used for any commercial or advertising purposes" without that person's written consent if that person's "name or likeness has commercial value." 42 Pa. Cons. Stat. § 8316 (2007). A well-known chef's name may have commercial value, <u>Lewis v. Marriott Int'l, Inc.</u>, 527 F. Supp. 2d 422, 428 (E.D. Pa. 2007), but a well-known intellectual property attorney could not prove that his name did, <u>Tillery v. Leonard & Sciolla, LLP</u>, 437 F. Supp. 2d 312, 318, 329 (E.D. Pa. 2006).

In this example, the first sentence (which starts with "Under Pennsylvania's right-of publicity statute") is a *textual* sentence. Notice that the sentence ends with a period. Immediately following this textual sentence is a citation to section 8316 of title 42 of the Pennsylvania Consolidated Statutes. It is a citation *sentence,* and the sentence ends with a period (after the publisher and year parenthetical). Following this citation sentence is another textual sentence with two citation *clauses* within that sentence—one to the <u>Lewis</u> case and one to the <u>Tillery</u> case. Notice that commas set off these citation clauses; the <u>Tillery</u> citation ends with a period instead of a comma because that citation is at the end of the entire sentence.

TAKE NOTE

Although the example above uses real legal authority, many examples and exercises in the book use fictional authority.

In addition, throughout this book, examples of citations, quotations, and text are in a monospaced font to enable you to determine more easily where there are, and are not, spaces. For example:

```
Burck v. Mars, Inc., 571 F. Supp. 2d 446,
453-54 (S.D.N.Y. 2008); see also Lombardo v.
Doyle, Dane & Bernbach, Inc., 396 N.Y.S.2d
661, 665 (App. Div. 1977).
```

E. Underlining or Italics

In the Bluepages rules, you will see examples with underlining. Similar examples in the Whitepages use italics. Although the Whitepages require italics in law reviews and journals, BP Rule B2 allows either italics or underlining in non-academic legal documents. Such documents, however, should consistently use one or the other (i.e., one such document should not use both italics and underlining).

TAKE NOTE

Although many readers prefer italics to underlining, this book uses underlining so that you can more easily see when text needs to be underlined or italicized. If your professor, supervisor, or any jurisdiction- or court-specific rules require italics, you should use italics in all instances where underlining is used in this book.

F. Common Rules & Tables

The following table provides the common Bluebook rules and tables for legal citations in general:

Rule or Table	Description
BP Rule B1.1	Citation Sentences & Clauses
BP Rule B2	Typeface Conventions (i.e., underlining & italics)
BP Table BT2	Jurisdiction- or Court-Specific Citation Rules & Style Guides

Part II

Basic Citation Information

Chapter 2
Cases: Full Citation

A. Introduction

Unless a short citation to a case is permitted (see Chapter 3), you should use a full citation. A citation is "full" when you include all of the information that the reader would want to know about the case. The basic information that is included in a full case citation is the following:

- who the parties to the case are (i.e., the case name);
- where the case can be found (i.e., the case location); and
- what the "weight," or precedential value, of the case is (i.e., the court and date).

A full case citation may also include other parenthetical information, if any, and the history of the case, if any. The descriptions, examples, and exercise in this chapter assume that no such additional information is required in the case citation.

NAVIGATE

Chapter 8 covers case history, and Chapter 10 covers parenthetical information.

Here is an example full case citation sentence (note: the period at the end of the citation represents the end of the citation sentence and is not otherwise part of the citation):

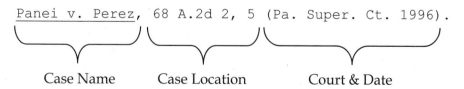

Panei v. Perez, 68 A.2d 2, 5 (Pa. Super. Ct. 1996).

Case Name   Case Location   Court & Date

TIP

When you are drafting a document, you should not stop to ensure perfect Bluebook format; otherwise, you will likely lose your writing momentum. Instead, use some shorthand notations that will enable you to go back and "Bluebook" your citations at the end. Be sure to leave enough time at the end for this task and, in your shorthand notations, include the appropriate pinpoint information so that you do not have to take time to hunt for it at the end. For example, for a case, your shorthand notation should include at least one of the party's names and the pinpoint page(s) for the specific information you are citing.

B. Case Name

The "case name" portion of a full citation includes the names of the parties in the case. Most case names that you will find in the caption of an opinion, however, contain more information than is necessary for a full citation. For example, if a party is an individual, you should use only the surname of the individual (see BP Rule B10.1.1(ii)). Likewise, you should use only the first party's name on each side of the "v." (see BP Rule B10.1.1(i)).

For example, if a case caption indicates Anna Hemingway, Ann Fruth, and David Raeker-Jordan, Plaintiffs, v. Amanda Smith and Jennifer Lear, Defendants, the case name would be the following:

    Hemingway v. Smith

TAKE NOTE

Always underline the entire case name (see BP Rule B2). Do not, however, underline the comma that belongs after the case name and before the case location in a citation.

You must also underline case names in textual sentences, even if they are used without an immediate citation. Do not, however, underline a party name when referring to the actual party, not the case. For example:

```
In Lear, the court held that the employer
wrongfully terminated Lear. [Citation
omitted.]
```

Recall that BP Rule B2 allows underlining or italics, but this book uses underlining so that you can more easily see when text needs to be underlined or italicized.

Rule 10.2 contains detailed rules for case names. It comprises two subsections. The first one (Rule 10.2.1) covers case names in textual sentences and citations. The second one (Rule 10.2.2) includes additional rules for case names in citations only. In other words, for case names in citations, you need to follow both subsections.

WARNING

Keep in mind that the examples of case names you see in Rule 10.2.1 may not be correct for case names in citations because case names in citations must also follow the additional rules in Rule 10.2.2.

Although using two subsections may seem confusing at first, the only distinction between case names in textual sentences and case names in citations is the level of abbreviation required. According to Rule 10.2.2, in citations, you need to abbreviate more words than in textual sentences.

There is a limited list of abbreviations that are appropriate for textual sentences (see BP Rule B10.1.1(vi) and Rule 10.2.1(c)). Along with widely known acronyms (see Rule 6.1(b)), the following eight words should be abbreviated in textual sentences, unless they are the first word of a party's name:

- and (&)
- Association (Ass'n)
- Brothers (Bros.)
- Company (Co.)
- Corporation (Corp.)
- Incorporated (Inc.)
- Limited (Ltd.)
- Number (No.)

According to Rule 10.2.2, for case names in citations, you must also abbreviate any word listed in Table T6, unless the word is part of a geographical location (e.g., a state or country) and that geographical location is the entire party name.

The following example illustrates the difference in the abbreviations used in a textual sentence versus a citation. In a case of Southern Hospital versus Medical Supplies, Incorporated, the following case names would be correct:

For a textual sentence:

```
Southern Hospital v. Medical Supplies, Inc.
```

For a citation:

```
S. Hosp. v. Med. Supplies, Inc.
```

TAKE NOTE

For case names in citations, Table T6 also allows, but does not require, you to abbreviate other words that are eight or more letters "if *substantial* space is thereby saved and the result is unambiguous in context." This book, however, does not use any such discretionary abbreviations.

In addition to abbreviating words according to Table T6, in citations (not textual sentences), you must abbreviate geographical locations listed in Table T10, unless that geographic location is the entire name of the party.

For example, in a case of Jennifer Dorfmeister versus the University of Pennsylvania, the following case names would be correct:

For a textual sentence:

Dorfmeister v. University of Pennsylvania

For a citation:

Dorfmeister v. Univ. of Pa.

But, in a case of Elliot Avidan versus the United States, the following case name would be correct in a textual sentence and a citation (because, although Table T10 indicates that "United States" should be abbreviated as "U.S.," United States is the entire party name):

Avidan v. United States

TIP

Rule 10.2.1 contains many other detailed rules for case names that apply to both textual sentences and citations. The exercise for this chapter will teach you many of these other rules by requiring you to apply them to answer the questions.

WARNING

Be aware that your word processor may auto-matically capitalize the first letter of any word after a period. Because many of the abbrevia-tions in Table T6 and Table T10 end with a period, this automatic capitalization may capitalize another word in the case name that should not be capitalized. For example:

Brown v. Bd. Of Educ. ✗ incorrect

Brown v. Bd. of Educ. ✓ correct

C. Case Location

The "case location" portion of a full citation indicates where the reader can find the case. This chapter covers cases published in reporters and in a public domain format.

NAVIGATE

Chapter 11 covers cases published only in elec-tronic sources.

Different jurisdictions have their cases published in different reporters, and many jurisdictions have their cases published in multiple reporters. Therefore, one case may be located in multiple reporters. Some states require that you use parallel citations for cases from that state that are located in multiple reporters. The descriptions, examples, and exercise in this chapter assume that a parallel citation to multiple reporters is not required.

NAVIGATE

Chapter 9 covers parallel citations involving multiple reporters.

Each reporter has many volumes to contain the numerous cases published in it. In addition, many reporters have a number of series. For example, the Atlantic Reporter has three series — Atlantic Reporter; Atlantic Reporter, Second Series; and Atlantic Reporter, Third Series. Each series of a reporter begins with volume 1.

For cases published in reporters, you must indicate the following information when specifying the location of a case in a basic full citation (see BP Rule B10.1.2 and Rule 10.3):

- volume number;
- reporter abbreviation;
- starting page number; and
- pinpoint information ("pincite") when citing material located on a specific page(s) of the case.

The first three pieces of information above allow the reader to find the case. The pinpoint information allows the reader to find the exact location in the case that supports the proposition for which you are citing the case. Not only will this information allow the reader to find the case in the print reporter, but it will also allow the reader to find the case in an electronic service (e.g., WestlawNext, Lexis Advance, and Bloomberg Law).

Let's look at the case location information from the example citation sentence from Section A:

Panei v. Perez, 68 A.2d 2, 5 (Pa. Super. Ct. 1996).

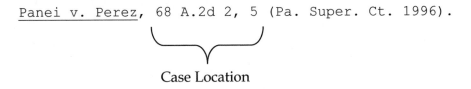

Case Location

"68" is the volume number, "A.2d" is the reporter abbreviation (it refers to the Atlantic Reporter, Second Series), "2" is the starting page number, and "5" is the pinpoint information. Therefore, the reader can find the case in volume 68 of the Atlantic Reporter, Second Series. The case starts on page 2 of that reporter, and page 5 contains the specific information being cited.

TAKE NOTE

Notice in the example above that the case location information immediately follows a comma and space after the case name.

1. Volume & Reporter

If a case is published in multiple reporters, you first need to determine which reporter to cite.[1] Table T1 provides that information and indicates the appropriate abbreviation for the reporter. Table T1 comprises four subparts arranged by jurisdiction. The first two subparts involve the federal jurisdiction—T1.1 for federal judicial and legislative material and T1.2 for federal administrative and executive material. T1.3 involves the states. Finally, T1.4 involves other U.S. jurisdictions, such as Puerto Rico and the Virgin Islands.

The example citation above is to a case from the Superior Court of Pennsylvania. Assume that this case is published in two reporters: (1) volume 68 of the Atlantic Reporter, Second Series, and (2) volume 454 of the Pennsylvania Superior Court Reports. The example citation uses the Atlantic Reporter, Second Series, because the entry for Pennsylvania in Table T1.3 indicates that the Atlantic Reporter is the preferred reporter.

Here is the entry for the Pennsylvania Superior Court in Table T1.3:

---

[1] As noted above, you will sometimes be required to include multiple reporters in one citation in a parallel citation, but this chapter assumes that a parallel citation is not required.

Superior Court (Pa. Super. Ct.): Cite to A., A.2d, or A.3d, if therein. For cases decided after December 31, 1998, use the following public domain citation format:

▶   Rapagnani v. Judas Co., 1999 PA Super 203.

▶   Atlantic Reporter   1931-date   A., A.2d, A.3d
▶   Pennsylvania Superior Court   1895-1997   Pa. Super.
    Reports

This entry in Table T1.3 indicates that you should cite to A., A.2d, or A.3d (i.e., Atlantic Reporter; Atlantic Reporter, Second Series; or Atlantic Reporter, Third Series) for a Pennsylvania Superior Court case, if the case is published there.[2] In addition, in the entry, that reporter is listed before the Pennsylvania Superior Court Reports (i.e., the other reporter that contains Pennsylvania Superior Court cases), so the Atlantic Reporter is the preferred reporter for a citation to a Pennsylvania Superior Court case.

TIP

Because each series of a particular reporter starts at volume 1, the volume number alone does not distinguish which series contains the case (e.g., all three series of the Atlantic Reporter contain a volume 10). You need to ensure that you indicate the correct series in the reporter abbreviation.

Some reporter abbreviations do not include spaces. For example:

```
A.2d
F.3d
```

Rule 6.1(a) indicates that you should not use spaces between words within an abbreviation that are adjacent single capital letters and that you should consider numerals and ordinals as a single capital letter.

---

[2] The entry also indicates that the public domain format should be used for cases decided after December 31, 1998 (note: Sections C.3 and D.3 below cover the public domain format).

Therefore, the two reporter abbreviations above do not contain any spaces.

The following are examples of reporter abbreviations that contain spaces between words because the abbreviations do not contain adjacent single capital letters (see Rule 6.1(a)):

```
Cal. App. 3d
F. Supp. 2d
```

TAKE NOTE

Rule 6.1(a) requires spaces between words in an abbreviation unless there are adjacent single capital letters, which includes numerals and ordinals. Even though the "F" and "S" in the second example above are adjacent single capital letters, there is a space between "F." and "Supp." because the abbreviation "Supp." does not contain only capital letters (see Rule 6.1(a)).

2. Starting Page & Pinpoint Information

Each volume of a reporter has many pages and cases, so your full citation to a case must indicate the page on which the case starts. It should also include the page(s) that contain the specific information you are citing.

TIP

Including the pinpoint information ("pincite") is very important for the reader. A case can be many pages, and the reader will want to be able to go directly to the information you are citing. By not including a pincite, you will force the reader to review the entire case to find the information. The reader will not be left with a good impression of you if you do not respect his or her time. In fact, you could be reprimanded, or worse, by a supervisor or court for a failure to pincite.

The format for including this information is to put the starting page number after the reporter abbreviation (note that there should be a space between the reporter abbreviation and the starting page number. To add pinpoint information, the starting page number is followed by a comma and space and then the pinpoint information. For example, if the starting page is 1152 and the pincite is to page 1155, the following would be correct after the reporter abbreviation and a space:

```
1152, 1155
```

The pincite can contain numerous pages. The following rules apply to pincites of multiple pages (see BP Rule B10.1.2 and Rule 3.2(a)).

For non-consecutive pinpoint pages, you should separate them by commas and spaces. Using 1152 as the starting page, if the pincite is to pages 1155, 1157, and 1160, the following would be correct after the reporter abbreviation and a space:

```
1152, 1155, 1157, 1160
```

For consecutive pinpoint pages, you should include the first and last page of the range, separated with a hyphen or en dash. If the last page number of a range is more than two digits, you should drop any repetitive digits except the last two. Using 1152 as the starting page, if the pincite is to pages 1159 through 1161, the following would be correct after the reporter abbreviation and a space:

```
1152, 1159-61
```

You can also have a combination of non-consecutive and consecutive pincites. Using 1152 as the starting page, if the pincite is to pages 1155 and 1159 through 1161, the following would be correct after the reporter abbreviation and a space:

```
1152, 1155, 1159-61
```

If the pincite is the same as the starting page number, you still need to include it:

```
1152, 1152
```

WARNING

Be careful pinciting to the initial page(s) of a case. If the case contains a summary and head-notes written by the publisher, those components are not part of the actual opinion (i.e., they are not the law) because they are not written by the court. Therefore, you should not cite them. In most jurisdictions, the actual opinion (i.e., what is written by the court) starts after the name(s) of the judge(s) who wrote the opinion.

NAVIGATE

Chapter 15 covers pinpoint information in more detail, including how to determine the pinpoint page(s) when you use the version of a case from an electronic database such as WestlawNext, Lexis Advance, or Bloomberg Law.

3. Public Domain Format

Some courts now use a public domain format for the case location. Table T1 indicates which jurisdictions and courts require a public domain format for cases decided after a certain date. For example, the Pennsylvania

Superior Court entry in Table T1.3 requires the following public domain format for cases decided after December 31, 1998:

`Smith v. Jones, 1999 PA Super 203.`

Unless a court's entry in Table T1 gives a different public domain format, the general public domain format is as follows (see Rule 10.3.3):

1. Case name;

2. Year of decision;

3. The jurisdiction's two-character postal code or abbreviation;

4. Court abbreviation from Table T7 (unless the court is the state's highest court);

5. Sequential number of the decision; and

6. If the decision is unpublished, a capital "U" after the sequential number of the decision.

TAKE NOTE

A court's entry in Table T1 will indicate whether that court requires a public domain format and, if so, what that format should be. If the format differs from the general public domain format above, you should follow the format listed in Table T1 for a particular court.

If a public domain is appropriate for a citation, Rule 10.3.3 indicates that a parallel citation to the regional reporter should be provided, if available. For example:

`Smith v. Jones, 1999 PA Super 203, ¶ 7, 690 A.2d 125, 128.`

The example above illustrates the parallel citation to the regional reporter (690 A.2d 125) and pinpoint information (¶ 7 for the public domain and page 128 for the regional reporter). Notice that the parallel citation to the regional reporter follows the public domain format (and is separated from it by a comma and space). According to Rule 10.3.3, when providing pinpoint information for a public domain format, you should refer to the paragraph number(s) after a paragraph symbol (¶) for one paragraph or two paragraph symbols (¶¶) for multiple paragraphs, unless the court's public domain listing in Table T1 indicates another format for pinpoint information.

TIP

You should always use a space between a paragraph symbol (¶) and the corresponding number. See Rule 6.2(c).

With this space, a paragraph symbol could be at the end of one line in your document and the paragraph number(s) at the beginning of the next line. To avoid this awkward split, you can use a non-breaking space between the paragraph symbol and the number(s).

Your word processor should allow you to add non-breaking spaces. For example, in Microsoft Word, a non-breaking space is a symbol, and you can find it in the "Special Characters" section when choosing to insert a symbol, or you can press Ctrl+Shift+Space (PC) or Option+Space (Mac) to insert a non-breaking space.

D. Court & Date

Along with the case name and location, a full citation to a case also includes information about the court and date. Let's look again at the example citation sentence from Section A:

Panei v. Perez, 68 A.2d 2, 5 (Pa. Super. Ct. 1996).

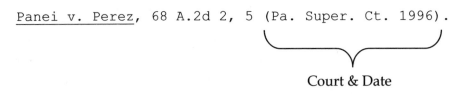

Court & Date

TAKE NOTE

Notice in the example above that the information about the court and date is contained in parentheses that immediately follow the case location and a space. If punctuation is required at the end of the court and date parenthetical (e.g., a period to end a citation sentence as in the example above), the punctuation should immediately follow the closing parenthesis (i.e., there should not be a space before the punctuation).

1. Court

The first piece of information in the court and date parenthetical is the court that decided the case (see BP Rule B10.1.3 and Rule 10.4), i.e., the court that issued the document you are citing. This court information generally includes abbreviations for (1) the jurisdiction and (2) the name of the court. Table T1 provides these abbreviations for all major U.S. jurisdictions, and such abbreviations are included in parenthesis after the name of the court. If you cannot find such abbreviations in Table T1, use Table T7 and Table T10 to determine the appropriate abbreviations.

Here is the entry in Table T1.3 for the Court of Appeals in North Carolina:

Court of Appeals (N.C. Ct. App.): . . . .

This entry indicates that a citation to a case decided by this court would include "N.C. Ct. App." in the court and date parenthetical, unless other Bluebook rules indicate that any part of this court information should be omitted (note: Sections D.1.a and D.1.b below cover these omission rules). This entry illustrates both parts of the court information: (1) "N.C." (for North Carolina) is the jurisdiction and (2) "Ct. App." (for Court of Appeals) is the name of the court.

TAKE NOTE

For a particular jurisdiction (e.g., North Carolina), Table T1 lists the courts in their hierarchical order, with the highest court (i.e., "court of last resort") first.

The rules for whether spaces are required between words of an abbreviation for the jurisdiction or name of court are the same as for reporter abbreviations (see Section C.1 above). As the following examples illustrate, you should not use spaces between words within an abbreviation that are adjacent single capital letters (see BP Rule B10.1.3 and Rule 6.1(a)):

```
S.D.N.Y.
D.N.J.
```

You should, however, use spaces between words within an abbreviation that are not adjacent single capital letters (see BP Rule B10.1.3 and Rule 6.1(a)). For example:

```
M.D. Pa.
D. Del.
```

Some court names include ordinals (e.g., 5th Cir.). Rule 6.2(b) contains information about using ordinals. For example, do not use superscript with ordinals:

5th ✘ incorrect
5th   ✓ correct

TAKE NOTE

Although ordinals ending in "st" and "th" are written as expected (e.g., 1st, 4th, 10th), ordinals ending in "nd" or "rd" are not. For example, you should use "2d" or "3d," not "2nd" or "3rd" (see Rule 6.2(b)).

Although the court information generally includes abbreviations for (1) the jurisdiction and (2) the name of the court, under certain circumstances, the jurisdiction and/or the name of the court are omitted. The basic rules for such omission are as follows (see BP Rule B10.1.3 and Rule 10.4):

- Omit the jurisdiction if the reporter abbreviation in the case location information unambiguously conveys the jurisdiction; and

- Omit the name of the court if the reporter abbreviation in the case location information unambiguously conveys the court or when the court is the highest court of the jurisdiction.

a. Jurisdiction Omission

The jurisdiction component of the court information should be omitted if the reporter abbreviation in the case location information unambiguously conveys the jurisdiction (see BP Rule B10.1.3 and Rule 10.4).

(1) Federal Cases

For federal cases, the U.S. jurisdiction is almost always unambiguously conveyed by the reporter abbreviation, and, therefore, the U.S. jurisdiction should be omitted in such situations (see BP Rule B10.1.3(i)-(iii) and Rule 10.4(a)). The reporters for U.S. District Court and Courts of Appeals cases—Federal Supplement (F. Supp. and F. Supp. 2d) and Federal Reporter (F., F.2d, and F.3d), respectively—unambiguously convey the U.S. jurisdiction, so case citations to these reporters should not include the jurisdiction. For example:

```
Bernard v. United States, 25 F.3d 98, 100-03
(2d Cir. 1994).

Blakeman v. Walt Disney Co., 613 F. Supp. 2d
288, 294 (E.D.N.Y. 2009).
```

The first two preferred reporters for U.S. Supreme Court cases — United States Reports (U.S.) and Supreme Court Reporter (S. Ct.) — also unambiguously convey the U.S. jurisdiction, so case citations to these reporters should not include the jurisdiction. In such instances, the second rule of omission regarding the highest court would also apply (see example below in the "Name of Court Omission" section).

(2) State Cases

For state cases, the preferred reporter for a citation is a regional reporter, which does not unambiguously convey the jurisdiction because many states' cases are published in a single regional reporter. If, however, a state case is not published in a regional reporter, the citation will be to the state's official reporter. A state's official reporter likely unambiguously conveys the jurisdiction (because the jurisdiction will be part of the reporter abbreviation), so a case citation to that reporter should not include the jurisdiction. See BP Rule B10.1.3(iv)-(v) and Rule 10.4(b). For example:

A regional reporter that does not unambiguously convey the jurisdiction (Md.):

```
Mitchell v. Balt. Sun Co., 883 A.2d 1008,
1015 (Md. Ct. Spec. App. 2005).
```

A state's official reporter that unambiguously conveys the jurisdiction (Md.):

```
Furman v. Sheppard, 130 Md. App. 67, 76,
78-79 (Ct. Spec. App. 2000).
```

b. Name of Court Omission

There are two instances when the name of the court component of the court information should be omitted. First, it should be omitted if the reporter abbreviation in the case location information unambiguously conveys the court. For example, the court — the Appellate Court of Connecticut — is omitted in the following citation because the reporter unambiguously conveys it:

`Branigan v. Cohen`, 3 Conn. App. 580, 581 (1985).

In the example above, not only is the name of the court omitted from the parenthetical, but the jurisdiction is also omitted because it is unambiguously conveyed by the reporter abbreviation (see Section D.1.a above). Therefore, only the year is included in the parenthetical.

The second instance that requires omission of the name of the court is when the court is the highest court of the jurisdiction. For example, a citation to a case decided by the U.S. Supreme Court would not include the name of the court in the court and date parenthetical:

`Brown v. Bd. of Educ.`, 347 U.S. 483, 495 (1954).

In the example above, not only is the name of the court omitted from the parenthetical, but the U.S. jurisdiction is also omitted because it is unambiguously conveyed by the reporter abbreviation (see Section D.1.a above). Therefore, only the year is included in the parenthetical.

In a citation to a case decided by a state's highest court, the name of the court should also be omitted. For the following two examples, assume that the Pennsylvania Supreme Court decided the case:

`Karoly v. Mancuso`, 65 A.3d 301, 311 (Pa. 2013).

`Welch v. Palka`, 603 Pa. 152, 154–55 (2009).

In both examples, the name of the court is omitted because it is the highest court of the jurisdiction. In the second example only, the jurisdiction is also omitted because it is unambiguously conveyed by the reporter abbreviation (see Section D.1.a above).

Some jurisdictions have more than one court at the highest appellate level. In such instances, the name of the court should be omitted only for the court listed first in Table T1. For example, Texas has two courts at the highest appellate level—the Supreme Court and the Court of Criminal Appeals. Here is the entry in Table T1.3 for Texas:

Supreme Court (Tex.): . . . .

. . . .

Court of Criminal Appeals (Tex. Crim. App.): . . . .

Because the Table T1.3 entry lists the Supreme Court first, only that court name should be omitted under the "highest court" omission rule.

TIP

As the Texas example illustrates, the court abbreviations in Table T1 indicate whether the court name should be included in a citation. For the first court listed under Texas, only the jurisdiction is listed in parentheses after the court name. For the second court listed, the abbreviation for the court name is also included.

This tip applies regardless of whether the jurisdiction has more than one court at the highest appellate level. For example, Pennsylvania has one court at the highest level, the Supreme Court, and its entry in Table T1.3 is as follows:

Supreme Court (Pa.): . . . .

2. Date

The second piece of information in the court and date parenthetical is the date. For cases that are published in reporters, you should use the year that the case was decided, if it is available (see BP Rule B10.1.3 and Rule 10.5(a)). At times, a case will indicate numerous dates (e.g., date argued and date decided). For your full citation, use the year of the date decided.

3. Public Domain Format

As you learned in Section C.3 above, some state courts require a public domain format, and, where possible, a parallel citation to the regional reporter at the end of a citation with a public domain (see Rule 10.3.3). Often, the information included for the public domain includes the jurisdiction, court abbreviation, and year of the decision. In such circumstances, the "court and date" parenthetical should not be included on the parallel citation to the regional reporter. For example:

Smith v. Jones, 1999 PA Super 203, ¶ 7, 690 A.2d 125, 128.

In the example above, the public domain information includes the jurisdiction (PA), the court abbreviation (Super), and the year of the decision (1999), so the "court and date" parenthetical is not included after the parallel citation to the regional reporter.

E. Common Rules & Tables

The following table provides the common Bluebook rules and tables for basic full case citations:

Rule or Table	Description
BP Rule B10.1.1	Case Names
BP Rule B10.1.2	Reporter & Pinpoint Citation (for case location)
BP Rule B10.1.3	Court & Year of Decision
Rule 3.2(a)	Pages, etc. (for pinpoint information)
Rule 6.1(a)	Spacing (for reporter & jurisdiction/court abbreviations)
Rule 6.2(b)	Ordinals
Rule 10.2	Case Names
Rule 10.3	Reporters and Other Sources (for case location)
Rule 10.4	Court & Jurisdiction
Rule 10.5	Date or Year

Rule or Table	Description
Table T1	Jurisdictions (information regarding courts & reporters)
Table T6	Abbreviations (for case names)
Table T10	Geographic Abbreviations (for case names & jurisdictions)

F. Exercise

Along with using the information in this chapter, you should use your Bluebook when answering these questions (note: do not use any jurisdiction- or court-specific citation rules, which are covered in Section C of Chapter 1 and are set forth in BP Table BT2). Some questions may require you to find and apply rules that were not specifically discussed in this chapter.

For all answers, use only ordinary or <u>underlined</u> typeface. That is, do not use *italics* or LARGE AND SMALL CAPS typeface.

As with some of the examples in this chapter, some of the legal authority used in these questions may be fictional authority designed to test various Bluebook rules.

This exercise is split into the following categories:

1. Case Name
2. Case Location
3. Court & Date
4. Full Citation

1. Case Name

1. What is the correct case name in a full citation for a case of Amanda L. Smith, et al., Plaintiffs v. Anna P. Hemingway, a/k/a The Director, Defendant?

   A. Amanda L. Smith, et al., Plaintiffs v. Anna P. Hemingway, a/k/a The Director, Defendant

   B. Amanda L. Smith, et al. v. Anna P. Hemingway, a/k/a The Director

   C. Amanda L. Smith v. Anna P. Hemingway

   D. Amanda Smith, et al. v. Anna Hemingway

   E. Amanda Smith v. Anna Hemingway

   F. Smith, et al. v. Hemingway

   G. Smith v. Hemingway

2. What is the correct case name in a full citation for a case of Amanda L. Smith & Jennifer M. Lear v. Anna P. Hemingway & Ann E. Fruth?

   A. Smith v. Hemingway

   B. Smith & Lear v. Hemingway & Fruth

   C. Smith-Lear v. Hemingway-Fruth

3. What is the correct case name in a full citation for a case of Lindsay Lohan v. The Miami Herald?

   A. Lohan v. The Miami Herald

   B. Lohan v. Miami Herald

4. What is the correct case name in a *textual* sentence for a case of David
    Raeker-Jordan v. Philadelphia Investment Company?

    A.   Raeker-Jordan v. Philadelphia Investment
         Company

    B.   Raeker-Jordan v. Philadelphia Investment Co.

    C.   Raeker-Jordan v. Philadelphia Investment

    D.   Raeker-Jordan v. Phila. Inv. Co.

    E.   Raeker-Jordan v. Phila. Inv.

5. What is the correct case name in a full citation for a case of Bella
    George v. Central Education Company, Incorporated?

    A.   George v. Central Education Co., Inc.

    B.   George v. Central Education Co.

    C.   George v. Cent. Educ. Co., Inc.

    D.   George v. Cent. Educ. Co.

6. What is the correct case name in a full citation for a case of Aaron
    Thomas v. International Services for Schools?

    A.   Thomas v. Int'l Servs. for Schs.

    B.   Thomas v. Int'l. Servs. for Schs.

    C.   Thomas v. Int'l Servs. for Sch.

    D.   Thomas v. Int'l. Servs. for Sch.

    E.   Thomas v. Int'l Serv. for Sch.

    F.   Thomas v. Int'l. Serv. for Sch.

7. What is the correct case name in a full citation for a case of Aaron Thomas on behalf of Ava Thomas v. Jackson Co.?

    A.   Thomas v. Jackson Co.

    B.   Thomas ex rel. Thomas v. Jackson Co.

8. What is the correct case name in a full citation for a case of Commonwealth of Pennsylvania v. Michael Howard, which was decided by the Superior Court of Pennsylvania?

    A.   Commonwealth of Pennsylvania v. Howard

    B.   Commonwealth of Pa. v. Howard

    C.   Commw. of Pa. v. Howard

    D.   Pennsylvania v. Howard

    E.   Pa. v. Howard

    F.   Commonwealth v. Howard

    G.   Commw. v. Howard

9. What is the correct case name in a full citation for a case of Common-
    wealth of Pennsylvania v. Jennifer Lear, which was decided by the
    United States Supreme Court?

    A.   Commonwealth of Pennsylvania v. Lear

    B.   Commonwealth of Pa. v. Lear

    C.   Commw. of Pa. v. Lear

    D.   Pennsylvania v. Lear

    E.   Pa. v. Lear

    F.   Commonwealth v. Lear

    G.   Commw. v. Lear

10. What is the correct case name in a full citation for a case of Mayor of
    the City of Harrisburg v. Patriot News?

    A.   Mayor of the City of Harrisburg v. Patriot News

    B.   Mayor of Harrisburg v. Patriot News

    C.   Mayor v. Patriot News

    D.   City of Harrisburg v. Patriot News

    E.   Harrisburg v. Patriot News

11. What is the correct case name in a full citation for a case of Cristina
    Perez v. City of Miami?

    A.   Perez v. City of Miami

    B.   Perez v. Miami

12. What is the correct case name in a full citation for a case of Cory Walsh v. City of Harrisburg, Pennsylvania?

    A.   Walsh v. City of Harrisburg, Pennsylvania

    B.   Walsh v. City of Harrisburg, Pa.

    C.   Walsh v. City of Harrisburg

    D.   Walsh v. Harrisburg, Pennsylvania

    E.   Walsh v. Harrisburg, Pa.

    F.   Walsh v. Harrisburg

13. What is the correct case name in a full citation for a case of Peter Anthony v. Board of Commissioners of Lancaster?

    A.   Anthony v. Bd. of Comm'rs of Lancaster

    B.   Anthony v. Bd. of Comm'rs

2. Case Location

14. You want to cite a case that was decided by the New York Court of Appeals. The case is published in the North Eastern Reporter, Second Series. How should you abbreviate that reporter?

    A.   N. E. 2d

    B.   N.E. 2d

    C.   N.E.2d

15. You want to cite a case that was decided by the Louisiana Supreme Court. The case is published in the Southern Reporter, Second Series. How should you abbreviate that reporter?

    A.   So. 2d

    B.   So.2d

16. You want to cite a case that is published in volume 71 of the Atlantic Reporter, Second Series, starting on page 113 (the specific information cited is on page 115). Which of the following is the correct case location information for the full citation?

    A.   71 A.2d 113

    B.   71 A.2d 115

    C.   71 A.2d 113, 115

    D.   71 A.2d 113-115

    E.   71 A.2d 113-15

    F.   71 A.2d 113-5

17. You want to cite a case that is published in volume 71 of the Atlantic Reporter, Second Series, starting on page 113 (the specific information cited is on page 113). Which of the following is the correct case location information for the full citation?

    A.   71 A.2d 113

    B.   71 A.2d 113, 113

18. You want to cite a case that is published in volume 71 of the Atlantic Reporter, Second Series, starting on page 113 (the specific information cited is on pages 115 and 117). Which of the following is the correct case location information for the full citation?

    A.   71 A.2d 113, 115, 117

    B.   71 A.2d 113, 115-117

    C.   71 A.2d 113, 115-17

    D.   71 A.2d 113, 115-7

19. You want to cite a case that is published in volume 71 of the Atlantic Reporter, Second Series, starting on page 113 (the specific information cited is on pages 115 through 117). Which of the following is the correct case location information for the full citation?

    A.   71 A.2d 113, 115, 116, 117

    B.   71 A.2d 113, 115-117

    C.   71 A.2d 113, 115-17

    D.   71 A.2d 113, 115-7

20. You want to cite a case that was decided by the Wisconsin Supreme Court. The case is published in two reporters: (1) volume 12 of the North Western Reporter, Second Series, starting on page 18 (the specific information cited is on page 20) and (2) volume 244 of the Wisconsin Reports, starting on page 251 (the specific information cited is on page 254). Which of the following should you use as the case location information in the full citation (assuming you will cite to only one reporter)?

    A.   12 N.W.2d 18, 20

    B.   244 Wis. 251, 254

    C.   Either of the above case locations can be used.

3. Court & Date

21. You want to cite a case that decided whether to grant the defendant's motion for summary judgment. The court heard oral argument on the motion on November 1, 2012, and decided to grant the motion on February 4, 2013. The case is published in the Southern Reporter, Third Series. Which date should you use in the court and date parenthetical at the end of the full case citation?

    A.   November 1, 2012

    B.   Nov. 1, 2012

    C.   2012

    D.   February 4, 2013

    E.   Feb. 4, 2013

    F.   2013

22. You want to cite a case that was decided by the Superior Court of Delaware in 2012. You will cite to the Atlantic Reporter, Third Series (A.3d). Which of the following is the court and date parenthetical you should use in the full citation?

    A.   (2012)

    B.   (Del. 2012)

    C.   (Super. Ct. 2012)

    D.   (Del. Super. Ct. 2012)

23. You want to cite a case that was decided by the Court of Appeals of Arizona in 1980. If you cite to the Arizona Reports (abbreviated as "Ariz."), which of the following is the court and date parenthetical you should use in the full citation?

    A.   (1980)

    B.   (Ariz. 1980)

    C.   (Ct. App. 1980)

    D.   (Ariz. Ct. App. 1980)

24. You want to cite a case that was decided by the Court of Appeals of New York in 2012. You will cite to the North Eastern Reporter, Second Series (N.E.2d). Which of the following is the court and date parenthetical you should use in the full citation?

    A.   (2012)

    B.   (N.Y. 2012)

    C.   (Ct. App. 2012)

    D.   (N.Y. Ct. App. 2012)

25. You want to cite a case that was decided by the California Supreme Court in 2012. You will cite to the California Reports, Fourth Series (Cal. 4th). Which of the following is the court and date parenthetical you should use in the full citation?

    A.   (2012)

    B.   (Cal. 2012)

    C.   (Sup. Ct. 2012)

    D.   (Cal. Sup. Ct. 2012)

26. You want to cite a case that was decided by the United States District Court for the District of Maryland. You will cite to the Federal Supplement, Second Series (F. Supp. 2d). Which of the following is the correct court for the court and date parenthetical in the full citation?

    A.   D. M.d.

    B.   D.M.D.

    C.   D. Md.

    D.   D. MD

    E.   D.Md.

    F.   D.MD

4. Full Citation

27. You want to cite the case of <u>Cecala v. Sharpe</u>. The Utah Court of Appeals decided the case on February 14, 2004. The case is published in volume 99 of the Pacific Reporter, Third Series, starting on page 152 (the specific information you are citing is in paragraph 11 of the opinion, which is on page 155). The case was given the sequential number 33 by the court. Which of the following is the correct full citation to the case?

    A. <u>Cecala v. Sharpe</u>, 99 P.3d 152, 155 (Utah Ct. App. 2004).

    B. <u>Cecala v. Sharpe</u>, 2004 UT Ct. App. 33, ¶ 11, 99 P.3d 152, 155.

    C. <u>Cecala v. Sharpe</u>, 2004 UT App 33, ¶ 11, 99 P.3d 152, 155.

    D. <u>Cecala v. Sharpe</u>, 2004 UT App 33, ¶ 11, 99 P.3d 152, 155 (Ct. App.).

    E. <u>Cecala v. Sharpe</u>, 2004 UT Ct. App. 33, ¶ 11.

    F. <u>Cecala v. Sharpe</u>, 2004 UT App 33, ¶ 11.

28. Which of the following is a correct full citation sentence to a case?

   A.   <u>Holbert v. Byrd</u>, 23 A.3d 43, 46-47 (Pa. 2012).

   B.   <u>Holbert v. Byrd</u>, 23 A.3d 43, 46-47 (Pa. 2012).

   C.   <u>Holbert v. Byrd</u>, 23 A.3d 43, 46-47 (Pa. 2012).

   D.   <u>Holbert v. Byrd,</u> 23 A.3d 43, 46-47 (Pa. 2012).

   E.   <u>Holbert v. Byrd</u>, 23 A.3d 43, 46-47 (Pa. 2012).

   F.   <u>Holbert v. Byrd,</u> 23 A.3d 43, 46-47 (Pa. 2012).

29. You want to cite the case of State of Maine versus Sean P. Lewis. The Supreme Judicial Court of Maine decided the case on July 17, 1992. The case is published in volume 611 of the Atlantic Reporter, Second Series, starting on page 69 (the specific information you are citing is on page 70). Provide the correct full citation sentence:

30. You want to cite the case of Kenneth R. Villanova versus Innovative Investments, Inc. The Intermediate Court of Appeals of Hawaii decided the case on July 9, 2001. The case is published in volume 96 of West's Hawaii Reports, starting on page 353 (the specific information you are citing is on pages 360 and 362 through 364). Provide the correct full citation sentence:

31. You want to cite the case of Gary Edward Brown versus Pennsylvania State Department of Health and Doylestown Hospital. The United States District Court for the Middle District of Pennsylvania decided the case on September 18, 2007. The case is published in volume 514 of the Federal Supplement, Second Series, starting on page 675 (the specific information you are citing is on pages 679 through 680). Provide the correct full citation sentence:

32. You want to cite the case of Robert Shaw versus Kevin Murphy. The United States Supreme Court decided the case on April 18, 2001. The case is published in volume 532 of the United States Reports, starting on page 223 (the specific information you are citing is on page 229). Provide the correct full citation sentence:

Chapter 3
Cases: Short Citation

A. When to Use a Short Citation

According to BP Rule B10.2, after you have provided a full citation to a case, subsequent citations to the same case can use a short form of the citation if the following conditions are met:

1. the reader will be able to identify the referenced case clearly;
2. the full citation to the case falls in the same general discussion; and
3. the reader will be able to locate the full citation to the case easily.

TIP

Although BP Rule B10.2 sets forth these conditions for when you *may* use a short citation, in practice, you *should* use a short citation when such conditions are met (i.e., do not use a full citation when a short citation is permitted).

By using the proper short form of the citation (discussed in Section B below), you can ensure that the first condition is met. The latter two conditions are similar and essentially involve how far away the short citation is from its corresponding full citation. In the types of documents that an attorney or law clerk write in practice (e.g., a brief, a memo, or an opinion), there is no predefined maximum number of pages that can separate a short and full citation. Generally, a short citation is appropriate if the corresponding full citation is in the same section/issue or the same sub-section/sub-issue of a document.

For example, assume that you separate the analysis of a particular situation into two distinct issues in a document, each with its own heading.

In addition, assume for each issue that you cite the <u>Lear</u> case. Whether you should use a full or short citation to <u>Lear</u> depends on the location of the citation. The first time you cite the case in your analysis of the first issue, you need to use a full citation. Subsequent citations to that case within your analysis of the first issue should use a short citation.[1] In your analysis of the second issue, you should use a full citation to the case again the first time you cite it in that issue.

TAKE NOTE

Even if your analysis of a particular issue is relatively short, you should still consider using a full citation again when addressing a distinct issue because the reader, at times, may read just one issue of your document or read the issues in a different order than you presented them. Therefore, the reader will be able to locate the corresponding full citation easily only if it is in your analysis of that issue.

B. How to Short Cite

After determining that a short citation is appropriate for your current case citation, you need to determine what form the short citation should take. Your answers to the following questions will determine the appropriate short form for your current case citation (see BP Rule B4, BP Rule B10.2, Rule 4.1, and Rule 10.9):

---

[1] An exception to this general rule requiring a short citation for subsequent citations to the same case throughout an entire section/issue would occur if that one section/issue in your document is particularly long and the reader will have a difficult time locating the corresponding full citation (i.e., if the third condition is not met). For the documents you will write for your legal research and writing class, each section/issue will likely be short enough that you can use a short citation for subsequent citations to the same case throughout an entire section/issue of your paper.

1. Does the immediately preceding citation in the document cite only one authority?

2. Is the immediately preceding citation in the document a citation (full or short) to the same authority as your current citation (i.e., is it to the same case as your current case citation)?

For question #1, the immediately preceding citation can include multiple authorities if it is a string citation.

NAVIGATE

Chapter 13 covers string citations.

A citation to a single case may list other authorities in two instances: (1) in the history of the case or (2) in a quoting/citing parenthetical or an explanatory parenthetical. Other authorities listed in these two instances, however, do not count as a separate authority when answering question #1.

NAVIGATE

Chapter 8 covers case history, and Chapter 10 covers the different types of parentheticals.

If you answer "yes" to both questions above, you should use the appropriate "id." form for your current citation (see Section B.1 below). If you answer "no" to either question, you cannot use any "id." form; you must use another short form, which is an abbreviated version of the full citation (see Section B.2 below).

For example, assume that (1) your current citation is to <u>Lear</u> and (2) you have already determined that a short citation is appropriate for the current citation. If the immediately preceding citation in your document contains only one authority and that one authority is the <u>Lear</u> case, you should use the appropriate "id." form. Otherwise, you need to use another short form for Lear.

1. Id.

If you have determined that you should use "id." for your short citation to a case, you then need to decide whether to use "id." alone or whether you need to use the "id. at X" form (where "X" is the pinpoint page(s)) — see BP Rule B4, BP Rule B10.2, Rule 4.1, and Rule 10.9. "Id." alone refers not only to the case in the immediately preceding citation, but it also refers to the same pinpoint page(s) as in the immediately preceding citation (see BP Rule B10.2(i)). If your current citation does not use the same pinpoint page(s) as the immediately preceding citation, you need to use the "id. at X" form (see BP Rule B10.2(ii)).

WARNING

You may have used "ibid." in other writing, but "ibid." is not a proper substitute for "id." under Bluebook rules.

For example, assume that the immediately preceding citation is to pinpoint page 77 in the Lear case (which starts on page 75) and that case is the only authority cited in the immediately preceding citation. If the specific information you are citing in your current citation is on page 77 in Lear, the short citation for it would be the following:

```
Id.
```

TAKE NOTE

According to BP Rule B10.2, the period in "<u>id.</u>" is always underlined (or italicized if you are using italics instead of underlining), and the "i" in "<u>id.</u>" should be capitalized only when the "<u>id.</u>" is the start of a citation sentence. If a sentence (textual or citation) ends with "<u>id.</u>," the period in "<u>id.</u>" also represents the period to end the sentence (i.e., do not add a second period after "<u>id.</u>"):

<u>Id.</u>.   ✗ incorrect punctuation to end sentence
<u>Id.</u>   ✓ correct punctuation to end sentence

Again, assume that the immediately preceding citation is to pinpoint page 77 in the <u>Lear</u> case (which starts on page 75) and that case is the only authority cited in the immediately preceding citation. If the specific information you are citing in your current citation is on page 79 in <u>Lear</u>, the short citation for it would be the following:

<u>Id.</u> at 79.

WARNING

The "a" in "at" should not be capitalized. Your word processor may automatically capitalize it because it follows a period, so be sure to correct any automatic capitalization.

Again, assume that the immediately preceding citation is to pinpoint page 77 in the <u>Lear</u> case (which starts on page 75) and that case is the only authority cited in the immediately preceding citation. If the specific information you are citing in your current citation is on pages 77 and 79 in <u>Lear</u>, the short citation for it would be the following:

<u>Id.</u> at 77, 79.

TAKE NOTE

All of the examples above use "id." at the beginning of a citation sentence; therefore, the "i" in "id." is capitalized. If "id." does not begin a citation sentence (e.g., when used in a citation clause), the "i" in "id." should not be capitalized.

2. Other Short Form

If an "id." form cannot be used (either because the immediately preceding citation cites to more than one authority or it is not a citation to the same authority as the current citation), you need to use another short form—an abbreviated version of the full citation. Here is an example of such a short form for a case published in a reporter (see BP Rule B10.2 and Rule 10.9):

```
Lear, 11 A.3d at 77-78.
```

Notice the following components of this short form:

- Shortened case name (only one party's name);
- Volume number;
- Reporter abbreviation;
- "at"; and
- Pinpoint page(s).

TIP

If you cannot use an "id." form for a short case citation, the short form you use for a case published in a reporter must include the volume number and reporter abbreviation. Therefore, the following citations are never correct:

```
Lear, at 77-78.  ✗
Lear at 77-78.   ✗
Lear, 77-78.     ✗
Lear 77-78.      ✗
```

Such shorthand notations are good for when you are drafting your document (so that you do not lose your writing momentum to set forth the correct citations), but you need to ensure that you correct them in the final version of your document.

a. Shortened Case Name

According to BP Rule B10.2 and Rule 10.9(a)(i), for the shortened case name, use the first party's name, unless that party is a geographical or governmental unit, a governmental official, or another common litigant. For example, if the full case name is <u>Cunfer v. Lear</u>, use <u>Cunfer</u> as the shortened case name in the short form citation. But, if the full case name is <u>Commonwealth v. Lear</u>, use <u>Lear</u> as the shortened case name in the short form citation.

TAKE NOTE

Not only can you use a shortened case name in a citation, but you may also do so in a textual sentence after you have given the full case name (see Rule 10.9(c)). The shortened case name you use for a citation and a textual sentence should be the same, except for possible differences in abbreviations. Recall that, if required by Rule 10.2.2, the words in the case name in a citation must be abbreviated according to Table T6 and Table T10, but the case name in a textual sentence will not be abbreviated according to these tables.

You may also shorten the case name further (beyond the entire party name), as long as the reader will be able to determine to which case you are referring (see BP Rule B10.2 and Rule 10.9(a)(i)). For example, if the full case name is <u>Capital Bakers & Chefs, Inc. v. Townsend</u>, you may use <u>Capital Bakers</u> as the shortened case name in the short form citation.

TIP

To determine how far to shorten a case name, you can see how other cases have referred to the case you are citing. For example, if other cases consistently refer to the case above as <u>Capital Bakers</u>, then that is the shortened case name you should use. But, if other cases consistently refer to the case as <u>Capital Bakers & Chefs</u>, then that is the shortened case name you should use because it will help the reader review your document in conjunction with the relevant cases.

Keep in mind, however, that the names that other cases use may not comply with Bluebook rules. Although you should try to be consistent with how other cases refer to a case, you must still follow Bluebook rules.

A shortened case name can be omitted entirely from the citation if there will be no confusion about the case to which the citation refers (see Rule 10.9(a)(i)). The following example (which includes a textual sentence and the corresponding citation sentence) illustrates this rule.

```
In Lear, the court held that the employer
wrongfully terminated the employee. 11 A.3d at
79.
```

TAKE NOTE

Notice in all of the examples that use a shortened case name that the case name (whether in a citation or textual sentence) is always underlined (see BP Rule B2) but the punctuation following the case name is not.

Recall that BP Rule B2 allows underlining or italics, but this book uses underlining so that you can more easily see when text needs to be underlined or italicized.

b. *Entire Decision*

If you are using a short case citation form but you are citing to the entire decision (rather than specific pinpoint pages), you should remove the "at" and include only the starting page number. In addition, you would not include a court and date parenthetical. See Rule 10.9(a)(i). For example, assume that the <u>Lear</u> case starts on page 75. The correct short form to the entire decision would be:

```
Lear, 11 A.3d 75.
```

WARNING

You will rarely, if ever, cite an entire decision; you should always attempt to indicate pinpoint pages to enable the reader to go directly to the specific information you are citing.

3. Pinpoint Page(s)

For the pinpoint page(s) in a short citation (whether an "id." or other short form), you should not include the page on which the case starts, unless it is a pinpoint page (i.e., a page on which information you are citing is located).

For example, assume that the Lear case starts on page 75. The correct "id." form to information on page 77 would be the following:

```
Id. at 77.
```

The correct other short form to information on page 77 would be the following:

```
Lear, 11 A.3d at 77.
```

NAVIGATE

Chapter 15 covers pinpoint information in more detail.

C. Common Rules & Tables

The following table provides the common Bluebook rules and tables for short case citations.

Rule or Table	Description
BP Rule B4	Id.
BP Rule B10.2	Cases: Short Form Citation
Rule 4.1	Id.
Rule 10.9	Short Forms for Cases

D. Exercise

Along with using the information in this chapter, you should use your Bluebook when answering these questions (note: do not use any jurisdiction- or court-specific citation rules, which are covered in Section C of Chapter 1 and are set forth in BP Table BT2). Some questions may require you to find and apply rules that were not specifically discussed in this chapter.

For all answers, use only ordinary or <u>underlined</u> typeface. That is, do not use *italics* or LARGE AND SMALL CAPS typeface.

As with some of the examples in this chapter, some of the legal authority used in these questions may be fictional authority designed to test various Bluebook rules.

1. The information you are citing is on page 723 of <u>Smith v. Cullen</u>, a case that starts on page 715 of the reporter you will cite. You have determined that a short citation is appropriate. Which of the following is the correct page information to include on the short citation?

    A. 715

    B. 723

    C. 715, 723

    D. 715-723

    E. 715-23

2. You currently want to cite to page 723 of <u>Smith v. Cullen</u>, 54 P.3d
    715 (Wash. 2011). Previously in the same section/issue of your doc-
    ument, you set forth the full citation to the case with 723 as the pin-
    point page. The immediately preceding citation to your current cita-
    tion is the following: <u>Hemingway v. Black</u>, 43 P.3d 926, 928 (Wash.
    Ct. App. 2010). Which of the following is the correct current citation
    sentence?

    A.   <u>Id.</u>

    B.   <u>Id.</u> at 723.

    C.   <u>Smith</u>, at 723.

    D.   <u>Smith</u>, 54 P.3d 715, 723.

    E.   <u>Smith</u>, 54 P.3d at 715, 723.

    F.   <u>Smith</u>, 54 P.3d 723.

    G.   <u>Smith</u>, 54 P.3d at 723.

    H.   <u>Smith v. Cullen</u>, 54 P.3d 715, 723 (Wash.
          2011).

3. You currently want to cite to page 723 of <u>Smith v. Cullen</u>, 54 P.3d
    715 (Wash. 2011). Previously in the same section/issue of your doc-
    ument, you set forth the full citation to the case. The immediately
    preceding citation to your current citation is the following: <u>Smith</u>, 54
    P.3d at 723. Which of the following is the correct current citation sen-
    tence?

    A.   <u>Id.</u>

    B.   <u>Id.</u> at 723.

    C.   <u>Smith</u>, 54 P.3d at 723.

    D.   <u>Smith v. Cullen</u>, 54 P.3d 715, 723 (Wash.
          2011).

4. You currently want to cite to page 723 of <u>Smith v. Cullen</u>, 54 P.3d 715 (Wash. 2011). In the same section/issue of your document, the immediately preceding citation to your current citation is the following: <u>Smith v. Cullen</u>, 54 P.3d 715, 724 (Wash. 2011). Which of the following is the correct current citation sentence?

A. <u>Id.</u>

B. <u>Id.</u> at 723.

C. <u>Smith</u>, 54 P.3d at 723.

D. <u>Smith v. Cullen</u>, 54 P.3d 715, 723 (Wash. 2011).

5. You currently want to cite to page 928 of <u>Hemingway v. Black</u>, 43 P.3d 926 (Wash. Ct. App. 2010). Previously in the same section/issue of your document, you set forth the full citation to the case. The immediately preceding citation to your current citation is the following: <u>Id.</u> at 928 (and the "<u>id.</u>" refers to the <u>Hemingway</u> case). Which of the following is the correct current citation sentence?

A. <u>Id.</u>

B. <u>Id.</u> at 928.

C. <u>Hemingway</u>, 43 P.3d at 928.

D. <u>Hemingway v. Black</u>, 43 P.3d 926, 928 (Wash. Ct. App. 2010).

6. You currently want to cite to pages 359 through 361 of <u>Fruth v. Wheeling</u>, 615 A.2d 352 (Pa. 1998). Previously in the same section/issue of your document, you set forth the full citation to the case. The immediately preceding citation to your current citation is the following: <u>Id.</u> at 928 (and the "<u>id.</u>" refers to the <u>Hemingway</u> case). Which of the following is the correct current citation sentence?

A. <u>Id.</u>

B. <u>Id.</u> at 359-61.

C. <u>Fruth</u>, 615 A.2d at 359-61.

D. <u>Fruth v. Wheeling</u>, 615 A.2d 352, 359-61 (Pa. 1998).

7. You currently want to cite the case of Jennifer Dorfmeister v. Elliot Avidan. Previously in the same section/issue of your document, you set forth the full citation to the case. Which of the following is the correct shortened case name for a short citation to the case?

A. <u>Dorfmeister</u>

B. <u>Avidan</u>

C. Either <u>Dorfmeister</u> or <u>Avidan</u>

8. You currently want to cite the case of State of Florida v. George Thomas. Previously in the same section/issue of your document, you set forth the full citation to the case. Which of the following is the correct shortened case name for a short citation to the case?

    A.   <u>State of Florida</u>

    B.   <u>Florida</u>

    C.   <u>State</u>

    D.   <u>Thomas</u>

    E.   Need the name of the court that decided the case to determine the correct shortened case name

9. You currently want to cite to page 6 of <u>Panei v. Perez</u>, 68 A.2d 2 (Pa. Super. Ct. 1996). Previously in the same section/issue of your document, you set forth the full citation to the case with 5 as the pinpoint page. The immediately preceding citation to your current citation is the following: <u>Welch v. Palka</u>, 603 Pa. 152, 154-55 (2009). Provide the correct citation sentence for the current citation (assume that in your corresponding textual sentence, you do not reference the <u>Panei v. Perez</u> case by name):

10. You currently want to cite to pages 1173 through 1174 of <u>United States v. Anderson</u>, 859 F.2d 1171 (3d Cir. 1988). Previously in the same section/issue of your document, you set forth the full citation to the case with 1175 as the pinpoint page. The immediately preceding citation to your current citation is the following: <u>United States v. Castro</u>, 776 F.2d 1118, 1128 (3d Cir. 1985). Provide the correct citation sentence for the current citation (assume that in your corresponding textual sentence, you do not reference the <u>United States v. Anderson</u> case by name):

11. You currently want to cite to page 294 of <u>Blakeman v. Walt Disney Co.</u>, 613 F. Supp. 2d 288 (E.D.N.Y. 2009). Previously in the same section/issue of your document, you set forth the full citation to the case. The immediately preceding citation to your current citation is the following: <u>Blakeman</u>, 613 F. Supp. 2d at 294. Provide the correct citation sentence for the current citation (assume that in your corresponding textual sentence, you do not reference the <u>Blakeman v. Walt Disney Co.</u> case by name):

12. You currently want to cite to page 294 of <u>Blakeman v. Walt Disney Co.</u>, 613 F. Supp. 2d 288 (E.D.N.Y. 2009). Previously in the same section/issue of your document, you set forth the full citation to the case. The immediately preceding citation to your current citation is the following: <u>Id.</u> at 293 (and the "<u>id.</u>" refers to the <u>Blakeman</u> case). Provide the correct citation sentence for the current citation (assume that in your corresponding textual sentence, you do not reference the <u>Blakeman v. Walt Disney Co.</u> case by name):

Chapter 4
Statutes

A. Full Citation

Unless a short citation to a statute is permitted (see Section B below), you should use a full citation. A citation to a statute is "full" when you include all of the information that the reader would want to know about the statute. When possible, you should cite to the official code.[1]

1. Federal Statutes

Federal statutes are organized by title number, with each title representing a particular topic (e.g., Title 18 involves crimes and criminal procedure and Title 35 involves patents). When citing to a particular federal statutory provision(s), the full citation includes the following information (see BP Rule B12.1.1 and Rule 12.3):

- title number;
- abbreviated name of code (found in Table T1.1);
- section symbol (§ or §§, depending on how many sections are cited);
- section number(s), including any relevant subsections; and
- year of the code edition.

For example, the full citation sentence to § 1332 of Title 28 in the 2006 edition of the United States Code would be the following:

```
28 U.S.C. § 1332 (2006).
```

---

[1] This chapter covers citations to codified statutes. For information on citing to session laws, see BP Rule B12.1.1 and Rule 12.4.

TAKE NOTE

When your citation is to all of the relevant sections of a particular act, you should include the name of the act at the beginning of the citation (e.g., Genetic Information Nondiscrimination Act of 2008). See BP Rule B12.1.1 and Rule 12.2.1. This chapter focuses on citations to particular provisions (i.e., sections).

The year in the parenthetical at the end of the citation is the year of the edition of the bound volume of the code, *not* the year the statute was passed, enacted, or amended. You should use the year on the spine of the book, the title page, or the copyright page, in that order of preference See Rule 12.3.2. Additional information may be necessary in this "year of code" parenthetical (see Section A.3 below).

TAKE NOTE

When citing to the Internal Revenue Code (which is located in Title 26 of the United States Code), you may replace "26 U.S.C." with "I.R.C." in the citation (see Rule 12.9.1). Thus, instead of 26 U.S.C. § 2001 (2006), the citation would be the following (assume that it is a citation sentence):

```
I.R.C. § 2001 (2006).
```

2. State Statutes

States have different organizations for their codified statutes. These organizations can be by title (like federal statutes), chapter, volume, or subject matter. Regardless of the type of organization, a full citation to a particular state statutory provision(s) includes the following information (see BP Rule B12.1.2 and Rule 12.3.1):

- abbreviated name of code (found in Table T1.3);
- section symbol (§ or §§, depending on how many sections are cited), if required for the particular state;
- section number(s), including any relevant subsections; and
- year of the code edition.

The full citation also includes the appropriate information regarding the organization of the code. For example, Pennsylvania organizes its statutes by title. A full citation sentence to section 8316 of title 42 in the 2007 edition of the Pennsylvania Consolidated Statutes would be the following:

    42 Pa. Cons. Stat. § 8316 (2007).

As another example, California organizes its statutes by subject matter. A full citation sentence to section 100 of California's Probate Code in the 2008 edition of West's Annotated California Codes would be the following:

    Cal. Prob. Code § 100 (West 2008).

TAKE NOTE

To determine the format and appropriate information (e.g., abbreviation of name of code and any required publisher information) for a full statute citation, you should look up the jurisdiction in Table T1 and review the statutory compilations section for that jurisdiction.

If a jurisdiction's statutory compilation is organized by subject matter, there will also be a listing of subject matter abbreviations to use in the citation. For example, the statutory compilations section in Table T1.3 for California indicates that the following is the general format for a citation to West's Annotated California Codes:

```
CAL. <subject> CODE § x (West <year>)
```

Below this general format are the subject matter abbreviations (e.g., PROB. for Probate).

Notice that "West" is included with the year in the ending parenthetical. West is the publisher of this statutory compilation, and you will at times need to include additional information in this "year of code" parenthetical (see Section A.3 below).

TIP

In the general format and abbreviation in the Take Note above, notice that the LARGE AND SMALL CAPS typeface is used. The examples in Table T1 (and in Rule 12) use this LARGE AND SMALL CAPS typeface. BP Rule B2 indicates that such a typeface is not required (it may be used for stylistic purposes) for the documents that the Bluepages cover (e.g., documents you write in your legal research and writing course and in practice). Prior to the 20th edition of the Bluebook (first published in 2015), this typeface was not permitted for these types of documents, so many current lawyers and judges will not be aware that this typeface is permitted for stylistic purposes. This book will not use the LARGE AND SMALL CAPS typeface for such documents.

Without the LARGE AND SMALL CAPS typeface, the general format above would change to the following:

```
Cal. <subject> Code § x (West <year>)
```

Likewise, the subject matter abbreviation would change from "PROB." to "Prob."

3. Year of Code Parenthetical

The "year of code" parenthetical in a full citation to a statute may include more information than just the year of the edition of the bound volume. First, as you saw in the example citations to state statutes, it may need to include the publisher (see Rule 12.3.1(d)). Table T1 indicates whether the publisher should be included in a citation to a particular statutory compilation. For example, the statutory compilations section of Table T1.1 for the United States jurisdiction indicates that (1) no publisher should be listed when citing to the United States Code (i.e., only the year will be included), (2) "West" should be listed as the publisher when citing to the United States Code Annotated, (3) "Lex-isNexis" should be listed as the publisher when citing to the United

States Code Service, and (4) "Gould" should be listed when citing to Gould's United States Code Unannotated.

TIP

As with case reporters, Table T1 also indicates the preferred statutory compilation to use for citations to statutes. For example, the statutory compilations section for the United States jurisdiction indicates that you should cite to U.S.C. (i.e., United States Code), if therein (i.e., if the statute you are citing is located in the United States Code).

When citing to statutes from the hardbound volumes (not from electronic sources such as WestlawNext, Lexis Advance, or Bloomberg Law), the "year of code" parenthetical will also include an indication if all or part of the statute cited is located in the supplement or pocket part to the main hardbound volume (see Rule 12.3.2).[2] For example, assume that you are citing to section 446.013 in the 2010 edition of Baldwin's Kentucky Revised Statutes Annotated and that this section is located entirely in the 2012 supplement to that edition. The full citation sentence (showing that this section is located only in the 2012 supplement) would be the following:

```
Ky. Rev. Stat. Ann. § 446.013 (West Supp. 2012).
```

As another example, assume that you are citing to section 17B:30-12 in the 2006 edition of the New Jersey Statutes Annotated and that part of that section is located only in the 2010 pocket part to that edition. The

---

[2] The hardbound volumes of statutes, like other authorities that are organized by subject, are often "out of date as soon as they [are] printed" because the law changes often. Amy E. Sloan, Basic Legal Research 15 (5th ed. 2012). Updates to statutes, like other authorities, are not immediately published in new hardbound volumes because of the high cost associated with publishing such volumes. Id. Instead, "softcover pamphlets" are published with the updated information. Id. at 15-16. "These supplementary pamphlets are often called 'pocket parts' because many of them fit into a 'pocket' in the inside back cover of the hardcover book." Id. at 16. If the supplementary pamphlet is too large to fit in the inside back cover, it will be a separate, softcover supplement to the hardbound volume.

full citation sentence (showing that part of the section is located in the main 2006 volume and part in the 2010 pocket part) would be the following:

```
N.J. Stat. Ann. § 17B:30-12 (West 2006 & Supp.
2010).
```

NAVIGATE

Section B.2 in Chapter 11 covers the "year of code" parenthetical when citing to statutes in commercial electronic databases such as WestlawNext, Lexis Advance, or Bloomberg Law.

4. Jurisdiction- or Court-Specific Citation Rules

As you learned in Chapter 1, some jurisdictions have jurisdiction- or court-specific citation rules that take precedence over Bluebook rules. If a jurisdiction has such rules, statutes are often included in them. This chapter covers citations using Bluebook rules, not any jurisdiction- or court-specific rules. Learning Bluebook rules will enable you to understand and apply any jurisdiction- or court-specific rules.

TIP

You can use BP Table BT2 to determine whether a jurisdiction has any specific citation rules and, if so, where to where to find such rules.

B. Short Citation

1. When to Short Cite

According to BP Rule B12.2, after you have provided a full citation to a statute, subsequent citations to the same statute can use a short form of the citation if the following conditions are met:

1. the reader will be able to identify the referenced statute clearly and
2. the full citation to the statute falls in the same general discussion.

TIP

Although BP Rule B12.2 sets forth these conditions for when you *may* use a short citation, in practice, you *should* use a short citation when such conditions are met (i.e., do not use a full citation when a short citation is permitted).

By using the proper short form of the citation (discussed in Section B.2 below), you can ensure that the first condition is met. The second condition essentially involves how far away the short citation is from its corresponding full citation. In the types of documents that an attorney or law clerk write in practice (e.g., a brief, a memo, or an opinion), there is no predefined maximum number of pages that can separate a short and full citation. Generally, a short citation is appropriate if the corresponding full citation is in the same section/issue or sub-section/sub-issue of a document.

For example, assume that you separate the analysis of a particular situation into two distinct issues in a document, each with its own heading. In addition, assume for each issue that you cite § 1332 of Title 28 of the United States Code. Whether you should use a full or short citation to § 1332 depends on the location of the citation. The first time you cite the statute, you need to use a full citation. Subsequent citations to that statute within your analysis of the first issue should use a short citation.[3] In your analysis of the second issue, you should use a full citation to the statute again the first time you cite it in that issue.

TAKE NOTE

Even if your analysis of a particular issue is relatively short, you should still consider using a full citation again when addressing a distinct issue because the reader, at times, may read just one issue of your document or read the issues in a different order than you presented them. Therefore, the reader will be able to locate the corresponding full citation easily if it is in your analysis of that issue.

2. How to Short Cite

After determining that a short citation is appropriate for your current statute citation, you need to determine what form the short citation should take. Your answers to the following questions will determine the appropriate short form for your current statute citation (see BP Rule B4, BP Rule B12.2, Rule 4.1, and Rule 12.10):

1. Does the immediately preceding citation in the document cite only one authority?

2. Is the immediately preceding citation in the document a citation (full or short) to the same authority as your current citation (i.e., is it to the same statute as your current statute citation)?

---

[3] An exception to this general rule requiring a short citation for subsequent citations to the same statute throughout an entire section/issue would occur if that one section/issue in your document is particularly long and the reader will have a difficult time locating the corresponding full citation (i.e., if the second condition is not met). For the documents you will write for your legal research and writing class, each section/issue will likely be short enough that you can use a short citation for subsequent citations to the same statute throughout an entire section/issue of your paper.

For question #1, the immediately preceding citation can include multiple authorities if it is a string citation.

NAVIGATE

Chapter 13 covers string citations.

A citation to a statute may list another authority in an explanatory parenthetical, but an authority cited (or referred) to in parentheticals does not count as separate authority when answering question #1.

NAVIGATE

Chapter 10 covers the different types of parentheticals.

For question #2, you would consider a statute within the same title or subject matter as the "same authority" (see BP Rule B12.2). For example, if you currently want to cite § 1332 of Title 28 of the United States Code, you would answer "yes" to question #2 if the immediately preceding citation in the document is a citation to any section of Title 28 of the United States Code.

You may still answer "yes" to question #2 in jurisdictions that do not organize their statutes by title number. For example, if you currently want to cite section 51 of New York's Civil Rights Law, you would answer "yes" to question #2 if the immediately preceding citation in the document is a citation to any section of New York's Civil Rights Law.

If you answer "yes" to both question #1 and question #2, you should use the appropriate "id." form for your current citation (see Section B.2.a below). If you answer "no" to either question, you cannot use any "id." form; you must use another short form, which is an abbreviated version of the full citation (see Section B.2.b below).

For example, assume that your current citation is to § 1332 of Title 28 of the United States Code and you have already determined that a short citation is appropriate for the current citation. If the immediately preceding citation in your document contains only one authority and that one authority is any section of Title 28 of the United States Code, you should use the appropriate "id." form. Otherwise, you need to use another short form for the statute.

a. *Id.*

If you have determined that you should use an "id." form for your short citation to a statute, you then need to decide whether to use "id." alone or whether you need to use the "id. § X" form (where "X" is the pinpoint information)—see BP Rule B12.2, Rule 4.1, and Rule 12.10.

TAKE NOTE

If your pinpoint information is to more than one section, the "id. § X" form would become "id. §§ X" (where "X" is the pinpoint information).

Two section symbols (§§) should always be used when citing to multiple sections, regardless of whether the citation is a full or short citation (see Rule 3.3(b)).

"Id." alone refers not only to the statute in the immediately preceding citation, but it also refers to the same pinpoint information (i.e., the same section(s) and any sub-section(s)) as in the immediately preceding citation. If your current citation does not use the same pinpoint information as the immediately preceding citation, you need to use the "id. § X" form.

WARNING

You may have used "ibid." in other writing, but "ibid." is not a proper substitute for "id." under Bluebook rules.

For example, assume that the immediately preceding citation is to § 1332(a) of Title 28 of the United States Code and that statute is the only authority cited in the immediately preceding citation. If your current citation is to § 1332(a) of Title 28 of the United States Code, the short citation sentence for it would be the following:

    Id.

TAKE NOTE

According to BP Rule B10.2, the period in "id." is always underlined (or italicized if you are using italics instead of underlining), and the "i" in "id." should be capitalized only when the "id." is the start of a citation sentence. If a sentence (textual or citation) ends with "id.," the period in "id." also represents the period to end the sentence (i.e., do not add a second period after "id."):

    Id..   ✗ incorrect punctuation to end sentence
    Id.   ✓ correct punctuation to end sentence

Again, assume that the immediately preceding citation is to § 1332(a) of Title 28 of the United States Code and that statute is the only authority cited in the immediately preceding citation. If your current citation is to § 1332(b) of Title 28 of the United States Code, the short citation sentence for it would be the following:

    Id. § 1332(b).

TAKE NOTE

Notice that you do not use an "at" before a section symbol (see BP Rule B12.2 and Rule 3.3).

Again, assume that the immediately preceding citation is to § 1332(a) of Title 28 of the United States Code and that statute is the only authority cited in the immediately preceding citation. If your current citation is to § 1331, the short citation sentence for it would be the following:

    Id. § 1331.

TAKE NOTE

All of the examples above use "id." at the beginning of a citation sentence; therefore, the "i" in "id." is capitalized. If "id." does not begin a citation sentence (e.g., when used in a citation clause), the "i" in "id." would not be capitalized.

---

b. Other Short Forms

If an "id." form cannot be used (either because the immediately preceding citation cites to more than one authority or it is not a citation to the same authority as the current citation), you need to use another short form—an abbreviated version of the full citation. Various short forms are acceptable, and they generally do not include the "year of code" parenthetical at the end of the citation.

For example, the following are acceptable short forms for the full citation to 28 U.S.C. § 1331 (2006):

    § 1331.
        or

    28 U.S.C. § 1331.

You can use such short forms even if the pinpoint information is different than the full citation. For example, the following would also be acceptable short forms given the previous full citation to 28 U.S.C. § 1331 (2006):

    § 1332(a).
        or

    28 U.S.C. § 1332(a).

You should review the table in Rule 12.10(b) to see other examples of short forms, including short forms for state statutes.

TIP

In choosing which short form to use, you should consider which one would allow the reader to identify the authority clearly.

For example, if you refer to only one title of the United States Code (e.g., Title 28) in a particular paragraph, section, or issue in your document, you can use the short form that does not include the title (e.g., § 1331) in that paragraph, section, or issue.

If, however, you refer to multiple titles (e.g., Titles 28 and 42) in a particular paragraph, section, or issue in your document, you should use the short form that includes the title (e.g., 28 U.S.C. § 1331) in that paragraph, section, or issue.

C. Pinpoint Information

When citing to a statute, you should provide as much pinpoint information as possible. For example, if the information you are citing comes from subsection (c)(1)(A) of § 1332, your citation sentence would be the following (assume that a short citation is appropriate):

    § 1332(c)(1)(A).

In the example above, there are no spaces between the parentheses of the subsections. If you cite to more than one *section*, you need to use two section symbols (§§). Do not, however, use two section symbols if you are citing to more than one *subsection* of the same section (e.g., § 1332(a), (c)). Rule 3.3 provides detailed information regarding pinpoint information with sections and subsections.

NAVIGATE

Section D of Chapter 15 covers pinpoint information with sections in more detail.

TIP

As you can see in all of the examples in this chapter, you should always use a space between a section symbol (§) and the corresponding number. See Rule 6.2(c).

With this space, a section symbol could be at the end of one line in your document and the section number(s) at the beginning of the next line. To avoid this awkward split, you can use a non-breaking space between the section symbol and the number(s).

Your word processor should allow you to add non-breaking spaces. For example, in Microsoft Word, a non-breaking space is a symbol, and you can find it in the "Special Characters" section when choosing to insert a symbol, or you can press Ctrl+Shift+Space (PC) or Option+Space (Mac) to insert a non-breaking space.

D. Statute References in Textual Sentences

When referring to statutes in a textual sentence (i.e., not a citation), you may use the section symbol (§) only when referring to a codified federal statute (i.e., a statute in the United States Code). For state statutes, you need to spell out the word "section" in textual sentences. See Rule 12.10(b), (c). Regardless of a statute's jurisdiction, you must spell out the word "section" if it is the first word of the sentence (see Rule 6.2(c)). The table in Rule 12.10(b) contains examples of referring to statutes in textual sentences.

E. Common Rules & Tables

The following table provides the common Bluebook rules and tables for full and short statute citations.

Rule or Table	Description
BP Rule B12.1.1	Federal Statutes: Full Citations
BP Rule B12.1.2	State Statutes: Full Citations
BP Rule B12.2	Statutes: Short Citations
Rule 3.3	Sections (for pinpoint information)
Rule 4.1	<u>Id.</u>
Rule 6.2(c)	Section (§) Symbol
Rule 12.1-12.3	Statutes: Full Citations
Rule 12.10	Statutes: Short Citations
Table T1	Jurisdictions (statutory compilations)

F. Exercise

Along with using the information in this chapter, you should use your Bluebook when answering these questions (note: do not use any juris-diction- or court-specific citation rules, which are covered in Section C of Chapter 1 and are set forth in BP Table BT2). Some questions may require you to find and apply rules that were not specifically discussed in this chapter.

For all answers, use only ordinary or <u>underlined</u> typeface. That is, do not use *italics* or Large and Small Caps typeface.

As with some of the examples in this chapter, some of the legal authority used in these questions may be fictional authority designed to test vari-ous Bluebook rules.

1. Which of the following is the correct full citation sentence to § 1983
    of Title 42 in the 2006 edition of the United States Code?

    A.   42 U.S.C. § 1983 (2006).

    B.   42 U.S.C. §1983 (2006).

    C.   42 U.S.C. 1983 (2006).

2. Which of the following is the correct full citation sentence to section
    3-419 of Maryland's Labor and Employment Law in the 2008 edition
    of Michie's Annotated Code of Maryland?

    A.   Md. Code Ann. § 3-419 (LexisNexis 2008).

    B.   Md. Code Ann. § 3-419 (West 2008).

    C.   Md. Code Ann. Lab. & Empl. § 3-419
          (LexisNexis 2008).

    D.   Md. Code Ann. Lab. & Empl. § 3-419 (West
          2008).

    E.   Md. Code Ann., Lab. & Empl. § 3-419
          (LexisNexis 2008).

    F.   Md. Code Ann., Lab. & Empl. § 3-419 (West
          2008).

3. Which of the following is the correct full citation sentence to section
    101 of Title 8 in the 2010 edition of the Delaware Code Annotated
    (LexisNexis)?

    A.   8 Del. Code Ann. § 101 (2010).

    B.   8 Del. Code Ann. § 101 (LexisNexis 2010).

    C.   Del. Code Ann. tit. 8, § 101 (2010).

    D.   Del. Code Ann. tit. 8, § 101 (LexisNexis
          2010).

4. Which of the following is the correct "year of code" parenthetical for a citation to § 22:1604 of West's Louisiana Statutes Annotated if part of the section you are citing is contained in the 2010 main volume and part is contained in the 2012 pocket part?

    A.   (2010)

    B.   (LexisNexis 2010)

    C.   (Supp. 2012)

    D.   (LexisNexis Supp. 2012)

    E.   (2010 & Supp. 2012)

    F.   (LexisNexis 2010 & Supp. 2012)

5. Which of the following is the correct "year of code" parenthetical for a citation to § 375.1306(3) of Vernon's Annotated Missouri Statutes if all of the subsection you are citing is contained in the 2008 supplement to the 2006 main volume?

    A.   (2006)

    B.   (West 2006)

    C.   (Supp. 2008)

    D.   (West Supp. 2008)

    E.   (2006 & Supp. 2008)

    F.   (West 2006 & Supp. 2008)

6. You currently want to cite section 8316 of title 42 of Pennsylvania
    Consolidated Statutes. Previously in the same section of your docu-
    ment, you set forth the full citation to section 8316 of title 42 in the
    2007 edition of Pennsylvania Consolidated Statutes. The immedi-
    ately preceding citation to your current citation is the following: 42
    Pa. Cons. Stat. § 8315. Which of the following is the correct current
    citation sentence?

    A. Id.

    B. Id. § 8316.

    C. Id. at § 8316.

    D. 42 Pa. Cons. Stat. § 8316.

    E. 42 Pa. Cons. Stat. § 8316 (2007).

    F. 42 Pa. Cons. Stat. § 8316 (West 2007).

7. You currently want to cite § 1332(a) of Title 28 of the United States
    Code. Previously in the same section of your document, you set
    forth the full citation to § 1331 of Title 28 in the 2006 edition of the
    United States Code, and you have not cited to any other statutes in
    this section of your document. The immediately preceding citation
    to your current citation is a citation to a case. Which of the following
    is the correct current citation sentence?

    A. Id.

    B. Id. § 1332(a).

    C. Id. at § 1332(a).

    D. 28 U.S.C. § 1332(a).

    E. 28 U.S.C. § 1332(a) (2006).

    F. § 1332(a).

    G. § 1332(a) (2006).

8. Provide the full citation sentence to section 21.402(a) of Texas's Labor Law in the 2010 edition of Vernon's Texas Codes Annotated:

9. Provide the full citation sentence to § 101 and § 103 of Title 35 in the 2012 edition of the United States Code:

10. Provide the full citation sentence to section 3A of chapter 214 in the 2010 edition of the General Laws of Massachusetts:

Chapter 5
Other Primary Authority

A. Introduction

Along with cases and statutes, you may also cite other primary authority (i.e., the law). Constitutions, rules, and administrative regulations are the most common other primary authorities you may cite.

As you learned in Chapter 1, some jurisdictions have jurisdiction- or court-specific citation rules that take precedence over Bluebook rules. If a jurisdiction has such rules, these other primary authorities are often included in them. This chapter covers citations using Bluebook rules, not any jurisdiction- or court-specific rules. Learning Bluebook rules will enable you to understand and apply any jurisdiction- or court-specific rules.

TIP

You can use BP Table BT2 to determine whether a jurisdiction has any specific citation rules and, if so, where to where to find such rules.

B. Constitutions

1. Full Citation

Unless a short citation to a constitution is permitted (see Section B.2 below), you should use a full citation. A full citation to a constitution includes the following information (see BP Rule B11 and Rule 11):

- abbreviation of the jurisdiction of the constitution cited;
- the abbreviation "Const."; and
- abbreviation of the cited subdivision(s) of the constitution.

For the abbreviation of the jurisdiction of the constitution cited, use "U.S." for the United States constitution or the abbreviation for the state in Table T10 for a state's constitution. For the abbreviation of the cited subdivision(s), use the abbreviations in Table T16.

For example, if you are citing to Article III, Section 1 of the United States Constitution, the full citation sentence would be the following:

    U.S. Const. art. III, § 1.

In the example above, the subdivision is abbreviated as "art." according to Table T16, and a section symbol (§) is used instead of an abbreviation of the word (see BP Rule B11 and Rule 11).

TAKE NOTE

Notice from the previous example that you use a comma to separate different subdivisions.

If you are citing to article I, section 8 of the Pennsylvania Constitution, the full citation sentence would be the following:

    Pa. Const. art. I, § 8.

In the example above, the jurisdiction (Pennsylvania) is abbreviated according to Table T10. As with the previous example, the subdivision is abbreviated according to Table T16, and a section symbol (§) is used.

NAVIGATE

Notice in the two examples above that the subdivision abbreviation in a citation is in lower case, regardless of whether the subdivision is capitalized in a textual sentence (e.g., "Article" for U.S. Constitution versus "article" for a state constitution in a textual sentence).

Chapter 16 covers the capitalization rules for textual sentences in more detail.

As the examples above illustrate, citations to constitutional provisions currently in force should not include a date (see Rule 11). For the "non-academic legal documents" you will write in your legal research and writing (LRW) courses and in practice (e.g., a brief, a memo, or an opinion), you will generally cite only constitutional provisions currently in force. If you cite a constitutional provision that has been repealed or subsequently amended, the citation should include such an indication, including the date (see Rule 11). For example:

```
U.S. Const. art. I, § 9, cl. 4 (amended 1913).
```

   or

```
U.S. Const. art. I, § 9, cl. 4, amended by
U.S. Const. amend. XVI.
```

Notice in the examples above that there is another level of subdivision—a clause within the section of the article. As when citing to other authorities, you should always include as much pinpoint detail as possible to enable the reader to find the information you are citing.

TAKE NOTE

You will notice in Rule 11 that the abbreviation "Const." is in the LARGE AND SMALL CAPS typeface. BP Rule B2 indicates that such a typeface is not required (it may be used for stylistic purposes) for the documents that the Bluepages cover (e.g., documents you write in your legal research and writing course and in practice). Prior to the 20th edition of the Bluebook (first published in 2015), this typeface was not permitted for these types of documents, so many current lawyers and judges will not be aware that this typeface is permitted for stylistic purposes. This book will not use the LARGE AND SMALL CAPS typeface for such documents.

2. Short Citation

Unlike with citations to some other types of authorities (e.g., cases and statutes), an abbreviated version of the full citation to a constitution does not exist. The only permitted short form for a citation to a constitution is an "id." short form (see BP Rule B11, Rule 4.1, and Rule 11). You may use an "id." short form if (1) the immediately preceding citation in the document cites to only one authority and (2) the immediately preceding citation in the document is a citation to the same authority—i.e., the same constitution (see BP Rule B4 and Rule 4.1). If either of these conditions is not met, you should use a full citation to the constitution.

C. Rules

1. Full Citation

Unless a short citation to a rule is permitted (see Section C.2 below), you should use a full citation. According to BP Rule B12.1.3 and Rule 12.9.3, full citations to rules (such as rules of procedure and evidence and court rules) use abbreviations for the title of the rules. You may find these abbreviations in a number of sources.

First, such abbreviations may be found in the rules themselves. For example, Rule 1 of the local rules of the United States Court of Appeals for the Sixth Circuit indicates that such rules should be cited as the following (note: the underlined spaces represent where you would indicate the rule number(s)):

```
6 Cir. R. ___ .
```

Second, such abbreviations may be found in jurisdiction- or court-specific citation rules. For example, Rule 9.800 of the Florida Rules of Appellate Procedure indicates that the Florida Rules of Procedure for Workers' Compensation should be abbreviated as the following (note: the underlined spaces represent where you would indicate the rule number(s)):

```
Fla. R. Work. Comp. P ___ .
```

Finally, if you cannot find an abbreviation in the first two sources, you should use the examples in the Bluebook. For example, the following are example citations to federal rules of procedure and evidence (see BP Rule B12.1.3 and Rule 12.9.3):

	Example Full Citation Sentence
Federal Rules of Civil Procedure:	Fed. R. Civ. P. 15(a).
Federal Rules of Criminal Procedure:	Fed. R. Crim. P. 11(a).
Federal Rules of Evidence:	Fed. R. Evid. 403.
Federal Rules of Appellate Procedure:	Fed. R. App. P. 26(a).

TAKE NOTE

You will notice that the example citations to rules in Rule 12.9.3 use the LARGE AND SMALL CAPS typeface. BP Rule B2 indicates that such a typeface is not required (it may be used for stylistic purposes) for the documents that the Bluepages cover (e.g., documents you write in your legal research and writing course and in practice). Prior to the 20th edition of the Bluebook (first published in 2015), this typeface was not permitted for these types of documents, so many current lawyers and judges will not be aware that this typeface is permitted for stylistic purposes. This book will not use the LARGE AND SMALL CAPS typeface for such documents.

For a state's rules of procedure and evidence, you should follow the same abbreviations as for the federal rules above and abbreviate the state according to Table T10, unless the state's rules or jurisdiction- or court-specific citation rules suggest otherwise (see Rule 12.9.3).

Citations to rules currently in force should not include a date, unless the state's rules or jurisdiction- or court-specific citation rules require it. If you cite a rule that has been repealed or subsequently amended, the citation should include such an indication, including the date (see Rule 12.9.3).

2. Short Citation

Like with citations to constitutions (see Section B.2 above), an abbreviated version of the full citation to a rule does not exist. The only permitted short form for a citation to a rule is an "id." short form (see Rule 4.1). You may use an "id." short form if (1) the immediately preceding citation in the document cites to only one authority and (2) the immediately preceding citation in the document is a citation to the same authority — i.e., the same rule (see BP Rule B4 and Rule 4.1). If either of these conditions is not met, you should use a full citation to the rule.

D. Administrative Regulations

1. Full Citation

Unless a short citation to an administrative regulation is permitted (see Section D.2 below), you should use a full citation. A basic full citation to a federal administrative regulation in the Code of Federal Regulations[1] includes the following information (see BP Rule B14 and Rule 14.2):

- title number;
- abbreviation "C.F.R.";
- section symbol (§) followed by a space;
- specific section(s) cited; and
- year of the most recent edition of the code cited.

For example, the following is a full citation sentence to section 900.12 of title 21 of the 2014 edition of the Code of Federal Regulations:

```
21 C.F.R. § 900.12 (2014).
```

You should include the name of a regulation in the full citation if the regulation is commonly referred to by its name. For example:

```
FCC Broadcast Radio Services, 47 C.F.R.
§ 73.609 (2014).
```

 TAKE NOTE

The "FCC" in the citation above represents the issuing agency. Rule 14.2 indicates that you may include the abbreviated name of the issuing agency, if such inclusion is helpful.

---

[1] Final federal administrative regulations are codified in the Code of Federal Regulations. Amy E. Sloan, <u>Basic Legal Research</u> 248 (5th ed. 2012). Prior to being codified, such regulations are published in the Federal Register, which is a daily publication of regulations, proposed regulations, and other activities of the executive branch. <u>Id.</u> For information on citing to regulations in the Federal Register, see Rule 14.2.

For a state's administrative regulations, the introduction to Rule 14 indicates that you should cite such materials "by analogy to the federal examples in this rule."

TIP

For a particular jurisdiction (e.g., a state), Table T1 lists the administrative compilation and register for that jurisdiction, along with the general citation format that you should use absent a jurisdiction- or court-specific citation rule.

2. Short Citation

According to Rule 14.5, after you have provided a full citation to an administrative regulation, you should use a short form of the citation if the regulation is already cited in the same general discussion.

TAKE NOTE

In the types of documents that an attorney or law clerk would write in practice (e.g., a brief, a memo, or an opinion), there is no predefined maximum number of pages that qualifies as the "same general discussion." Generally, a short citation is appropriate if the corresponding full citation is in the same section/issue or sub-section/sub-issue of a document.

Even if your analysis of a particular issue is relatively short, you should still consider using a full citation again when addressing a distinct issue because the reader, at times, may read just one issue of your document or read the issues in a different order than you presented them. Therefore, the reader will be able to locate the corresponding full citation easily if it is in your analysis of that issue.

If a short form is appropriate, you need to determine whether to use an "<u>id.</u>" short form or an abbreviated version of the full citation. You should use an "<u>id.</u>" short form if (1) the immediately preceding citation in the document cites to only one authority and (2) the immediately preceding citation in the document is a citation to the same authority — i.e., the same regulation (see BP Rule B4 and Rule 4.1). Otherwise, the short form should be an abbreviated version of the full citation (see Rule 14.5). For example, the following are acceptable short forms for the full citation to 21 C.F.R. § 900.12 (2014):

§ 900.12.
   <u>or</u>

21 C.F.R. § 900.12.

Such short forms can be used even if the pinpoint information is different from the full citation. For example, the following would also be acceptable short forms given the previous full citation to 21 C.F.R. § 900.12 (2014):

§ 900.13(a).
   <u>or</u>

21 C.F.R. § 900.13(a).

TIP

In choosing which short form to use, you should consider which one would allow the reader to identify the authority clearly. For example, if you refer to only one title of the Code of Federal Regulations (e.g., Title 21) in a particular paragraph, section, or issue in your document, you can use the short form that does not include the title (e.g., § 900.12) in that paragraph, section, or issue. If, however, you refer to multiple titles (e.g., Titles 21 and 42) in a particular paragraph, section, or issue in your document, you should use the short form that includes the title (e.g., 21 C.F.R. § 900.12) in that paragraph, section, or issue.

E. Common Rules & Tables

The following table provides the common Bluebook rules and tables for full and short citations to constitutions, rules, and administrative regulations.

Rule or Table	Description
BP Rule B4	<u>Id.</u>
BP Rule B11	Constitutions
BP Rule B12.1.3	Rules
BP Rule B14	Administrative Regulations: Full Citations
Rule 4.1	<u>Id.</u>
Rule 11	Constitutions
Rule 12.9.3	Rules
Rule 14.2	Administrative Regulations: Full Citations
Rule 14.5	Administrative Regulations: Short Citations
Table T1	Jurisdictions (administrative compilation & register)
Table T10	Geographic Abbreviations
Table T16	Subdivision Abbreviations (for parts of constitution)

F. Exercise

Along with using the information in this chapter, you should use your Bluebook when answering these questions (note: do not use any jurisdiction- or court-specific citation rules, which are covered in Section C of Chapter 1 and are set forth in BP Table BT2). Some questions may require you to find and apply rules that were not specifically discussed in this chapter.

For all answers, use only ordinary or <u>underlined</u> typeface. That is, do not use *italics* or LARGE AND SMALL CAPS typeface.

As with some of the examples in this chapter, some of the legal authority used in these questions may be fictional authority designed to test various Bluebook rules.

1. Which of the following is the correct full citation sentence to Section 1 of the Fifteenth Amendment to the United States Constitution?

    A.   U.S. Const. amend. XV § 1.

    B.   U.S. Const. Amend. XV § 1.

    C.   U.S. Const. amend. XV, § 1.

    D.   U.S. Const. Amend. XV, § 1.

    E.   U.S. Const. amend. XV sec. 1.

    F.   U.S. Const. Amend. XV Sec. 1.

    G.   U.S. Const. amend. XV, sec. 1.

    H.   U.S. Const. Amend. XV, Sec. 1.

2. You currently want to cite the First Amendment of the United States Constitution. Previously in the same section of your document, you set forth the full citation to this Amendment. The immediately preceding citation to your current citation is a citation to a case. Which of the following is the correct current citation sentence?

    A.   <u>Id.</u>

    B.   Amend. I.

    C.   amend. I.

    D.   U.S. Const. amend. I.

    E.   U.S. Const. Amend. I.

3. Which of the following is the correct full citation sentence to Rule 56(a) of the Federal Rules of Civil Procedure?

   A.   Fed. R. Civ. P. 56(a).

   B.   Fed. R. Civ. P. R. 56(a).

   C.   Fed. R. Civ. P. Rule 56(a).

   D.   A or B.

   E.   A, B, or C.

4. Which of the following is the correct full citation sentence to Rule 24 of the Rules of the United States Supreme Court?

   A.   Sup. Ct. 24.

   B.   Sup. Ct. R. 24.

   C.   Sup. Ct. Rule 24.

   D.   A or B.

   E.   A, B, or C.

5. Which of the following is the correct full citation sentence to section 1604.3 of title 29 of the 2014 edition of the Code of Federal Regulations?

   A.   C.F.R. § 29-1604.3.

   B.   C.F.R. § 29-1604.3 (2014).

   C.   29 C.F.R. § 1604.3.

   D.   29 C.F.R. § 1604.3 (2014).

6. You currently want to cite section 1604.4 of title 29 of the 2014 edition of the Code of Federal Regulations. The immediately preceding citation to your current citation is a citation to section 1604.3 of title 29 of the 2014 edition of the Code of Federal Regulations. Which of the following is the correct current citation sentence?

   A.   Id.

   B.   Id. at § 1604.4.

   C.   Id. § 1604.4.

   D.   § 29-1604.4.

   E.   § 1604.4.

7. Provide the full citation sentence to the Fifth and Eighth Amendments to the United States Constitution:

8. Provide the full citation sentence to Rule 801(c) of the Pennsylvania Rules of Evidence (assume that the Pennsylvania Rules of Evidence do not contain a rule indicating how to cite them, nor are there any jurisdiction- or court-specific rules):

9. Provide the full citation sentence to rule 4604.0430 of the 2013 version of the Minnesota Rules, which contains Minnesota's administrative regulations.

Chapter 6
Court & Litigation Documents

A. Introduction

For a particular case, the parties generally submit many documents in court (i.e., court and litigation documents).[1] For example, a plaintiff initiates a lawsuit by filing a complaint. The defendant would then file an appropriate response (e.g., an answer or a motion to dismiss). After discovery, a party may file a motion for summary judgment with accompanying evidence (e.g., an affidavit, deposition transcript, admissions, and documents produced by the opposing party). When using information in such documents, you must cite the documents.

TAKE NOTE

This chapter covers how to cite court and litigation documents from your current case, not from another case. For example, assume you represent the plaintiff in Prior v. Matthews and you file a brief in support of a motion for summary judgment. In that brief, you cite a deposition transcript that you also filed in that case (i.e., the current case of Prior v. Matthews), and you cite a document from another case (e.g., a document from Eaton v. Eaton).

BP Rule B17 covers how to cite the deposition transcript from the current case; Rule 10.8.3 covers how to cite the document from another case. This chapter focuses on the former because you will commonly cite documents from your current case (e.g., when citing facts in a Statement of Facts section); you will not often cite documents from another case.

---

[1] If an attorney represents a party, the attorney files such documents.

B. Full Citation

The first time you cite a particular court and litigation document from the current case, you should use a full citation. A citation is "full" when you include all of the information that the reader would want to know about the document.

The basic information that is included in a full citation to a court and litigation document is the following (see BP Rule B17.1):

- document name/title and
- pinpoint information.

Information that may be required for a full citation is the following (see BP Rule B17.1):

- date and
- electronic case filing (ECF) number.

The following are example full citation sentences:

```
Compl. ¶ 13.
Answer ¶ 13.
Eaton Dep. 20:11-14.
Black Aff. ¶ 7.
R. at 22.
```

TAKE NOTE

Note that the period at the end of each of the example citations above is not part of the actual citation; it is the end of the citation sentence.

TIP

As you can see in the examples above, for the court and litigation documents that are organized by paragraphs (e.g., complaint, answer, and affidavit), you should always use a space between a paragraph symbol (¶) and the corresponding number. See Rule 6.2(c).

With this space, a paragraph symbol could be at the end of one line in your document and the paragraph number(s) at the beginning of the next line. To avoid this awkward split, you can use a non-breaking space between the paragraph symbol and the number(s).

Your word processor should allow you to add non-breaking spaces. For example, in Microsoft Word, a non-breaking space is a symbol, and you can find it in the "Special Characters" section when choosing to insert a symbol, or you can press Ctrl+Shift+Space (PC) or Option+Space (Mac) to insert a non-breaking space.

1. Document Name/Title

In the example citations above, the name/title of the document is often abbreviated—"Compl." for Complaint, "Dep." for Deposition, "Aff." for Affidavit, and "R." for Record. You should use abbreviations from BP Table BT1, unless doing so in a particular citation would confuse the reader (see BP Rule B17.1.1).

For example, BP Table BT1 indicates that you should abbreviate "Petitioner's" as "Pet'r's" and "Brief" as "Br." Therefore, if you cite a document titled "Petitioner's Brief," you should abbreviate it as "Pet'r's Br."

TIP

Not only does BP Table BT1 include abbreviations for common words in court and litigation documents, but it also contains words that should not be abbreviated. For example, BP Table BT1 indicates that the abbreviation for "Answer" is "Answer" (i.e., do not abbreviate the word in a citation to this court and litigation document).

BP Table BT1 also indicates that you may abbreviate other words that are seven or more letters, "so long as the abbreviation is unambiguous."

2. Pinpoint Information

As with all citations, you should include as much pinpoint information as possible. Unlike with citations to other types of authority, when citing to a page(s) in a court and litigation document, you generally do not precede the page number(s) with "at" (see BP Rule B17.1.2). For example, if the information you are citing comes from page 8 of a document titled "Petitioner's Brief," your full citation sentence would be the following:

```
Pet'r's Br. 8.
```

You should, however, precede the page number(s) with "at" in references to an appellate record — often titled "Record" or "Joint Appendix" (see BP Rule B17.1.2). For example:

```
R. at 5-6.
J.A. at 11.
```

Although you should not use "p." before page numbers, other types of pinpoint information should be identified (see BP Rule B17.1.2). For example, if the information you are citing comes from page 2 of Exhibit A to Susan Black's affidavit, your full citation sentence would be the following:

```
Black Aff. Ex. A, at 2.
```

TAKE NOTE

Notice that the example above is another instance where "at" precedes the page number(s).

When citing to documents that are organized by paragraphs using the paragraph symbol (¶), use a single paragraph symbol (¶) to introduce one paragraph and two paragraph symbols (¶¶) to introduce multiple paragraphs. As with the section symbol (§), an "at" should not precede a paragraph symbol (see Rule 3.3). For example:

```
Answer ¶ 13.
Answer ¶¶ 13-14.
Answer ¶¶ 13, 15.
```

Rule 3.3 provides detailed information regarding pinpoint information with paragraphs.

NAVIGATE

Chapter 15 covers pinpoint information in more detail.

When citing to a transcript (e.g., deposition, trial, or hearing), provide as much detail as possible. If the transcript contains line numbers on each page, use a colon to separate references to page and line numbers (see BP Rule B17.1.2). For example, if the information you are citing comes from lines 14 through 16 on page 7 of Thomas Eaton's deposition transcript, your full citation sentence would be the following:

```
Eaton Dep. 7:14-16.
```

As another example, if the information you are citing comes from line 28 on page 7 through line 4 on page 8 of Thomas Eaton's deposition transcript, your full citation sentence would be the following:

```
Eaton Dep. 7:28-8:4.
```

3. Date

Generally, you do not include the date of a document in a citation to it. In certain circumstances, however, you should include the date. BP Rule B17.1.3 indicates that you should include the date when one of the following is true:

- more than one document has the same name/title;
- the date is relevant; or
- the date is needed to avoid confusion.

For example, assume that Thomas Eaton was deposed over the course of two days—October 23 and 24, 2013. If the information you are citing comes from lines 14 through 16 on page 7 of the first day of his deposition, your full citation sentence would be the following:

```
Eaton Dep. 7:14-16, Oct. 23, 2013.
```

TIP

The example above uses the abbreviation for October. Table T12 contains the abbreviation for each month.

4. Electronic Case Filing (ECF) Number

Documents filed with an electronic case management system (e.g., PACER for federal cases) are assigned document numbers. Such numbers—the electronic case filing (ECF) numbers—should be included at the end of citations to these documents. For example:

```
Compl. ¶ 13, ECF No. 1.
Eaton Dep. 7:14-16, Oct. 23, 2013, ECF No. 35.
```

C. Short Citation

1. When to Short Cite

According to BP Rule B17.2, after you have provided a full citation to a particular court and litigation document, subsequent citations to the same document can use a short form of the citation if the following conditions are met:

1. the reader will be able to identify the referenced document clearly;
2. the full citation to the document falls in the same general discussion; and
3. the reader will be able to locate the full citation to the document easily.

By using the proper short form of the citation (discussed in Section C.2 below), you can ensure that the first condition is met. The latter two conditions are similar and essentially involve how far away the short citation is from its corresponding full citation. In the types of documents that an attorney or law clerk write in practice (e.g., a brief, a memo, or an opinion), there is no predefined maximum number of pages that can separate a short and full citation. Generally, a short citation is appropriate if the corresponding full citation is in the same section/issue or the same sub-section/sub-issue of a document.

For example, assume that you separate the analysis of a particular situation into two distinct issues in a document, each with its own heading. In addition, assume for each issue that you cite a particular court and litigation document. Whether you should use a full or short citation to that document depends on the location of the citation. The first time you cite the document in your analysis of the first issue, you need to use a full citation. Subsequent citations to that document within your analysis of the first issue should use a short citation.[2] In your analysis of the second issue, you should use a full citation to the document again the first time you cite it in that issue.

TAKE NOTE

Even if your analysis of a particular issue is relatively short, you should still consider using a full citation again when addressing a distinct issue because the reader, at times, may read just one issue of your document or read the issues in a different order than you presented them. Therefore, the reader will be able to locate the corresponding full citation easily only if it is in your analysis of that issue.

2. How to Short Cite

After determining that a short citation is appropriate for your current citation, you need to determine what form the short citation should take. Generally, your answers to the following questions will determine the appropriate short form for your current citation (see BP Rule B4, BP Rule B17.2, and Rule 4.1):

1. Does the immediately preceding citation cite only one authority?[3]

2. Is the immediately preceding citation a citation (full or short) to the same authority as your current citation (i.e., is

---

[2] An exception to this general rule requiring a short citation for subsequent citations to the same case throughout an entire section/issue would occur if that one section/issue in your document is particularly long and the reader will have a difficult time locating the corresponding full citation (i.e., if the third condition is not met). For the documents you will write for your legal research and writing class, each section/issue will likely be short enough that you can use a short citation for subsequent citations to the same case throughout an entire section/issue of your paper.

[3] The immediately preceding citation can include multiple authorities if it is a string citation. Chapter 13 covers string citations. Likewise, a citation may list another authority in an explanatory parenthetical. Chapter 10 covers this additional information, but such an addition to a citation does *not* count as a separate authority for this question.

it to the same court and litigation document as your current citation)?

If you answer "yes" to both questions, you may use the appropriate "id." form for your current citation "only . . . if significant space will be saved" (see BP Rule B17.2). In other words, you do not always use an "id." form for court and litigation documents, even if you answer "yes" to both questions. For example:

Immediately Preceding Citation	Current Citation to Same Document
Pet'r's Br. 8-10.	Id. at 7.
R. at 34.	R. at 35.

TAKE NOTE

Note that "at" precedes page numbers in "id." even if it does not do so in the immediately preceding citation to the same document.

If you answer "no" to either question above, you cannot use an "id." form; you must use another short form, which is an abbreviated version of the full citation. Unlike with citations to other authorities, the Bluebook does not have specific rules for how to abbreviate such a full citation; you should ensure that you comply with the three rules for when to short cite (see Section C.1 above). For example:

Full Citation	Short Citation
App. to Pet'r's Br. 8, ECF No. 14	App. 18-19, ECF No. 14.
	or
	App. 18-19.

The bottom line for such a short citation is that it must clearly convey to the reader the referenced document. When in doubt, include more information for the reader.

D. Parentheses

You may enclose full and short citations to court and litigation documents from the current case in parentheses (see BP Rule B17.1.1). There is no space after the beginning parenthesis or before the ending parenthesis. For example:

```
(Eaton Dep. 20:11-14.)
(Black Aff. ¶ 7.)
(R. at 22.)
```

TAKE NOTE

Note that the period ending the citation sentence is inside the ending parenthesis.

TIP

Prior to the 19th edition of the Bluebook (first published in 2010), parentheses were required for citations to court and litigation documents from the current case. Therefore, many current lawyers and judges will expect such citations to be in parentheses because they are unaware of the change to the Bluebook rules and/or they prefer parentheses to distinguish such citations from other citations.

In your legal research and writing course, follow the course or professor instructions. In the absence of such instructions, ensure that you are consistent with such citations — either put all such citations, including any corresponding "id." citations, in parentheses or none of them in parentheses.

E. Common Rules & Tables

The following table provides the common Bluebook rules and tables for full and short citations to court and litigation documents.

Rule or Table	Description
BP Rule B17.1	Full Citations
BP Rule B17.1.1	Abbreviations
BP Rule B17.1.2	Pinpoint Citation
BP Rule B17.1.3	Date
BP Rule B17.1.4	Electronic Case Filings (ECF)
BP Rule B17.2	Short Citations
BP Table BT1	Abbreviations for Court and Litigation Documents
Rule 3.3	Paragraphs (for pinpoint information)
Rule 6.2(c)	Paragraph (¶) Symbol
Table T12	Abbreviations for Months

F. Exercise

Along with using the information in this chapter, you should use your Bluebook when answering these questions (note: do not use any jurisdiction- or court-specific citation rules, which are covered in Section C of Chapter 1 and are set forth in BP Table BT2). Some questions may require you to find and apply rules that were not specifically discussed in this chapter.

For all answers, use only ordinary or underlined typeface. That is, do not use *italics* or LARGE AND SMALL CAPS typeface.

As with some of the examples in this chapter, some of the legal authority used in these questions may be fictional authority designed to test various Bluebook rules.

1. What is the correct full citation sentence for a citation to the following document in your current case: paragraphs 9 through 10 of Plaintiff's Complaint?

    A.   Complaint 9-10.

    B.   Complaint ¶ 9-10.

    C.   Complaint ¶¶ 9-10.

    D.   Compl. 9-10.

    E.   Compl. ¶ 9-10.

    F.   Compl. ¶¶ 9-10.

2. What is the correct full citation sentence for a citation to the following document in your current case: lines 22 through 25 on page 6 of Carl Prior's deposition (note: the deposition took place on October 25, 2013 and that was the only day he was deposed)?

    A.   Prior Dep. 6.

    B.   Prior Dep. 22-25.

    C.   Prior Dep. 6:22-25.

    D.   Prior Dep. 6, Oct. 25, 2013.

    E.   Prior Dep. 22-25, Oct. 25, 2013.

    F.   Prior Dep. 6:22-25, Oct. 25, 2013.

3. What is the correct full citation sentence for a citation to the following document in your current case: line 27 on page 9 through line 5 on page 10 of Carl Prior's deposition (note: the deposition took place on October 25, 2013 and that was the only day he was deposed)?

    A.   Prior Dep. 9:27-10:5.

    B.   Prior Dep. 9-10:27-5.

    C.   Prior Dep. 9-10.

    D.   Prior Dep. 9:27-10:5, Oct. 25, 2013.

    E.   Prior Dep. 9-10:27-5, Oct. 25, 2013.

    F.   Prior Dep. 9-10, Oct. 25, 2013.

4. What is the correct full citation sentence for a citation to the following document in your current case: lines 22 through 25 on page 6 and lines 11 through 12 on page 7 of Carl Prior's deposition (note: the deposition took place on October 25, 2013 and that was the only day he was deposed)?

    A.   Prior Dep. 6:22-7:12.

    B.   Prior Dep. 6:25-7:12.

    C.   Prior Dep. 6:22-25, 7:11-12.

    D.   Prior Dep. 6:22-7:12, Oct. 25, 2013.

    E.   Prior Dep. 6:25-7:12, Oct. 25, 2013.

    F.   Prior Dep. 6:22-25, 7:11-12, Oct. 25, 2013.

5. What is the correct full citation sentence for a citation to the following document in your current case: lines 13 through 14 on page 22 of Thomas Eaton's deposition (note: along with this deposition, the deposition of Mark Eaton is also filed in your current case)?

    A.   Eaton Dep. 22:13-14.

    B.   T. Eaton Dep. 22:13-14.

6. What is the correct full citation sentence for a citation to the following document in your current case: page 113 through 115 of the Joint Appendix?

    A.   Joint App. at 113-15.

    B.   Joint App. 113-15.

    C.   J.A. at 113-15.

    D.   J.A. 113-15.

7. What is the correct full citation sentence for a citation to the following document in your current case: page 5 of Exhibit C to Carl Prior's deposition?

    A.   Prior Dep. 5, Ex. C.

    B.   Prior Dep. at 5, Ex. C.

    C.   Prior Dep. Ex. C, 5.

    D.   Prior Dep. Ex. C, at 5.

8. You want to cite to paragraph 11 of Defendant Sharpe's Answer to Plaintiff's Complaint (note: Defendant Langon filed a separate Answer). Provide the correct citation sentence:

9. You want to cite to lines 8 through 14 on page 8 of Defendant Langon's Deposition (note: the deposition you are citing took place on November 21, 2013, and he was also deposed on November 22, 2013). Provide the correct citation sentence:

10. You want to cite to line 21 on page 10 through line 5 on page 11 of Defendant Sharpe's Deposition (note: the deposition you are citing took place on November 21, 2013 and that was the only day he was deposed). Provide the correct citation sentence:

11. You want to cite to line 21 on page 10 through line 5 on page 11 of Defendant Sharpe's Deposition (note: the deposition you are citing took place on November 21, 2013 and that was the only day he was deposed). These deposition pages are on pages 114 through 115 of the Record at the appellate court. Provide the correct citation sentence:

12. You currently want to cite to page 33 of the Joint Appendix. The immediately preceding citation to your current citation is the following (and it is in the same section/issue of your document): (J.A. at 34.) Provide the correct citation sentence for the current citation:

Chapter 7
Secondary Authority

A. Introduction

Along with citing to primary authority (e.g., cases, statutes, constitutions, rules, and administrative regulations), you may also cite secondary authority. This chapter covers how to cite some of the most commonly cited secondary authorities: books and periodicals.[1]

> **TIP**
>
> Although you may use secondary authority as you are researching a legal issue, you should not often cite such authority in the types of documents that you will write in a legal research and writing (LRW) course or in practice (e.g., a memorandum, brief, or opinion). Instead, you should cite the relevant primary authority (i.e., the law), some of which you may have found through your review of secondary authority.

B. Books

1. Full Citation

Unless a short citation to a book is permitted (see Section B.2 below), you should use a full citation. A full citation to a book includes the following information (see BP Rule B15.1 and Rule 15):

---

[1] To find the specific Bluebook rule(s) on how to cite other secondary authorities (e.g., legal encyclopedias, American Law Reports, Restatements, and Uniform Laws and Model Acts), consult the index in the Bluebook.

- volume number, if citing a multi-volume compilation;
- full name(s) of author(s);
- title of book;
- pinpoint information; and
- parenthetical with (i) edition, if more than one; (ii) editor(s) or translator(s), if any; and (iii) year of publication.

For example, the following is a full citation sentence to a book with one author:

```
Ronald D. Rotunda, Legal Ethics in a Nutshell
13-15 (4th ed. 2012).
```

In the example above, "13-15" is the pinpoint information (i.e., the pages of the book where the cited information is located).

TAKE NOTE

You will notice that the example citations to books in Rule 15 use the LARGE AND SMALL CAPS typeface for author names and book titles. BP Rule B2 indicates that such a typeface may be used for stylistic purposes, but is not required, in the documents that the Bluepages cover (e.g., documents you write in your LRW course and in practice). Prior to the 20th edition of the Bluebook (first published in 2015), this typeface was not permitted for these types of documents, so many current lawyers and judges will not be aware that this typeface is permitted for stylistic purposes. This book will not use the LARGE AND SMALL CAPS typeface for such documents.

a. Authors

If a book has two authors, they should be listed in the order in which they are listed in the book and should be separated by an ampersand

(&) (see BP Rule B15.1 and Rule 15.1(a)). For example, the following is a full citation sentence to a book with two authors:

```
Jill Barton & Rachel H. Smith, The Handbook
for the New Legal Writer 40 (2014).
```

If a book has more than two authors, either (1) use only the first author's full name, followed by "et al." or (2) use all authors' names separated by commas, except the last one, which should use an ampersand (&) instead of a comma. When saving space is important, choose the first option; when listing all of the authors is particularly relevant, choose the second option. See BP Rule B15.1 and Rule 15.1(a). For example, the following are full citation sentences to a book with three authors:

```
Laurel Currie Oates et al., Just Briefs 141-42
(3d ed. 2013).
```

or

```
Laurel Currie Oates, Anne Enquist & Connie
Krontz, Just Briefs 141-42 (3d ed. 2013).
```

TAKE NOTE

A book may have an institutional author (e.g., Federal Judicial Center). In such cases, abbreviate the institutional author's name according to Table T6 and Table T10 (see Rule 15.1(c) and Rule 15.1(d)).

b. Title

Notice in the examples above that the title of the book is underlined (see BP Rule B15.1).

TAKE NOTE

Recall that BP Rule B2 allows underlining or italics (i.e., in all instances where this book uses underlining, italics would be appropriate), but this book uses underlining so that you can more easily see when text needs to be underlined or italicized.

In addition to underlining a book's title, follow these rules (see Rule 15.3):

- omit a subtitle unless it is particularly relevant;
- do not abbreviate any words;
- do not omit articles; and
- for titles in English, capitalize the words of a title except articles, conjunctions, and prepositions when they are four or fewer letters, unless such words begin the title or immediately follow a colon (see Rule 8(a)).

2. Short Citation

After you have provided a full citation to a book, you should use a short form of the citation (see BP Rule B15.2 and Rule 15.10).

TAKE NOTE

Although the Bluebook rules for short citations of books do not specify that such citations are appropriate only in the same general discussion (as do the short citation rules for many other types of authorities), you may also want to follow the "same general discussion" rule as you do for cases, which is covered in Section A in Chapter 3.

If a short form is appropriate, you need to determine whether to use an "id." or "supra" short form.

You should use an "id." short form if (1) the immediately preceding citation in the document cites to only one authority and (2) the immediately preceding citation in the document is a citation to the same authority—i.e., the same book (see BP Rule B4, BP Rule B15.2, Rule 4.1, and Rule 15.10). As with all "id." citations, "id." alone refers to the same pinpoint information as the immediately preceding citation. If the pinpoint information is different than the immediately preceding citation, you need to use an "id. at X" form to indicate the different pinpoint page(s).

If an "id." short form is not appropriate, you should use a "supra" short form (see BP Rule B4, BP Rule B15.2, Rule 4.2, and Rule 15.10). A "supra" short form generally includes (1) the last name(s) of the author(s), (2) the underlined word "supra," and (3) the pinpoint information (see BP Rule B15.2). Note that "supra" is separated by commas and that these commas are not underlined. The last name(s) of the author(s) should mirror the name(s) used in the full citation. For example, the following citations are the appropriate short citation sentences for the full citations in Section B.1 above (note: assume that the "et al." version of the full citation with three authors was used):

```
Rotunda, supra, at 17.

Barton & Smith, supra, at 42-44.

Oates et al., supra, at 122-23.
```

TAKE NOTE

The example "supra" citations in Rule 4.2 and Rule 15.10 include "note X" after "supra." Such an indication is appropriate only when the full citation is in a footnote. According to BP Rule B1.1, for the types of documents that you will write in your LRW course and in practice, your citations should appear directly within the main text of your document, not in footnotes, so you will not include a "note X" indication on a "supra" short citation.

C. Periodicals

1. Full Citation

The term "periodicals" refers to authorities such as law reviews, journals, magazines, and newspapers. Unless a short citation to a periodical is permitted (see Section C.2 below), you should use a full citation. A full citation to a periodical generally includes the following information (see BP Rule B16.1 and Rule 16):

- full name(s) of author(s);
- title of material;
- abbreviated name of periodical;
- starting page number;
- pinpoint information; and
- date of publication.

The exact format for such a citation depends on the type of periodical cited—consecutively paginated or non-consecutively paginated.

TAKE NOTE

A consecutively paginated periodical is one in which multiple issues are included in one volume and the pagination in each subsequent issue in a volume continues from the previous issue. For example, if the first issue of a volume ends on page 142, the first page number of the second issue of that volume would be 143. By contrast, each issue of a non-consecutively paginated periodical starts on page 1.

a. Consecutively Paginated Periodical

A full citation to material in a consecutively paginated periodical includes the following (in this order): (1) full name(s) of author(s), (2) title of material, (3) volume number, (4) abbreviated name of periodical, (5) starting page of material, (6) pinpoint information, and (7) year of publication in a parenthetical (see BP Rule B16.1.1 and Rule 16.4). For example, the following is a full citation sentence to a consecutively paginated periodical:

> Anna P. Hemingway, Making Effective Use of Practitioners' Briefs in the Law School Curriculum, 22 St. Thomas L. Rev. 417, 421-24 (2010).

In the example above, "22" is the volume number of the St. Thomas Law Review where you can find the article, "417" is the page on which the article starts in that volume, and "421-24" is the pinpoint information.

b. Non-Consecutively Paginated Periodical

In contrast, a full citation to material in a non-consecutively paginated periodical includes the following (in this order): (1) full name(s) of author(s), (2) title of material, (3) abbreviated name of periodical, (4) date of issue as it appears on the cover of the periodical, (5) starting page of material (preceded by "at"), and (6) pinpoint information (see BP Rule B16.1.2 and Rule 16.5). For example, the following is a full citation sentence to a non-consecutively paginated periodical:

> Haley Sweetland Edwards, Dangerous Cases, Time, Dec. 1 / Dec. 8, 2014, at 54, 58.

In the example above, "54" is the page on which the article starts in the Dec. 1 / Dec. 8, 2014, issue of Time magazine, and "58" is the pinpoint information.

c. Authors & Title

The rules for author names with periodicals are the same as for author names with books (see Section B.1.a above and Rule 16.2). Likewise, the rules for titles of articles are the same as for titles of books (see Section B.1.b above and Rule 16.3).

d. *Abbreviation for Name of Periodical*

To determine the appropriate overall abbreviation for the name of a periodical, you should use Table T13 and Table T10. Table T13 comprises two subparts. The first subpart (T13.1) includes abbreviations for common words in institutional names of periodicals. The second subpart (T13.2) includes abbreviations for other common words in periodical names. To determine the overall abbreviation, use both of these subparts and Table T10, which includes abbreviations for geographical terms.

The introduction to Table T13 indicates that you should omit the following words from the overall abbreviation: "a," "at," "in," "of," and "the." In addition, if only one word remains in the name of the periodical after such omission, you should not abbreviate the remaining word, even if it appears in Table 13.

TIP

The introduction to Table T13 contains other detailed rules regarding the overall abbreviation of the name of a periodical.

For example, the following would be the correct overall abbreviation for the University of Pennsylvania Law Review:

```
U. Pa. L. Rev.
```

For the example above, Table T13.2 provides the following abbreviations: "U." for "University"; "L." for "Law"; and "Rev." for "Review" (note that Table T13.2 indicates that you should not abbreviate "Law" if it is the first word in the name). The introduction to Table T13 indicates that you should also abbreviate according to Table T10, which contains geographical terms and lists "Pa." as the abbreviation for "Pennsylvania." The introduction to Table T13 also indicates that you should omit the word "of" in the overall abbreviation.

In the example above, the overall abbreviation (U. Pa. L. Rev.) contains spaces between each word because there are no adjacent single capital letters. Even though the "U" and "P" in the beginning are adjacent single capital letters, there is a space between "U." and "Pa." because the abbreviation "Pa." does not contain only capital letters. See Rule 6.1(a).

As another example, the following would be the correct overall abbreviation for the Georgetown Law Journal:

```
Geo. L.J.
```

For the example above, Table T13.1 indicates that you should abbreviate "Georgetown" as "Geo." In addition, Table T13.2 provides the following abbreviations: "L." for "Law" and "J." for "Journal" (note that Table T13.2 indicates that you should not abbreviate "Law" if it is the first word in the name).

In the example above, the overall abbreviation (Geo. L.J.) contains a space between "Geo." and "L." but no space between "L." and "J." You should use a space between "Geo." and "L." because there are no adjacent single capital letters. You should not use a space between "L." and "J." because they are adjacent single capital letters. See Rule 6.1(a).

TAKE NOTE

You will notice that the example citations to periodicals in Rule 16 use the LARGE AND SMALL CAPS typeface for the overall abbreviation for the name of the periodical. BP Rule B2 indicates that such a typeface may be used for stylistic purposes, but is not required, in the documents that the Bluepages cover (e.g., documents you write in your LRW course and in practice). Prior to the 20th edition of the Bluebook (first published in 2015), this typeface was not permitted for these types of documents, so many current lawyers and judges will not be aware that this typeface is permitted for stylistic purposes. This book will not use the LARGE AND SMALL CAPS typeface for such documents.

2. Short Citation

After you have provided a full citation to a periodical, you should use a short form of the citation (see BP Rule B16.2 and Rule 16.9).

TAKE NOTE

Although the Bluebook rules for short citations of periodicals do not specify that such citations are appropriate only in the same general discussion (as do the short citation rules for many other types of authorities), you may also want to follow the "same general discussion" rule as you do for cases, which is covered in Section A in Chapter 3.

If a short form is appropriate, you need to determine whether to use an "id." or "supra" short form. You should use an "id." short form if (1) the immediately preceding citation in the document cites to only one authority and (2) the immediately preceding citation in the document is a citation to the same authority—i.e., the same article from the periodical (see BP Rule B4, BP Rule B16.2, Rule 4.1, and Rule 16.9(a)). Otherwise, you should use a "supra" short form (see BP Rule B16.2, Rule 4.2, and Rule 16.9(b)). The rules for "id." and "supra" with periodicals are the same as with books (see Section B.2 above).

D. Common Rules & Tables

The following table provides the common Bluebook rules and tables for full and short citations to secondary authority.

Rule or Table	Description
BP Rule B4	Id. & Supra
BP Rule B15.1	Books: Full Citations
BP Rule B15.2	Books: Short Citations
BP Rule B16.1	Periodicals: Full Citations
BP Rule B16.2	Periodicals: Short Citations
Rule 4.1	Id.
Rule 4.2	Supra
Rule 6.1(a)	Spacing (for abbreviations)
Rule 8(a)	Capitalization of Titles
Rule 15	Books
Rule 16	Periodicals
Table T10	Geographic Abbreviations
Table T13	Periodical Abbreviations

E. Exercise

Along with using the information in this chapter, you should use your Bluebook when answering these questions (note: do not use any jurisdiction- or court-specific citation rules, which are covered in Section C of Chapter 1 and are set forth in BP Table BT2). Some questions may require you to find and apply rules that were not specifically discussed in this chapter.

For all answers, use only ordinary or <u>underlined</u> typeface. That is, do not use *italics* or LARGE AND SMALL CAPS typeface.

As with some of the examples in this chapter, some of the legal authority used in these questions may be fictional authority designed to test various Bluebook rules.

1. You want to cite the fourth edition of the book titled "Scholarly Writing for Law Students" by Elizabeth Fajans and Mary R. Falk, which was published in 2011 by West Academic Publishing (note: assume that the first three editions were also published by West Academic Publishing). Which of the following is the correct full citation sentence to page 25 in this book?

    A. Elizabeth Fajans et al., <u>Scholarly Writing for Law Students</u> 25 (4th ed. 2011).

    B. Elizabeth Fajans & Mary R. Falk, <u>Scholarly Writing for Law Students</u> 25 (4th ed. 2011).

    C. Elizabeth Fajans et al., <u>Scholarly Writing for Law Students</u> 25 (West Academic Publishing, 4th ed. 2011).

    D. Elizabeth Fajans & Mary R. Falk, <u>Scholarly Writing for Law Students</u> 25 (West Academic Publishing, 4th ed. 2011).

    E. Elizabeth Fajans et al., <u>Scholarly Writing for Law Students</u> 25 (West Academic Publ'g, 4th ed. 2011).

    F. Elizabeth Fajans & Mary R. Falk, <u>Scholarly Writing for Law Students</u> 25 (West Academic Publ'g, 4th ed. 2011).

2. Which of the following is the correct title in a citation to a book titled "American Law and the American Legal System"?

    A. <u>American Law and the American Legal System</u>

    B. <u>American Law And The American Legal System</u>

    C. <u>Am. Law & the Am. Legal Sys.</u>

    D. <u>Am. Law & The Am. Legal Sys.</u>

    E. <u>American Law and American Legal System</u>

    F. <u>American Law And American Legal System</u>

    G. <u>Am. Law & Am. Legal Sys.</u>

    H. <u>Am. Law & Am. Legal Sys.</u>

3. You want to cite the article "The Complexities of Judicial Takings" by D. Benjamin Barros. The article, published in March 2011, starts on page 903 of volume 45 of the University of Richmond Law Review, which is a consecutively paginated journal. Which of the following is the correct full citation sentence to pages 913 through 915 of this article?

    A. D. Benjamin Barros, <u>The Complexities of Judicial Takings</u>, 45 U. Rich. L. Rev. 903, 913-15 (2011).

    B. D. Benjamin Barros, <u>The Complexities of Judicial Takings</u>, 45 U.Rich.L.Rev. 903, 913-15 (2011).

    C. D. Benjamin Barros, <u>The Complexities of Judicial Takings</u>, 45 U. Rich. L. Rev. 903, 913-15 (Mar. 2011).

    D. D. Benjamin Barros, <u>The Complexities of Judicial Takings</u>, 45 U.Rich.L.Rev. 903, 913-15 (Mar. 2011).

4. You want to cite the student-written comment "Urinating on the Pennsylvania Constitution? Drug Testing of High School Athletes and Article I, Section 8 of the Pennsylvania Constitution" by Amanda L. Harrison. The article, published in 2000, starts on page 379 of volume 140 of the Dickinson Law Review, which is a consecutively paginated journal. Which of the following is the correct full citation sentence to page 403 of this comment?

A. Amanda L. Harrison, <u>Urinating on the Pennsylvania Constitution? Drug Testing of High School Athletes and Article I, Section 8 of the Pennsylvania Constitution</u>, 140 Dick. L. Rev. 379, 403 (2000).

B. Amanda L. Harrison, Comment, <u>Urinating on the Pennsylvania Constitution? Drug Testing of High School Athletes and Article I, Section 8 of the Pennsylvania Constitution</u>, 140 Dick. L. Rev. 379, 403 (2000).

5. You currently want to Christopher J. Robinette's article titled "Two Roads Diverge for Civil Recourse Theory." You previously cited to this article in the same general discussion with the following full citation: Christopher J. Robinette, <u>Two Roads Diverge for Civil Recourse Theory</u>, 88 Ind. L.J. 543, 546 (2013). The immediately preceding citation to your current citation is a citation to a case. Which of the following is the correct current citation sentence to page 551 of the article?

A. <u>Id.</u>

B. <u>Id.</u> at 551.

C. Robinette, <u>supra</u>, at 551.

D. Robinette, 88 Ind. L.J. at 551.

E. Christopher J. Robinette, <u>Two Roads Diverge for Civil Recourse Theory</u>, 88 Ind. L.J. 543, 551 (2013).

Part III

Additional Citation Information

Chapter 8
Cases: Prior & Subsequent History

A. Introduction

At times, full case citations require more than just the basic information covered in Chapter 2—case name, case location, and court and date. One such instance is when a case has history (see BP Rule B10.1.6 and Rule 10.7). There are two general kinds of history for a case: (1) direct history and (2) indirect history.[1] In Basic Legal Research, Amy Sloan describes these two kinds of history:

> Direct history refers to all of the opinions issued in conjunction with a single piece of litigation. . . . Indirect history refers to an opinion generated from a different piece of litigation than the original case. Every unrelated case that cites the original case is part of the indirect history of the original case.[2]

Direct history of a case you wish to cite includes prior or subsequent history to that case. For example, if you are citing to a case decided by an intermediate appellate court, its prior history would include an opinion from the trial court in that particular litigation, and its subsequent history would include an opinion from the highest appellate court in that particular litigation. Indirect history is always subsequent history because it involves any unrelated authority (e.g., a statute or a case that is not part of that litigation) that cites the case you wish to cite. See Figure 8.1 below.

---

[1] Amy E. Sloan, Basic Legal Research 145 (5th ed. 2012).
[2] Id.

Figure 8.1: Direct vs. Indirect History & Prior vs. Subsequent History

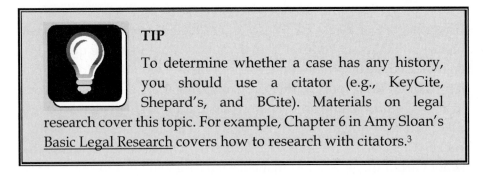

When providing a full citation to a case, you first need to determine whether that case has any history — direct and/or indirect.

> **TIP**
>
> To determine whether a case has any history, you should use a citator (e.g., KeyCite, Shepard's, and BCite). Materials on legal research cover this topic. For example, Chapter 6 in Amy Sloan's Basic Legal Research covers how to research with citators.[3]

If the case you wish to cite has any history, you must then determine (1) whether Bluebook rules require that the history be included on the full citation to the case and, if so, (2) how that history should be included on the full citation.

---

[3] Id. at 143–71.

TAKE NOTE

If a case has relevant history and Bluebook rules require that it be included in the citation to the case, you should include it only on the full citation to the case, not any short citations.

B. Direct History

1. Direct Subsequent History

a. When to Include Direct Subsequent History

The general Bluebook rule for whether to include direct subsequent history of a case is that you should include it on the full citation to the case unless one of the following exceptions applies (see BP Rule B10.1.6 and Rule 10.7):

- It is a denial of a discretionary appeal (e.g., a denial of certiorari), the denial is not "particularly relevant," and the case you are citing is at least two years old;
- It is the history on remand or a denial of a rehearing, and it is not "relevant to the point for which the case is cited"; or
- It is a withdrawn disposition.

For example, a denial of certiorari should be included if the case you are citing is less than two years old. For the following example, assume that the current date is October 15, 2007:

```
Lear v. Raeker-Jordan, 684 F.3d 707, 709 (3d
Cir. 2006), cert. denied, 571 U.S. 91 (2007).
```

But, if the current date is October 15, 2014 (i.e., the case cited above from 2006 is at least two years old), you should not include the denial of certiorari unless it was "particularly relevant."

TAKE NOTE

The jurisdiction and court name are not included in the court and date parenthetical of the subsequent history in the example above because (1) the jurisdiction is unambiguously conveyed by the reporter (U.S.) and (2) the court is the highest court in the jurisdiction. See Section D in Chapter 2 for details on the court and date parenthetical and when the jurisdiction and court name should be omitted from it.

TIP

You may wonder why there is this two-year rule for denials of discretionary appeals. Consider the reader. If you cite a recent case (i.e., one that is less than two years old), the reader may wonder whether the case still has a chance of being reversed. By indicating the denial of a discretionary appeal for a case less than two years old, you inform the reader that the case will not be reversed on appeal.

b. Basic Citation Format

If the Bluebook requires that direct subsequent history be included on a full case citation, it is included following a comma and an explanatory phrase after the basic full citation (see BP Rule B10.1.6, Rule 10.7, and Rule 10.7.1(a)). For example:

```
Hemingway v. Smith, 518 A.2d 14, 18 (Pa. Super.
Ct. 1986), aff'd, 538 A.2d 100 (Pa. 1988).
```

This example illustrates a full citation to a case from the Pennsylvania Superior Court in 1986 that was affirmed by the Pennsylvania Supreme Court in 1988 (note: the "aff'd" explanatory phrase stands for "affirmed").

The explanatory phrase indicates the effect of the subsequent decision on the case you are citing (e.g., affirmed, reversed, modified, or vacated). You can find a list of common explanatory phrases, including any appropriate abbreviations, in Table T8.

TAKE NOTE

Notice that the explanatory phrase in a citation is underlined and followed by a comma.

In Table T8, the explanatory phrases are italicized. Recall that BP Rule B2 allows underlining or italicizing and that this book uses underlining.

The comma after the explanatory phrase is appropriate in the example above (i.e., when introducing subsequent history) because the phrase "introduce[es] a case citation for the action indicated by the explanatory phrase" (see Table T8). This comma should not be underlined (or italicized). Table T8 includes the commas with the phrases when they are required.

---

c. *Years of Decisions*

If you include direct subsequent history on a full case citation and the years of the decisions are the same, you should omit the year from the parenthetical of the primary case citation, i.e., the case you are citing (see Rule 10.5(d) and Rule 10.7.1(a)).[4] For example, if you are citing to a U.S. Court of Appeals case decided in 2012 and the U.S. Supreme Court reversed that case in the same year, the following would be the correct full citation sentence:

```
Fruth v. Raeker-Jordan, 683 F.3d 800, 802 (3d
Cir.), rev'd, 569 U.S. 13 (2012).
```

---

[4] In certain circumstances (e.g., decisions not published in reporters), the court and date parenthetical of a full citation includes the exact date (i.e., month, day, and year) of the decision, not just the year (see Rule 10.5(b)). When including history on a full case citation, you should not omit the year if either case includes the exact date (see Rule 10.5(d)).

2. Direct Prior History

a. *When to Include Direct Prior History*

The general rule for whether to include direct prior history is the opposite of the general rule for whether to include direct subsequent history: do not include prior history unless one of the following exceptions applies (see BP Rule B10.1.6 and Rule 10.7):

- The prior history is "significant to the point for which the case is cited"; or
- The case "cited does not intelligibly describe the issues in the case."

The bottom line is that you will not often include prior history in a full case citation.

b. *Basic Citation Format*

If the Bluebook requires that direct prior history be included on a full case citation, it is included following a comma and an explanatory phrase after the basic full citation (see BP Rule B10.1.6, Rule 10.7, and Rule 10.7.1(a)). For example:

> Hemingway v. Smith, 538 A.2d 100, 102 (Pa. 1988), aff'g 518 A.2d 14 (Pa. Super. Ct. 1986).

This example illustrates a full citation to a case from the Pennsylvania Supreme Court in 1988 that affirmed the Pennsylvania Superior Court decision in 1986 (note: the "aff'g" explanatory phrase stands for "affirming").

As with subsequent history, you can find a list of common explanatory phrases, including any appropriate abbreviations, in Table T8.

TAKE NOTE

Notice that there is no comma after the explanatory phrase in the example above, as there was for subsequent history. No comma is used here because the citation that follows the explanatory phrase is the "direct object" of the phrase (see Table T8). Table T8 includes the commas with the phrases when they are required.

a. Years of Decisions

As with direct subsequent history, if you include direct prior history on a full case citation and the years of the decisions are the same, you should omit the year from the parenthetical of the primary case citation, i.e., the case you are citing (see Rule 10.5(d) and Rule 10.7.1(a)).[5] For example, if you are citing to a U.S. Court of Appeals case decided in 1992 that affirmed a U.S. District Court case decided in the same year and you have determined that you should include the prior history, the following would be the correct full citation sentence:

```
Sharpe v. Laettner, 692 F.3d 32, 37 (4th Cir.),
aff'g 800 F. Supp. 56 (M.D.N.C. 1992).
```

3. Prior & Subsequent History

If a case you are citing includes both prior and subsequent history that should be included in the full citation to the case, you should include the prior history first (see Rule 10.7.1(a)). For example:

---

[5] In certain circumstances (e.g., decisions not published in reporters), the court and date parenthetical of a full citation includes the exact date (i.e., month, day, and year) of the decision, not just the year (see Rule 10.5(b)). When including history on a full case citation, you should not omit the year if either case includes the exact date (see Rule 10.5(d)).

> Perez v. Alverez, 102 F.3d 778, 782 (11th Cir.
> 2004), aff'g 455 F. Supp. 2d 23 (S.D. Fla. 2003),
> rev'd, 545 U.S. 254 (2005).

4. Changes to Case Names

If the case name changes in the direct prior or subsequent history, the changed name should generally be included in the citations (see BP Rule B10.1.6 and Rule 10.7.2).

For subsequent history, you should provide the changed name after the phrase "sub nom." Both "sub nom." and the changed case name should precede the comma that normally follows the explanatory phrase. See Rule 10.7.2(a). For example:

> Dorfmeister v. Sorieno, 798 F. Supp. 233, 235
> (M.D. Pa. 1992), aff'd sub nom. Anthony v.
> Simon, 973 F.2d 15 (3d Cir. 1993).

For prior history, you should not use the phrase "sub nom." As with any full case citation, a comma should follow the case name, even though a comma would not normally follow the explanatory phrase. See Rule 10.7.2(b). For example:

> Anthony v. Simon, 973 F.2d 15, 18 (3d Cir.
> 1993), aff'g Dorfmeister v. Sorieno, 798 F.
> Supp. 233 (M.D. Pa. 1992).

In certain circumstances, you should not indicate a change to the case name (see Rule 10.7.2(c)). For example, you should not provide the changed case name if the only change is to the order of the party names (e.g., Hemingway v. Smith to Smith v. Hemingway) or if the subsequent history is a denial of a discretionary appeal or a rehearing. See Rule 10.7.2(c) for other exceptions to providing the changed case name.

C. Indirect History

Section B involves direct history of a case, but a case also often has indirect history. A full case citation generally does not include such indirect history; it includes only relevant indirect history (i.e., indirect history that affects the validity of the law in the case you are citing). For example, a case may be overruled or abrogated by an unrelated case decided by the same or higher court (see Rule 10.7.1(c)(i)-(ii)), or a case may be superseded by a statute or constitutional amendment (see Rule 10.7.1(c)(iii)). Such indirect history should be included on a full citation to a case. For example:

> Bowers v. Hardwick, 478 U.S. 186, 194 (1986), overruled by Lawrence v. Texas, 539 U.S. 558 (2005).

Because indirect history involves unrelated authority, you should include the case name of the subsequent case. As with direct history, you can find many explanatory phrases in Table T8.

D. Common Rules & Tables

The following table provides the common Bluebook rules and tables for citing history in full case citations:

Rule or Table	Description
BP Rule B10.1.6	Prior or Subsequent History
Rule 10.5(d)	Multiple Decisions Within a Single Year
Rule 10.7	Prior & Subsequent History
Rule 10.7.1	Explanatory Phrases & Weight of Authority
Rule 10.7.2	Different Case Name on Appeal
Table T8	Explanatory Phrases

E. Exercise

Along with using the information in this chapter, you should use your Bluebook when answering these questions (note: do not use any juris-diction- or court-specific citation rules, which are covered in Section C of Chapter 1 and are set forth in BP Table BT2). Some questions may require you to find and apply rules that were not specifically discussed in this chapter.

For all answers, use only ordinary or <u>underlined</u> typeface. That is, do not use *italics* or LARGE AND SMALL CAPS typeface.

As with some of the examples in this chapter, some of the legal authority used in these questions may be fictional authority designed to test various Bluebook rules.

1. Look up the following case in an electronic database (e.g., WestlawNext, Lexis Advance, or Bloomberg Law): <u>Williams v. Consovoy</u>, 333 F. Supp. 2d 297 (D.N.J. 2004). Does this case have any history that should be included in a full citation to the case (note: assume that any denial of a discretionary appeal is not particularly relevant)?

    A. Yes, it has direct prior history that should be included in the full case citation.

    B. Yes, it has direct subsequent history that should be included in the full case citation.

    C. Yes, it has indirect history that should be included in the full case citation.

    D. No, it does not have any history that should be included in the full case citation.

2. Look up the following case in an electronic database (e.g., WestlawNext, Lexis Advance, or Bloomberg Law): United States v. Gibbs, 656 F.3d 180 (3d Cir. 2011). Does this case have any history that should be included in a full citation to the case (note: assume that any denial of a discretionary appeal is not particularly relevant)?

    A. Yes, it has direct prior history that should be included in the full case citation.

    B. Yes, it has direct subsequent history that should be included in the full case citation.

    C. Yes, it has indirect history that should be included in the full case citation.

    D. No, it does not have any history that should be included in the full case citation.

3.   You want to cite <u>Thomas v. Ads, Inc.</u>, 522 A.2d 32, 34 (Pa. Super. Ct. 1988), for a particular issue. The case was reversed on other grounds (i.e., the reversal did not involve the issue for which you want to cite the case) by <u>Thomas v. Ads, Inc.</u>, 541 A.2d 105 (Pa. 1989). Which of the following is the correct full citation to the case?

A.   <u>Thomas v. Ads, Inc.</u>, 522 A.2d 32, 34 (Pa. Super. Ct. 1988).

B.   <u>Thomas v. Ads, Inc.</u>, 522 A.2d 32, 34 (Pa. Super. Ct. 1988), <u>rev'd</u>, 541 A.2d 105 (Pa. 1989).

C.   <u>Thomas v. Ads, Inc.</u>, 522 A.2d 32, 34 (Pa. Super. Ct. 1988), <u>rev'd</u>, <u>Thomas v. Ads, Inc.</u>, 541 A.2d 105 (Pa. 1989).

D.   <u>Thomas v. Ads, Inc.</u>, 522 A.2d 32, 34 (Pa. Super. Ct. 1988), <u>rev'd on other grounds</u>, 541 A.2d 105 (Pa. 1989).

E.   <u>Thomas v. Ads, Inc.</u>, 522 A.2d 32, 34 (Pa. Super. Ct. 1988), <u>rev'd on other grounds</u>, <u>Thomas v. Ads, Inc.</u>, 541 A.2d 105 (Pa. 1989).

4.   In your document, you previously had the following full citation: <u>Hemingway v. Smith</u>, 518 A.2d 14, 18 (Pa. Super. Ct. 1986), <u>aff'd</u>, 538 A.2d 100 (Pa. 1988). Which of the following would be an appropriate short citation later in the document?

A.   <u>Hemingway</u>, 518 A.2d at 18, <u>aff'd</u>, 538 A.2d 100 (Pa. 1988).

B.   <u>Hemingway</u>, 518 A.2d at 18.

C.   A short citation cannot be used when a case has relevant prior or subsequent history.

5. You want to cite <u>Byrd v. Holbert</u>, 533 A.2d 145, 150 (Pa. Super. Ct. 1991). The case was affirmed by <u>Cecala v. Raymund</u>, 545 A.2d 307 (Pa. 1993). Which of the following is the correct full citation to the case?

A. <u>Byrd v. Holbert</u>, 533 A.2d 145, 150 (Pa. Super. Ct. 1991).

B. <u>Byrd v. Holbert</u>, 533 A.2d 145, 150 (Pa. Super. Ct. 1991), <u>Cecala v. Raymund</u>, 545 A.2d 307 (Pa. 1993).

C. <u>Byrd v. Holbert</u>, 533 A.2d 145, 150 (Pa. Super. Ct. 1991), <u>aff'd</u> <u>Cecala v. Raymund</u>, 545 A.2d 307 (Pa. 1993).

D. <u>Byrd v. Holbert</u>, 533 A.2d 145, 150 (Pa. Super. Ct. 1991), <u>aff'd sub nom.</u> <u>Cecala v. Raymund</u>, 545 A.2d 307 (Pa. 1993).

E. <u>Byrd v. Holbert</u>, 533 A.2d 145, 150 (Pa. Super. Ct. 1991), <u>aff'd,</u> <u>Cecala v. Raymund</u>, 545 A.2d 307 (Pa. 1993).

F. <u>Byrd v. Holbert</u>, 533 A.2d 145, 150 (Pa. Super. Ct. 1991), <u>aff'd sub nom.,</u> <u>Cecala v. Raymund</u>, 545 A.2d 307 (Pa. 1993).

6. Look up the following case in an electronic database (e.g., WestlawNext, Lexis Advance, or Bloomberg Law): <u>Wolf v. Colorado</u>, 338 U.S. 25 (1949). Which of the following is the correct full citation to the case (without a pincite)?

A.   <u>Wolf v. Colorado</u>, 338 U.S. 25 (1949).

B.   <u>Wolf v. Colorado</u>, 338 U.S. 25 (1949), <u>rev'd</u>, <u>Mapp v. Ohio</u>, 367 U.S. 643 (1961).

C.   <u>Wolf v. Colorado</u>, 338 U.S. 25 (1949), <u>rev'd</u> <u>Mapp v. Ohio</u>, 367 U.S. 643 (1961).

D.   <u>Wolf v. Colorado</u>, 338 U.S. 25 (1949), <u>overruled</u>, <u>Mapp v. Ohio</u>, 367 U.S. 643 (1961).

E.   <u>Wolf v. Colorado</u>, 338 U.S. 25 (1949), <u>overruled</u> <u>Mapp v. Ohio</u>, 367 U.S. 643 (1961).

F.   <u>Wolf v. Colorado</u>, 338 U.S. 25 (1949), <u>overruled by</u>, <u>Mapp v. Ohio</u>, 367 U.S. 643 (1961).

G.   <u>Wolf v. Colorado</u>, 338 U.S. 25 (1949), <u>overruled by</u> <u>Mapp v. Ohio</u>, 367 U.S. 643 (1961).

7. Look up the <u>United States v. Laboy-Torres</u> case in an electronic database (e.g., WestlawNext, Lexis Advance, or Bloomberg Law)—its basic full citation, without any history, is 614 F. Supp. 2d 531 (M.D. Pa. 2007). Provide the correct full citation sentence to this case (the specific information you are citing is on page 534), assuming that (1) if there is any direct prior history, it is not significant and the case being cited intelligibly describe the issues in the case and (2) any denials of certiorari or rehearing are not relevant:

8. Look up the <u>Bender v. Dudas</u> case in an electronic database (e.g., WestlawNext, Lexis Advance, or Bloomberg Law)—its basic full citation, without any history, is 490 F.3d 1361 (Fed. Cir. 2007). Provide the correct full citation sentence to this case (the specific information you are citing is on page 1369), assuming that (1) if there is any direct prior history, it is not significant and the case being cited intelligibly describe the issues in the case and (2) any denials of certiorari or rehearing are not relevant:

9. Look up the <u>Booth v. Maryland</u> case in an electronic database (e.g., WestlawNext, Lexis Advance, or Bloomberg Law)—its basic full citation, without any history, is 482 U.S. 496 (1987). Provide the correct full citation sentence to this case (the specific information you are citing is on page 502), assuming that (1) if there is any direct prior history, it is not significant and the case being cited intelligibly describe the issues in the case and (2) any denials of certiorari or rehearing are not relevant:

Chapter 9
Cases: Parallel Citation

A. Introduction

A case citation includes information about where the case is located (see Section C in Chapter 2 for general information about case location). Many state cases are located in multiple reporters, and some states require that you use a parallel citation in which you indicate location information for multiple reporters for the case.

Instead of requiring a parallel citation to multiple reporters, some states require that you use a public domain format combined with a parallel citation to one reporter.

NAVIGATE

Sections C.3 and D.3 in Chapter 2 cover the public domain format, including the use of a parallel citation to one reporter with it.

The descriptions, examples, and exercise in this chapter assume that a public domain format is not required (i.e., this chapter covers parallel citations to multiple reporters, not a public domain format).

B. When to Use a Parallel Citation

If a case is located in multiple reporters, a parallel citation is required when the following two conditions are met (see BP Rule B10.1.3 and Rule 10.3.1(a)):

1. The document containing the citation is submitted to a state court (e.g., a brief in support of a motion);

2. That state or court requires parallel citations to multiple reporters.

TIP

To determine whether a state or court requires parallel citations, you should consult that state's or court's local rules (i.e. the jurisdiction- or court-specific rules). BP Table BT2 directs you to these rules, and you can often find them on the court's website.

Although not explicitly set forth in BP Rule B10.1.3 or Rule 10.3.1, another condition for using a parallel citation exists in practice given the second condition above regarding whether a state or court requires parallel citations. If a state or court requires parallel citations, it does so for cases decided only by its own state's courts. Therefore, if the two conditions above are met, you will use parallel citations in a document submitted to a state court for cases decided only by that state's courts.

For example, assume that you are submitting a document to the Hawaii Supreme Court and that you have determined that the court's rules require parallel citations to cases decided by its state's courts (note: also assume that Hawaii and this court do not have a public domain format):

Case Cited	Use Parallel Citation?
Case decided by Hawaii's Supreme Court	Yes, if case is located in multiple reporters
Case decided by Hawaii's Intermediate Court of Appeals	Yes, if case is located in multiple reporters
Case decided by California's Supreme Court	No
Case decided by U.S. District Court for the District of Hawaii	No

Notice in the example above that in a document submitted to a Hawaii state court, you should use parallel citations for cases decided only by Hawaii's state courts. In such a document, you should not use a parallel citation for a case decided by a California court. Nor should you use a parallel citation for a case decided by a federal court in Hawaii because a federal court located in a particular state is not one of that state's courts.

Now assume that instead of submitting the document to the Hawaii Supreme Court, you are submitting the document to the U.S. District Court for the District of Hawaii:

Case Cited	Use Parallel Citation?
Case decided by Hawaii's Supreme Court	No
Case decided by Hawaii's Intermediate Court of Appeals	No
Case decided by California's Supreme Court	No
Case decided by U.S. District Court for the District of Hawaii	No

In the example above, parallel citations are not appropriate because you are submitting the document to a federal, not state, court.

TIP

Although Bluebook rules require parallel citations only in documents submitted to a state court, you should consider including parallel citations in other documents as well. For example, assume you are drafting an objective/predictive office memorandum. Because such a document would not be submitted to a court, parallel citations would not be appropriate according to Bluebook rules. If, however, you may later use all or part of that memorandum in a document submitted to a state court and that state requires parallel citations, including them in your memorandum would be helpful so that you do not need to determine the parallel citations later.

C. How to Include a Parallel Citation

When a parallel citation to multiple reporters is required for a case, it should be included in the full and short citations to that case.

1. Full Citation

According to BP Rule B10.1.3 and Rule 10.3.1(a), states that require parallel citations typically require such a citation to include the location information for the state's official reporter first, followed by the location information for the regional reporter. In addition, you should include the court and date parenthetical only once, after both reporters' information. For example, the following is a parallel citation sentence (without any pinpoint information) to a case decided by the Hawaii Supreme Court:

> Murasko v. Loo, 125 Haw. 39, 252 P.3d 58 (2011).

The following is an example of a parallel citation sentence (without any pinpoint information) to a case decided by Hawaii's Intermediate Court of Appeals:

> Justice v. Fuddy, 125 Haw. 104, 253 P.3d 665
> (Ct. App. 2011).

In both examples above, the location information (i.e., the volume number, the reporter abbreviation, and the page on which the case starts) for the state's official reporter—West's Hawaii Reports—is listed before the location information for the regional reporter—the Pacific Reports, Third Series. Also in both examples, the jurisdiction abbreviation (Haw.) is omitted from the court and date parenthetical because the jurisdiction is unambiguously conveyed by the abbreviation for the state's official reporter (see BP Rule B10.1.3 and Rule 10.4).

In the first example above, the abbreviation for the name of the court (Sup. Ct.) is omitted from the court and date parenthetical because the court is the highest court of the jurisdiction. The abbreviation for the name of the court in the second example above, however, is included because the court is not the highest court of the jurisdiction and it is not unambiguously conveyed by the reporter abbreviation. See BP Rule B10.1.3 and Rule 10.4.

NAVIGATE

Section D.1 in Chapter 2 covers the rules for the omission of the jurisdiction and/or name of court in more detail. As both examples above illustrate, such rules also apply for parallel citations.

Although both examples above do not include any pinpoint information, you should always include this information, when possible. For a parallel citation, you need to include the pinpoint information for each reporter (see BP Rule B10.1.3). For example:

Murasko v. Loo, 125 Haw. 39, 43, 252 P.3d
58, 62 (2011).

Justice v. Fuddy, 125 Haw. 104, 107, 253
P.3d 665, 668 (Ct. App. 2011).

In the first example above, the pinpoint information is page 43 in West's
Hawaii Reports and page 62 in the Pacific Reporter, Third Series. In the
second example above, the pinpoint information is page 107 in West's
Hawaii Reports and page 668 in the Pacific Reporter, Third Series.

TIP

A tip in Chapter 2 recommended that you not
stop to ensure perfect Bluebook format as you
are drafting a document. Instead, you should
use shorthand notations that you can fix at the end of your
drafting process. In such shorthand notations, be sure to include
the pinpoint information for each reporter if you will use a
parallel citation.

2. Short Citation

You should use a parallel citation on a short citation to a case if you used
a parallel citation on the full citation to that case.

NAVIGATE

Chapter 3 covers when to use short citations to
cases and what form of short citation to use — an
"id." form or the other short form (i.e., an
abbreviated version of the full citation).

If you have determined that a non-"id." short form is appropriate for
your case citation and that it requires a parallel citation, you must include the information for both reporters on the short citation, and it
should be in the same order as in the full citation (see BP Rule B10.2). In

addition, you must specify the pinpoint information for both reporters. For example, the following would be appropriate non-"id." short citations for the two examples in Section C.1 above):

> Murasko, 125 Haw. at 44, 252 P.3d at 63.

> Justice, 125 Haw. at 108, 253 P.3d at 669.

If you have determined that an "id." short form is appropriate for your case citation and that it requires a parallel citation, the "id." refers to the reporter listed first on the full citation, and you must also include the information for the reporter listed second (see BP Rule B10.2(iv) and Rule 10.9(b)(ii)). In addition, you must specify the pinpoint information for both reporters. For example, the following would be appropriate "id." citations for the two examples above):

> Id. at 43, 252 P.3d at 62.

> Id. at 107, 253 P.3d at 668.

TAKE NOTE

Recall from Chapter 3 that "id." alone refers to the same authority and pinpoint information from the immediately preceding citation (see BP Rule B10.2(i)). Therefore, if the pinpoint information is the same for the first reporter listed as in the immediately preceding citation, it would not be included after the "id." The pinpoint information for the second reporter, however, should be included regardless of whether it is the same as in the immediately preceding citation. For example:

> Id., 252 P.3d at 62.
> Id., 253 P.3d at 668.

D. Common Rules & Tables

The following table provides the common Bluebook rules and tables for parallel citations.

Rule or Table	Description
BP Rule B10.1.3	Parallel Citations in State Court Documents
BP Rule B10.2	Cases: Short Form Citation
BP Table BT2	Jurisdiction- or Court-Specific Citation Rules & Style Guides
Rule 10.3.1(a)	Parallel Citations in State Court Documents
Rule 10.4	Court & Jurisdiction
Rule 10.9(b)(ii)	<u>Id.</u> for Parallel Citations
Table T1	Jurisdictions (information regarding courts and reporters)

E. Exercise

Along with using the information in this chapter, you should use your Bluebook when answering these questions (note: do not use any jurisdiction- or court-specific citation rules, which are covered in Section C of Chapter 1 and are set forth in BP Table BT2). Some questions may require you to find and apply rules that were not specifically discussed in this chapter.

For all answers, use only ordinary or <u>underlined</u> typeface. That is, do not use *italics* or LARGE AND SMALL CAPS typeface.

As with some of the examples in this chapter, some of the legal authority used in these questions may be fictional authority designed to test various Bluebook rules.

1. You want to cite the case of <u>Olson v. Toretti</u>. The case was decided in 2007 by the Arizona Supreme Court. It is located in volume 177 of the Pacific Reporter, Third Series, starting on page 207, and in volume 217 of the Arizona Reports, starting on page 97. The information you want to cite is on page 212 in the Pacific Reporter, Third Series, and page 100 in the Arizona Reports. You have determined that the Arizona court rules require parallel citations for citations to cases decided by its courts and that such citations should include the state reporter before the regional reporter. Which of the following is the correct full citation sentence to the case in a brief that you will submit to the Arizona Supreme Court?

   A.   <u>Olson v. Toretti</u>, 177 P.3d 207, 212 (Ariz. 2007).

   B.   <u>Olson v. Toretti</u>, 217 Ariz. 97, 100 (2007).

   C.   <u>Olson v. Toretti</u>, 177 P.3d 207, 212, 217 Ariz. 97, 100 (2007).

   D.   <u>Olson v. Toretti</u>, 217 Ariz. 97, 100, 177 P.3d 207, 212 (2007).

   E.   <u>Olson v. Toretti</u>, 177 P.3d 207, 212, 217 Ariz. 97, 100 (Ariz. 2007).

   F.   <u>Olson v. Toretti</u>, 217 Ariz. 97, 100, 177 P.3d 207, 212 (Ariz. 2007).

   G.   <u>Olson v. Toretti</u>, 177 P.3d 207, 212, 217 Ariz. 97, 100 (Ariz. Sup. Ct. 2007).

   H.   <u>Olson v. Toretti</u>, 217 Ariz. 97, 100, 177 P.3d 207, 212 (Ariz. Sup. Ct. 2007).

2. You want to cite the case of <u>Olson v. Toretti</u>. The case was decided in 2007 by the Arizona Supreme Court. It is located in volume 177 of the Pacific Reporter, Third Series, starting on page 207, and in volume 217 of the Arizona Reports, starting on page 97. The information you want to cite is on page 212 in the Pacific Reporter, Third Series, and page 100 in the Arizona Reports. You have determined that the Arizona court rules require parallel citations for citations to cases decided by its courts and that such citations should include the state reporter before the regional reporter. Which of the following is the correct full citation sentence to the case in a brief that you will submit to the U.S. District Court for the District of Arizona?

A. <u>Olson v. Toretti</u>, 177 P.3d 207, 212 (Ariz. 2007).

B. <u>Olson v. Toretti</u>, 217 Ariz. 97, 100 (2007).

C. <u>Olson v. Toretti</u>, 177 P.3d 207, 212, 217 Ariz. 97, 100 (2007).

D. <u>Olson v. Toretti</u>, 217 Ariz. 97, 100, 177 P.3d 207, 212 (2007).

E. <u>Olson v. Toretti</u>, 177 P.3d 207, 212, 217 Ariz. 97, 100 (Ariz. 2007).

F. <u>Olson v. Toretti</u>, 217 Ariz. 97, 100, 177 P.3d 207, 212 (Ariz. 2007).

G. <u>Olson v. Toretti</u>, 177 P.3d 207, 212, 217 Ariz. 97, 100 (Ariz. Sup. Ct. 2007).

H. <u>Olson v. Toretti</u>, 217 Ariz. 97, 100, 177 P.3d 207, 212 (Ariz. Sup. Ct. 2007).

3. You want to cite the case of <u>Olson v. Toretti</u>. The case was decided in 2007 by the Arizona Supreme Court. It is located in volume 177 of the Pacific Reporter, Third Series, starting on page 207, and in volume 217 of the Arizona Reports, starting on page 97. The information you want to cite is on page 212 in the Pacific Reporter, Third Series, and page 100 in the Arizona Reports. You have determined that the Arizona court rules require parallel citations for citations to cases decided by its courts and that such citations should include the state reporter before the regional reporter. Which of the following is the correct non-"<u>id.</u>" short citation sentence to the case in a brief that you will submit to the Arizona Supreme Court?

A. <u>Olson</u>, 177 P.3d at 212.

B. <u>Olson</u>, 217 Ariz. at 100.

C. <u>Olson</u>, 177 P.3d 212, 217 Ariz. 100.

D. <u>Olson</u>, 217 Ariz. 100, 177 P.3d 212.

E. <u>Olson</u>, 177 P.3d at 212, 217 Ariz. at 100.

F. <u>Olson</u>, 217 Ariz. at 100, 177 P.3d at 212.

G. <u>Olson</u>, 177 P.3d at 212, 100.

H. <u>Olson</u>, 217 Ariz. at 100, 212.

4. You want to cite the case of <u>Olson v. Toretti</u>. The case was decided in 2007 by the Arizona Supreme Court. It is located in volume 177 of the Pacific Reporter, Third Series, starting on page 207, and in volume 217 of the Arizona Reports, starting on page 97. The information you want to cite is on page 213 in the Pacific Reporter, Third Series, and page 101 in the Arizona Reports. You have determined that the Arizona court rules require parallel citations for citations to cases decided by its courts and that such citations should include the state reporter before the regional reporter. Which of the following is the correct "<u>id.</u>" short citation sentence to the case in a brief that you will submit to the Arizona Supreme Court?

A.   <u>Id.</u> at 213.

B.   <u>Id.</u> at 101.

C.   <u>Id.</u> at 213, 217 Ariz. at 101.

D.   <u>Id.</u> at 101, 177 P.3d at 213.

E.   <u>Id.</u> at 213, <u>id.</u> at 101.

F.   <u>Id.</u> at 101, <u>id.</u> at 213.

G.   <u>Id.</u> at 213, 101.

H.   <u>Id.</u> at 101, 213.

5. You have determined that the Arizona court rules require parallel citations for citations to cases decided by its courts. In a brief that you will submit to the Arizona Supreme Court, should you use a parallel citation for a case decided by the Arizona Court of Appeals that is located in state and regional reporters?

A.   Yes

B.   No

6. You have determined that the Arizona court rules require parallel citations for citations to cases decided by its courts. In a brief that you will submit to the Arizona Supreme Court, should you use a parallel citation for a case decided by the Oregon Supreme Court that is located in state and regional reporters?

    A. Yes

    B. No

7. You have determined that the Arizona court rules require parallel citations for citations to cases decided by its courts. You have also determined that the Oregon court rules require parallel citations to cases decided by its courts. In a brief that you will submit to the Oregon Supreme Court, should you use a parallel citation for a case decided by the Arizona Supreme Court that is located in state and regional reporters?

    A. Yes

    B. No

8. You want to cite the case of <u>Teris, LLC v. Chandler</u>, decided in 2008 by the Arkansas Supreme Court. It is located in volume 375 of the Arkansas Reports, starting on page 70, and in volume 289 of the South Western Reporter, Third Series, starting on page 63. The information you want to cite is on page 77 in the Arkansas Reports and page 68 in the South Western Reporter, Third Series. You found the following Arkansas rule: "Decisions included in the Arkansas Reports and Arkansas Appellate Reports shall be cited in all court papers by referring to the volume and page where the decision can be found and the year of the decision. Parallel citations to the regional reporter, if available, are required." Provide the correct full citation sentence to the case in a brief that you will submit to the Arkansas Supreme Court:

9. You want to cite the case of <u>Teris, LLC v. Chandler</u>, decided in 2008 by the Arkansas Supreme Court. It is located in volume 375 of the Arkansas Reports, starting on page 70, and in volume 289 of the South Western Reporter, Third Series, starting on page 63. The information you want to cite is on page 78 in the Arkansas Reports and page 69 in the South Western Reporter, Third Series. You found the following Arkansas rule: "Decisions included in the Arkansas Reports and Arkansas Appellate Reports shall be cited in all court papers by referring to the volume and page where the decision can be found and the year of the decision. Parallel citations to the regional reporter, if available, are required." You have determined that a non-"<u>id.</u>" short citation is appropriate. Provide the correct short citation sentence to the case in a brief that you will submit to the Arkansas Supreme Court:

10. You want to cite the case of <u>Teris, LLC v. Chandler</u>, decided in 2008 by the Arkansas Supreme Court. It is located in volume 375 of the Arkansas Reports, starting on page 70, and in volume 289 of the South Western Reporter, Third Series, starting on page 63. The information you want to cite is on page 77 in the Arkansas Reports and page 68 in the South Western Reporter, Third Series. You found the following Arkansas rule: "Decisions included in the Arkansas Reports and Arkansas Appellate Reports shall be cited in all court papers by referring to the volume and page where the decision can be found and the year of the decision. Parallel citations to the regional reporter, if available, are required." You have determined that an "<u>id.</u>" short citation is appropriate. Provide the correct short citation sentence to the case in a brief that you will submit to the Arkansas Supreme Court:

Chapter 10
Parentheticals

A. Introduction

Along with the basic information that belongs on a citation to a particular authority, additional information may be added (and is sometimes required to be added) parenthetically to the citation. The general types of parentheticals are the following:

- weight of authority (for case citations only);
- quoting/citing; and
- explanatory.

TAKE NOTE

Most of the examples in this chapter show parentheticals on full citations, but these three types of parentheticals may be added to (and sometimes may be required on) short citations (including the "id." short form).

The examples and exercise in this chapter use parentheticals on citations to cases, but keep in mind that quoting/citing and explanatory parentheticals can be used on citations to all types of authority (weight of authority parentheticals are appropriate for case citations only).

TIP

A space should always precede the opening parenthesis of a parenthetical, even if it follows another parenthetical. A space should not come after the opening parenthesis (i.e., the text of the parenthetical should immediately follow this parenthesis), nor should one precede the closing parenthesis (i.e., this parenthesis should immediately follow the end of the text of the parenthetical). E.g.:

```
United States v. Windsor, 133 S. Ct. 2675,
2696 (2013) (holding that DOMA violated the
Fifth Amendment).
```

B. Weight of Authority Parenthetical (Case Citations Only)

The weight of authority of the information you want to cite from a case (i.e., the strength of the information's precedential value) can be affected in numerous ways. The most common way is by the court that decided the case (i.e., the court information that tells the reader whether a case is binding/mandatory authority). Because all cases contain this court information (the jurisdiction and name of court), it is included on full citations to cases (see BP Rule B10.1.3 and Rule 10.4). The weight of authority can also be affected by the subsequent history of case (e.g., a case may be reversed or overruled) (see BP Rule B10.1.6, Rule 10.7, Rule 10.7.1(a), and Rule 10.7.1(c)).

NAVIGATE

Section D.1 in Chapter 2 covers the court information on a full case citation and Chapter 8 covers the history of a case.

The weight of authority of the information you want to cite from a case can also be affected in other ways, and you may, and are sometimes required to, indicate these other ways parenthetically (see BP Rule B10.1.5

and Rule 10.6.1). This section covers these other ways that the weight of authority can be affected.

1. Types of Weight of Authority

a. *General Weight of Authority Information*

General weight of authority information may, but is not required to be, indicated parenthetically (see Rule 10.6.1). Examples of this general weight of authority information include the following:

- 5-4 decision (or other distribution);
- en banc;
- per curiam; and
- unpublished table decision.

If you decide to include such information, you should include it in a parenthetical after the "court and date" parenthetical of a full case citation (see BP Rule B10.1.5 and Rule 10.6.1(a)). For example, the following is a full citation sentence with a weight of authority parenthetical:

```
Dada v. Mukasey, 554 U.S. 1, 20 (2007) (5-4
decision).
```

b. *Not a Single, Clear Holding of Majority*

If you are citing to information in a case "that is not the single, clear holding of a majority of the court" (e.g., information in a concurring or dissenting opinion), Rule 10.6.1(a) requires that you include a weight of authority parenthetical indicating that fact (see also BP Rule B10.1.5).

TIP

You will not often cite concurring or dissenting opinions (or any information "that is not the single, clear holding of a majority of the court"), but, at times, such information can be helpful. For example, if you are advocating that your jurisdiction should adopt a particular rule, you may use policy rationale from a concurrence or dissent.

As with the general weight of authority information, you should include such parenthetical information after the "court and date" parenthetical of a full case citation (see BP Rule B10.1.5 and Rule 10.6.1(a)). For example, the following are full citation sentences, each with a weight of authority parenthetical:

Abrams v. United States, 250 U.S. 616, 626–27 (1919) (Holmes, J., dissenting).

Montejo v. Louisiana, 556 U.S. 778, 801 (2009) (Alito, J., concurring).

United States v. Navedo, 694 F.3d 463, 476 (3d Cir. 2012) (Hardiman, J., dissenting).

TIP

The "J." in each weight of authority parenthetical above stands for "Justice" (for the U.S. Supreme Court cases) or "Judge" (for the U.S. Court of Appeals for the Third Circuit case); it does not represent the first initial of the first name. You will always use "J." in such parentheticals to stand for either "Justice" or "Judge." If you need to list more than one judge or justice in a parenthetical, use "JJ." (see BP Rule B9 and Rule 9)—e.g., (Sotomayor & Kagan, JJ.).

TAKE NOTE

If you are citing to a "single, clear holding of a majority of the court," you may also include the name of the justice or judge who wrote the majority opinion if it will help the reader better evaluate the weight of the authority cited (see Rule 10.6.1(a)). In such a case, you should include only the last name of the justice or judge and the "J." abbreviation. For example:

(Marshall, J.)

The "not a single, clear holding of a majority of the court" situation is typically encountered when citing to a concurring or dissenting opinion as illustrated above, but it can also arise in other circumstances (e.g., dictum, plurality opinion). In such circumstances, you must also use a weight of authority parenthetical (see BP Rule B10.1.5 and Rule 10.6.1). For example:

Regents of the Univ. of Cal. v. Bakke, 438 U.S. 265, 287-91 (1978) (5-4 decision) (plurality opinion).

Notice that the example above includes a weight of authority parenthetical indicating that the information cited is "not a single, clear holding of a majority of the court" (plurality opinion) and a general weight of authority parenthetical (5-4 decision). Both types of weight of authority parentheticals are permitted on one citation. As another example, assume you want to cite a dissenting opinion in a 5-4 decision. The following is the full citation sentence that you could use:

Dada v. Mukasey, 554 U.S. 1, 24-25 (2007) (5-4 decision) (Scalia, J., dissenting).

Although the general weight of authority parenthetical in the example above (i.e., the "(5-4 decision)" parenthetical) is not required, it helps the reader understand that you are citing to a dissent from a close case, not an 8-1 decision.

WARNING

Be careful when using information from a dissenting or concurring opinion (or any information "that is not the single, clear holding of a majority of the court"). If you do so, you cannot present the information as though it is the law. Although the weight of authority parenthetical will alert the reader to this fact, your textual sentence(s) should not mislead the reader otherwise.

2. Weight of Authority & Short Citations

All of the example weight of authority parentheticals above use full citations. BP Rule B10.1.5 and Rule 10.6.1 show only full citations, but, at times, weight of authority parentheticals should be included on short citations as well. Rule 10.9(b)(i) covers the use of the "id." short form when citing to different opinions of the same case (i.e., majority, concurrence, and dissent).

NAVIGATE

Chapter 3 covers short citations to cases, including when and how to use the "id." and non-"id." short forms in general.

According to Rule 10.9(b)(i), a weight of authority parenthetical must be used with an "id." short form when the "id." refers to a different opinion than the immediately preceding citation, including when it refers to the majority opinion. For example, assume that (1) the following citation sentences are in this order in your document, separated only by the corresponding textual sentences, without any other intervening citations and (2) citation #1 below is the first citation to this case in your document (i.e., it must be a full citation to the case):

1. Friends of the Earth, Inc. v. Laidlaw Envtl.
    Servs. (TOC), Inc., 528 U.S. 167, 173 (2000).

2. Id. at 188.

3. Id. at 195 (Stevens, J., concurring).

4. Id. at 196.

5. Id. at 197 (Kennedy, J., concurring).

6. Id. at 187-88 (majority opinion).

Citation #1 above does not include a weight of authority parenthetical because the information cited on pinpoint page 173 comes from the majority opinion. Likewise, the information cited on pinpoint page 188 comes from the majority opinion, so citation #2 does not include a weight of authority parenthetical because it does not cite a different opinion. The information cited on pinpoint page 195 comes from the concurrence written by Justice Stevens. Because this concurring opinion is a different opinion than the one in the immediately preceding citation, citation #3 includes the appropriate weight of authority parenthetical. The information cited on pinpoint page 196 also comes from the concurrence written by Justice Stevens; therefore, citation #4 does not include a weight of authority parenthetical because it does not cite a different opinion. Because the information cited on pinpoint page 197 comes from the concurrence written by Justice Kennedy and this opinion is different from the one in the immediately preceding citation, citation #5 includes the appropriate weight of authority parenthetical. Finally, the information cited on pinpoint pages 187 through 188 comes from the majority opinion. Therefore, citation #6 includes a weight of authority parenthetical because the majority opinion was not cited in the immediately preceding citation.

Although Bluebook rules do not specifically cover weight of authority parentheticals and the non-"id." short form, you may still need to use a weight of authority parenthetical on such a short citation. If you are using such a short citation that cites information that is "not a single, clear holding of a majority of the court," you should include the appropriate weight of authority parenthetical because the reader will need to know this fact. For example, assume that (1) the following citation sentences are in this order in your document, separated only by the corresponding textual sentences without any other intervening citations and (2) citations #1 and #2 below are the first citations to these cases in your document (i.e., they must be full citations to the cases):

1.   Friends of the Earth, Inc. v. Laidlaw Envtl. Servs. (TOC), Inc., 528 U.S. 167, 173 (2000).

2.   City of L.A. v. Lyons, 461 U.S. 95, 101 (1983).

3.   Friends of the Earth, 528 U.S. at 195 (Stevens, J., concurring).

The weight of authority parenthetical is necessary on citation #3 above because without it, the reader would not know that the citation is to information in the concurrence written by Justice Stevens.

3. Weight of Authority of Case History

For some cases, you need to include relevant prior or subsequent case history on the full citation.

NAVIGATE

Chapter 8 covers prior and subsequent history on case citations.

If the relevant case history includes information that would typically be included in a weight of authority parenthetical (e.g., per curiam) but is part of the relevant explanatory phrase from Table T8 (e.g., aff'd per curiam or rev'd per curiam), you should use the explanatory phrase, not a weight of authority parenthetical, to include this information (see Rule 10.6.1). For example:

Harrah Indep. Sch. Dist. v. Martin, 440 U.S. 194 (1979) (per curiam).

Martin v. Harrah Indep. Sch. Dist., 579 F.2d 1192, 1200 (10th Cir. 1978), rev'd per curiam, 440 U.S. 194 (1979).

The first example above illustrates a full citation to a case where the opinion was issued "by the court" (i.e., per curiam) rather than by a particular judge; therefore, the citation includes "per curiam" in a weight of authority parenthetical. The second example illustrates a full citation to the case that was reversed by the per curiam decision from the first example. Notice that instead of a weight of authority parenthetical, the "per curiam" information is included on the explanatory phrase for the case history (see Rule 10.6.1).

C. Quoting/Citing Parenthetical

When the authority you are citing quotes or cites another authority for the proposition stated in your textual sentence, you should generally indicate the other authority in a quoting or citing parenthetical (see Rule 1.6(c), Rule 5.2(e), and Rule 10.6.2). On a basic citation without other parentheticals, a quoting or citing parenthetical would follow the "date" parenthetical of the authority cited (see Section E below for information on the order of parentheticals).

TIP

Recall that you can use this type of parenthetical on citations to all types of authorities, not just on citations to cases.

For example, assume that (1) in your textual sentence, you use a direct quotation from <u>Windsor</u> and (2) within that quotation, the <u>Windsor</u> court quoted another case. The citation sentence after your textual sentence would be the following (assuming that full citations are required for both cases):

> United States v. Windsor, 133 S. Ct. 2675, 2693
> (2013) (quoting U.S. Dep't of Agric. v. Moreno,
> 413 U.S. 528, 534 (1973)).

If, on the other hand, the information in your textual sentence comes from a portion of Windsor where the Supreme Court cited, not quoted, another case, the citation sentence after your textual sentence would be the following (assuming that full citations are required for both cases):

> United States v. Windsor, 133 S. Ct. 2675, 2695
> (2013) (citing Bolling v. Sharpe, 347 U.S. 497,
> 499-500 (1954)).

TAKE NOTE
You need to include only one level of quoting or citing (see Rule 10.6.2). In other words, assume that (1) the information you cite from Windsor came from Moreno and (2) for that information, the Moreno court quoted or cited another case (i.e., the second level case from the original Windsor case). You should not include a nested quoting/citing parenthetical for the second-level case in your citation to Windsor; you should include only a quoting/citing parenthetical to Moreno.

TIP

Rule 10.6.2 indicates that a quoting/citing parenthetical is "appropriate" when the case you are citing for your proposition quotes or cites another case. In practice, however, you will not always include a *citing* parenthetical (you will generally include a *quoting* parenthetical). Even when not directly quoting another authority, cases often include citations to other authority. Therefore, if you always use citing parentheticals, your document may include many long citations with information that does not help the reader.

When deciding whether to include a citing parenthetical, consider whether that information will help the reader or help you make your point better. For example, you may want to use a citing parenthetical if the cited case is from a higher court (to add "weight" to your citation) or is an older case (to show that your proposition—e.g., your rule—has not changed over a period of time).

D. Explanatory Parenthetical

You should use an explanatory parenthetical if you want, or need, to explain the relevance of the cited authority beyond what you have already included in your textual sentence (see BP Rule B1.3). When using certain introductory signals, explanatory parentheticals are encouraged or strongly recommended (see Rule 1.2).

NAVIGATE

Chapter 14 covers introductory signals.

Even when not encouraged or strongly recommended, explanatory parentheticals can be useful to add relevant information about the cited authority that is not contained in the textual sentence.

TIP

Recall that you can use this type of parenthetical on citations to all types of authorities, not just on citations to cases.

On a basic citation without other parentheticals, an explanatory parenthetical should follow the "date" parenthetical of the authority cited (see Section E below for information on the order of parentheticals). An explanatory parenthetical should be in one of three forms (see BP Rule B1.3 and Rule 1.5(a)):

1.   quoted sentence(s);

2.   present participial phrase; or

3.   short statement.

1. Quoted Sentence(s) Form

If the information you want to use in an explanatory parenthetical quotes one or more full sentences from the cited authority or quotes a portion of the cited authority that reads as a full sentence, the information in the parenthetical should (1) be enclosed in quotation marks, (2) begin with a capital letter, and (3) include the appropriate ending punctuation (see BP Rule B1.3 and Rule 1.5(a)(ii)). For example, the following are full and short case citation sentences, each with the same explanatory parenthetical:

<u>United States v. Windsor</u>, 133 S. Ct. 2675, 2694 (2013) ("The class to which DOMA directs its restrictions and restraints are those persons who are joined in same-sex marriages made lawful by the State.").

<u>Windsor</u>, 133 S. Ct. at 2694 ("The class to which DOMA directs its restrictions and restraints are those persons who are joined in same-sex marriages made lawful by the State.").

<u>Id.</u> at 2694 ("The class to which DOMA directs its restrictions and restraints are those persons who are joined in same-sex marriages made lawful by the State.").

TAKE NOTE

In each of the examples above, notice that the first letter of the information in the explanatory parenthetical is capitalized. Notice also that ending punctuation is included within the explanatory parenthetical quotation (i.e., at the end of the quotation) and at the end of the citation sentence.

As with quotations in textual sentences, you need to indicate any alterations to the quoted language, and you may need to indicate omissions from the quoted language.

NAVIGATE

Chapter 12 covers quotations in general, including alterations and omissions.

2. Present Participial Phrase Form

If the information you want to use in an explanatory parenthetical does not quote one or more full sentences from the cited authority and does not quote a portion of the cited authority that reads as a full sentence, the explanatory parenthetical can take one of two forms. One such form involves using a present participial phrase (i.e., a phrase that starts with a verb ending in "ing") (see BP Rule B1.3 and Rule 1.5(a)(i)). For example, the following are full and short case citation sentences, each with the same explanatory parenthetical:

```
United States v. Windsor, 133 S. Ct. 2675, 2696
(2013) (holding that DOMA violated the Fifth
Amendment).

Windsor, 133 S. Ct. at 2696 (holding that DOMA
violated the Fifth Amendment).

Id. at 2696 (holding that DOMA violated the
Fifth Amendment).
```

TIP

BP Rule B1.3 allows you to omit extraneous words such as "the" to save space in explanatory parentheticals, so long as the omission would not confuse the reader. Therefore, the explanatory parenthetical above could be as follows: (holding that DOMA violated Fifth Amendment).

This present participial phrase form can also use a quoted phrase that does not read as a full sentence. For example:

```
United States v. Windsor, 133 S. Ct. 2675, 2694
(2013) (recognizing that the class of people
restricted by DOMA are those "joined in same-
sex marriages made lawful by the State").
```

Windsor, 133 S. Ct. at 2694 (recognizing that
the class of people restricted by DOMA are
those "joined in same-sex marriages made lawful
by the State").

Id. at 2694 (recognizing that the class of
people restricted by DOMA are those "joined in
same-sex marriages made lawful by the State").

TAKE NOTE

Each of the present participial phrase examples
above (with and without quoted phrases)
complies with the formatting requirements of
BP Rule B1.3 and Rule 1.5(a)(i). First, notice that the first letter of
the information in the explanatory parenthetical is not
capitalized. Notice also that there is no ending punctuation
within the explanatory parenthetical. Such ending punctuation
is appropriate only in the quoted sentence(s) form (see Section
D.1 above). The only ending punctuation is the period to end the
citation sentence, which belongs outside the parenthetical.

Although the quoted phrase in the examples above appears at
the end of the explanatory parenthetical, a quoted phrase may
appear elsewhere in an explanatory parenthetical.

As with quotations in textual sentences, if you use a quoted phrase in
the present participial phrase form, you need to indicate any alterations
to the quoted language, and you may need to indicate omissions from
the quoted language.

NAVIGATE

Chapter 12 covers quotations in general,
including alterations and omissions.

3. Short Statement Form

In circumstances where a present participial phrase form is appropriate for an explanatory parenthetical (see Section D.2 above), you can instead use the short statement form (see BP Rule B1.3 and Rule 1.5(a)(i)). This form is appropriate when the information you want to use in the explanatory parenthetical is very brief. For example, the following are full and short case citation sentences, each with the same explanatory parenthetical:

> United States v. Windsor, 133 S. Ct. 2675, 2696 (2013) (same-sex married couples).

> Windsor, 133 S. Ct. at 2696 (same-sex married couples).

> Id. at 2696 (same-sex married couples).

TAKE NOTE

As with the present participial phrase form (see Section D.2 above), each of the examples above complies with the formatting requirements of BP Rule B1.3 and Rule 1.5(a)(i). First, notice that the first letter of the information in the explanatory parenthetical is not capitalized. Notice also that there is no ending punctuation within the explanatory parenthetical. Such ending punctuation is appropriate only in the quoted sentence(s) form (see Section D.1 above). The only ending punctuation is the period to end the citation sentence, which belongs outside the parenthetical.

E. Order of Parentheticals

You may need to use multiple parentheticals on one citation. For example, on a case citation, you may have a weight of authority parenthetical, a quoting or citing parenthetical, and an explanatory parenthetical. If you use multiple parentheticals on a citation, you should list them in the following order (see Rule 1.5(b) and Rule 10.6.3):

1. weight of authority;
2. quoting/citing; and
3. explanatory.

TAKE NOTE

If you need to use multiple parentheticals on a citation, consult Rule 1.5(b) for a more detailed order of specific parentheticals.

For a full case citation, all of these types of parentheticals should precede any prior or subsequent case history information.

NAVIGATE

Chapter 8 covers prior and subsequent history on case citations.

At times, you may include information on a citation about where the cited authority is located on the Internet. Any weight of authority parentheticals and a quoting/citing parenthetical should precede any such Internet information. An explanatory parenthetical should follow any such Internet information.

NAVIGATE

Chapter 11 covers citations to Internet sources.

F. Common Rules & Tables

The following table provides the common Bluebook rules and tables for parentheticals.

Rule or Table	Description
BP Rule B1.3	Explanatory Parentheticals
BP Rule B10.1.5	Weight of Authority & Explanatory Parentheticals for Case Citations
Rule 1.5(a)	Explanatory Parentheticals
Rule 1.5(b)	Order of Parentheticals
Rule 1.6(c)	Related Authority
Rule 5.2(e)	Quotations within Quotations
Rule 10.6.1	Weight of Authority for Case Citations
Rule 10.6.2	Quoting/Citing Parentheticals in Case Citations
Rule 10.6.3	Order of Parentheticals
Rule 10.9(b)(i)	Id. for Different Opinions

G. Exercise

Along with using the information in this chapter, you should use your Bluebook when answering these questions (note: do not use any jurisdiction- or court-specific citation rules, which are covered in Section C of Chapter 1 and are set forth in BP Table BT2). Some questions may require you to find and apply rules that were not specifically discussed in this chapter.

For all answers, use only ordinary or underlined typeface. That is, do not use italics or LARGE AND SMALL CAPS typeface.

As with some of the examples in this chapter, some of the legal authority used in these questions may be fictional authority designed to test various Bluebook rules.

1. You want to cite a decision by the U.S. Supreme Court. The information you plan to cite on page 248 is from the dissent written by Justice Sandra Day O'Connor. Which of the following is the correct full citation sentence?

    A. United States v. Gen. Dynamics Corp., 481
        U.S. 239, 248 (1987).

    B. United States v. Gen. Dynamics Corp., 481
        U.S. 239, 248 (1987) (O'Connor, J.,
        dissenting).

    C. United States v. Gen. Dynamics Corp., 481
        U.S. 239, 248 (1987)(O'Connor, J.,
        dissenting).

    D. United States v. Gen. Dynamics Corp., 481
        U.S. 239, 248 (1987) (O'Connor, S.,
        dissenting).

    E. United States v. Gen. Dynamics Corp., 481
        U.S. 239, 248 (1987)(O'Connor, S.,
        dissenting).

2. You want to cite a 5-4 decision by the U.S. Supreme Court. The information you plan to cite on page 54 is from the concurrence written by Justice John Paul Stevens. Which of the following is the correct full citation sentence?

A. Hess v. Port Auth. Trans-Hudson Corp., 513 U.S. 30, 54 (1994).

B. Hess v. Port Auth. Trans-Hudson Corp., 513 U.S. 30, 54 (1994) (Stevens, J., concurring) (5-4).

C. Hess v. Port Auth. Trans-Hudson Corp., 513 U.S. 30, 54 (1994) (Stevens, J., concurring) (5-4 decision).

D. Hess v. Port Auth. Trans-Hudson Corp., 513 U.S. 30, 54 (1994) (5-4) (Stevens, J., concurring).

E. Hess v. Port Auth. Trans-Hudson Corp., 513 U.S. 30, 54 (1994) (5-4 decision) (Stevens, J., concurring).

3. You currently want to cite to page 247 of Plaut v. Spendthrift Farm, Inc., 514 U.S. 211 (1995). Page 247 is part of the dissent written by Justice John Paul Stevens. In the same section/issue of your document, the immediately preceding citation to your current citation is to page 238 of the same case. Page 238 is part of the majority decision. Which of the following is the correct current citation sentence?

Id. at 247.

+ 247 (Stevens, J., dissenting).

4. You currently want to cite to page 247 of <u>Plaut v. Spendthrift Farm,</u> <u>Inc.</u>, 514 U.S. 211 (1995). Page 247 is part of the dissent written by Justice John Paul Stevens. In the same section/issue of your document, the immediately preceding citation to your current citation is to page 248 of the same case. Page 248 is part of the dissent written by Justice John Paul Stevens. Which of the following is the correct current citation sentence?

   A.   <u>Id.</u> at 247.

   B.   <u>Id.</u> at 247 (Stevens, J., dissenting).

5. You currently want to cite to page 248 of <u>Plaut v. Spendthrift Farm,</u> <u>Inc.</u>, 514 U.S. 211 (1995). Page 248 is part of the dissent written by Justice John Paul Stevens. In the same section/issue of your document, the immediately preceding citation to your current citation is the following: <u>Id.</u> at 247. This "<u>id.</u> at 247" citation is to the dissent written by Justice John Paul Stevens from the same case as your current citation. Which of the following is the correct current citation sentence?

   A.   <u>Id.</u> at 248.

   B.   <u>Id.</u> at 248 (Stevens, J., dissenting).

6. You currently want to cite to page 238 of <u>Plaut v. Spendthrift Farm,</u> <u>Inc.</u>, 514 U.S. 211 (1995). Page 238 is part of the majority opinion. In the same section/issue of your document, the immediately preceding citation to your current citation is the following: <u>Id.</u> at 247. This "<u>id.</u> at 247" citation is to the dissent written by Justice John Paul Stevens from the same case as your current citation. Which of the following is the correct current citation sentence?

   A.   <u>Id.</u> at 238.

   B.   <u>Id.</u> at 238 (majority opinion).

7. You currently want to cite to page 238 of <u>Plaut v. Spendthrift Farm,</u> <u>Inc.</u>, 514 U.S. 211 (1995). Page 238 is part of the majority opinion. In the same section/issue of your document, the immediately preceding citation to your current citation is the following: <u>Id.</u> at 235. This "<u>id.</u> at 235" citation is to the majority opinion from the same case as your current citation. Which of the following is the correct current citation sentence?

    A.   <u>Id.</u> at 238.

    B.   <u>Id.</u> at 238 (majority opinion).

8. You currently want to cite to page 606 of <u>Barker v. Kansas</u>, 503 U.S. 594 (1992). Page 606 is part of the concurrence written by Justice John Paul Stevens. Previously in the same section/issue of your document, you set forth the full citation to the case with 604 as the pinpoint page. Page 604 is part of the majority opinion. The immediately preceding citation to your current citation is the following: <u>Plaut v. Spendthrift Farm, Inc.</u>, 514 U.S. 211, 238 (1995). Which of the following is the correct current citation sentence?

    A.   <u>Barker</u>, 503 U.S. at 606.

    B.   <u>Barker</u>, 503 U.S. at 606 (Stevens, J., concurring).

9. You want to cite to page 38 of <u>Fruth v. Lear</u>, 688 A.2d 35 (Pa. 1998). As part of the citation, you want to explain that the court held that the defendant breached the contract. Which of the following is the correct full citation sentence?

A. <u>Fruth v. Lear</u>, 688 A.2d 35, 38 (Pa. 1998), held that the defendant breached the contract.

B. <u>Fruth v. Lear</u>, 688 A.2d 35, 38 (Pa. 1998), holding that the defendant breached the contract.

C. <u>Fruth v. Lear</u>, 688 A.2d 35, 38 (Pa. 1998) (held that the defendant breached the contract).

D. <u>Fruth v. Lear</u>, 688 A.2d 35, 38 (Pa. 1998) (holding that the defendant breached the contract).

10. You want to cite to page 18 of <u>Raeker v. Jordan</u>, 691 A.2d 15 (Pa. 2000). As part of the citation, you want to explain that the court stated that the defendant's conduct did not meet the standard for intentional infliction of emotional distress. Your explanation will use part of the following language from the case: "The conduct must be so outrageous in character, and so extreme in degree, as to go beyond all possible bounds of decency, and to be regarded as atrocious, and utterly intolerable in a civilized society." Which of the following is the correct short (non-"<u>id.</u>") citation sentence?

A. <u>Raeker</u>, 691 A.2d at 18 (stating that the defendant's conduct was not "utterly intolerable in a civilized society.").

B. <u>Raeker</u>, 691 A.2d at 18 (stating that the defendant's conduct was not "utterly intolerable in a civilized society.")

C. <u>Raeker</u>, 691 A.2d at 18 (stating that the defendant's conduct was not "utterly intolerable in a civilized society").

D. <u>Raeker</u>, 691 A.2d at 18 (stating that the defendant's conduct was not "utterly intolerable in a civilized society")

E. An explanation cannot be included on a short citation.

11. You want to cite to page 18 of <u>Raeker v. Jordan</u>, 691 A.2d 15 (Pa. 2000). As part of the citation, you want to explain what meets the standard for intentional infliction of emotional distress. Your explanation will use the following language from the case: "Cases which have found a sufficient basis for a cause of action of intentional infliction of emotional distress have presented only the most egregious conduct." Which of the following is the correct short ("<u>id.</u>") citation sentence?

A. <u>Id.</u> at 18 ("Cases which have found a sufficient basis for a cause of action of intentional infliction of emotional distress have presented only the most egregious conduct.").

B. <u>Id.</u> at 18 ("Cases which have found a sufficient basis for a cause of action of intentional infliction of emotional distress have presented only the most egregious conduct").

C. <u>Id.</u> at 18 (stating that "[c]ases which have found a sufficient basis for a cause of action of intentional infliction of emotional distress have presented only the most egregious conduct.").

D. <u>Id.</u> at 18 (stating that "[c]ases which have found a sufficient basis for a cause of action of intentional infliction of emotional distress have presented only the most egregious conduct").

E. Both A and C are correct.

F. Both A and D are correct.

G. Both B and C are correct.

H. Both B and D are correct.

I. An explanation cannot be included on a short citation.

12. You want to cite to page 18 of <u>Hemingway v. Smith</u>, 518 A.2d 14 (Pa. Super. Ct. 1986). This case has relevant case history — it was affirmed in 1988 by the Pennsylvania Supreme Court at 538 A.2d 100. As part of the citation, you want to inform the reader that the cited authority involves an employment contract (compared to other cases that you have previously cited that involve other types of contracts). Which of the following is the correct full citation sentence?

    A.   <u>Hemingway v. Smith</u>, 518 A.2d 14, 18 (employment contract) (Pa. Super. Ct. 1986), <u>aff'd</u>, 538 A.2d 100 (Pa. 1988).

    B.   <u>Hemingway v. Smith</u>, 518 A.2d 14, 18 (Pa. Super. Ct. 1986) (employment contract), <u>aff'd</u>, 538 A.2d 100 (Pa. 1988).

    C.   <u>Hemingway v. Smith</u>, 518 A.2d 14, 18 (Pa. Super. Ct. 1986), <u>aff'd</u>, 538 A.2d 100 (employment contract) (Pa. 1988).

    D.   <u>Hemingway v. Smith</u>, 518 A.2d 14, 18 (Pa. Super. Ct. 1986), <u>aff'd</u>, 538 A.2d 100 (Pa. 1988) (employment contract).

13. You want to cite to page 262 of <u>Plaut v. Spendthrift Farm, Inc.</u>, 514 U.S. 211 (1995). Page 262 is part of the dissent written by Justice John Paul Stevens. As part of the citation, you want to explain part of his reasoning for his dissent by using only the following language from the case: "The majority's rigid holding unnecessarily hinders the Government from addressing difficult issues that inevitably arise in a complex society." Provide the correct full citation sentence:

14. You want to cite to page 732 of <u>Locke v. Davey</u>, 540 U.S. 712 (2004). Page 732 is part of the dissent written by Justice Antonin Scalia. For the information you are citing, Justice Scalia cited the following case: <u>United States v. Virginia</u>, 518 U.S. 515, 549-51 (1996). You decide to inform the reader that Justice Scalia cited <u>United States v. Virginia</u>. Assume that you have not previously cited <u>United States v. Virginia</u> in your document (i.e., you need to use a full citation to it). Provide the correct full citation sentence (recall that you are citing to <u>Locke v. Davey</u>):

Chapter 11
Nonprint Sources

A. Introduction

At times, you may want to cite authority located in nonprint sources such as commercial electronic databases, the Internet, videos, and audio recordings. This chapter will cover citations to cases and statutes in commercial electronic databases (e.g., WestlawNext, Lexis Advance, or Bloomberg Law) and citations to Internet sources.[1]

B. Citations to Cases & Statutes in Commercial Electronic Databases

1. Cases

If a case is unreported (i.e., it is not available in a reporter) but is available in a commercial electronic database (e.g., WestlawNext, Lexis Advance, or Bloomberg Law), you may cite the case in the electronic database (see Rule 10.8.1(a)).

WARNING

Often, cases available only in commercial electronic databases are non-precedential decisions (i.e., they are not binding/mandatory authority for any court). Some jurisdictions may not allow the use of, or citation to, such cases, so you should check the rules of the jurisdiction and court to which you plan to submit a document.

---

[1] Consult Rule 18 for information on how to cite other nonprint sources.

a. Full Citation

A full citation to a case in a commercial electronic database follows the same structure as a full citation to a case in a reporter: (1) case name, (2) case location, and (3) court and date. The differences in a full citation to a case in an electronic database are in the case location and the date (see Rule 10.8.1(a)). The case location includes the docket number of the case (preceded by "No.") and the database identifier. The date is the full date, not just the year, and you should abbreviate the month according to Table T12. For the other portions of the full citation (i.e., the case name and court), you should follow the same rules as for citations to cases available in reporters.

NAVIGATE

Chapter 2 covers basic full citations to cases available in reporters.

A full citation to a case in a commercial electronic database should also include any appropriate prior or subsequent history.

NAVIGATE

Chapter 8 covers when and how to include such history on full citations to cases available in reporters.

The following are full citation sentences to cases located in WestlawNext, Lexis Advance, and Bloomberg Law, respectively, and not available in reporters (see BP Rule B10.1.4(i) and Rule 10.8.1(a)):

Javaid v. Weiss, No. 4:11-CV-1084, 2011 WL 6339838, at *6 (M.D. Pa. Dec. 19, 2011).

Therrien v. Sullivan, No. 04-31-SM, 2005 U.S. Dist. LEXIS 3935, at *11 (D.N.H. Mar. 14, 2005).

Banks v. Barnes, No. 1:04CV199, 2005 BL 83217, at *3 (M.D.N.C. June 8, 2005).

In the first example above for the case location information, "4:11-CV-1084" is the docket number of the cited case (notice that "No." precedes it), and "2011 WL 6339838" is the database identifier.

TIP

You can use the database identifier to retrieve the case in the appropriate electronic database. For example, entering "2011 WL 6339838" in the search box in WestlawNext (or Westlaw) will retrieve the Javaid v. Weiss case.

In the first example above, the date for the "court and date" parenthetical is the full date (Dec. 19, 2011) of the court's decision, with the month abbreviated according to Table T12. The other two examples above follow the same format for the case location and date.

TAKE NOTE

Notice the pinpoint information in the examples above—the "at *X" (where "X" represents the pinpoint page number).

According to Rule 10.8.1(a), when an electronic database uses screen or page numbers, you should precede such numbers with an asterisk (*) and use an "at" to introduce the pinpoint information. When an electronic database uses paragraph numbers, you should precede such numbers with a paragraph symbol (¶) without an "at" (recall that you should always use a space between a paragraph symbol and the paragraph number—see Rule 6.2(c)).

b. *Short Citation*

To determine when to use a short citation to a case, follow the same rules as for citations to cases available in reporters.

NAVIGATE

Section A in Chapter 3 covers how to determine when to use a short citation to a case.

If you determine that you should use a short citation and that the "id." short form is not appropriate (i.e., the abbreviated version of the full citation is appropriate), you should use the unique database identifier in the short citation to a case in an electronic database (see Rule 18.8(b)). The following are the short citation sentences for the full citations in Section B.1.a above:

```
Javaid, 2011 WL 6339838, at *6.

Therrien, 2005 U.S. Dist. LEXIS 3935, at *11.

Banks, 2005 BL 83217, at *3.
```

TAKE NOTE

As with short citations to cases available in reporters, you should use shortened case names in short citations to unreported cases available in commercial electronic databases. Notice, however, that unlike with short citations to cases available in reporters, you should use a comma before the pinpoint information (i.e., before the "at") in short citations to unreported cases available in commercial electronic databases. See Rule 18.8(b).

2. Statutes

The only difference when citing to a statute in a commercial electronic database, compared to citing to the print version, occurs in the "year of code" parenthetical. Because you do not include the "year of code" parenthetical in a short citation to a statute, only the full citation will be different.

NAVIGATE

Chapter 4 covers full and short citations to statutes, including the "year of code" parenthetical on full citations.

In a full citation to a statute in a commercial electronic database, the "year of code" parenthetical includes the name of the database and how current the database is (see Rule 12.5(a)). For example, the following is a full citation sentence to a statute in a commercial electronic database:

```
Wis. Stat. Ann. § 41.15 (West, Westlaw through
2015 Act 20).
```

The "Westlaw through 2015 Act 20" in the example above is the name of the database (Westlaw) and how current the database is (through 2015 Act 20). The "West" at the beginning of the parenthetical is the publisher; as with citations to statutes in the print volumes, the "year of code" parenthetical should still include any necessary publisher information (see Rule 12.3.1(d)).

C. Citations to Internet Sources

When you want to cite information located on the Internet (not in a commercial electronic database), you need to determine whether to include the uniform resource locator (URL), i.e., the Internet address, in the citation.

TIP

You should capitalize the URL as the actual source does (see Rule 8(b)) because Internet addresses are case-sensitive.

WARNING

Before using (and citing) information from the Internet, you should first determine whether a print source for the same information is available (see Rule 18.2, which "requires the use and citation of traditional print sources when available" except in certain circumstances). If not, you should evaluate the Internet source and determine whether the information is accurate and reliable before using and citing it.

1. When to Include the URL in a Citation

You should include the URL in a full citation in any of the following situations:

- the print source is obscure, i.e., when the print source is "practically unavailable" or when including the URL "will substantially improve access to the source" (see Rule 18.2.1(b)(i));
- the Internet source has the characteristics of a print source and could be cited according to the corresponding Bluebook rule for that print source (see Rule 18.2.1(b)(ii)); or
- the Internet source is the only source of the information.

TAKE NOTE

An Internet source has the characteristics of a print source only when it is "a version permanently divided into pages with permanent page numbers, as in a PDF, and [has] the elements that characterize a given print source." An Internet source can be considered as such even if it is not also published in print. See Rule 18.2.1(b)(ii).

According to BP Rule B18.2, you may (but do not need to) also include the URL if the print source you are citing is also located on the Internet.

On the other hand, you are not required to include the URL when citing information from an Internet source that is an exact copy of an original print source or an authenticated or official source of the information (see Rule 18.2.1(a), which includes examples of such sources).

TAKE NOTE

If you include the URL, you do so in only a full citation, not any subsequent short citations (see BP Rule B18.2 and Rule 18.8(a)).

A short citation would be a typical "id." form (see BP Rule B4 and Rule 4.1) or "supra" form (see BP Rule B4, BP Rule B18.2, Rule 4.2, and Rule 18.8(a)). For example, assume that (1) you have previously used a full citation, with the URL, to an Internet blog post by Ashby Jones and (2) an "id." short form is not appropriate (i.e., the immediately preceding citation is not to only one source or is not to the blog post by Ashby Jones). The short citation sentence to the blog post would be the following:

```
Jones, supra.
```

If the source is divided into pages or other sections that you can pinpoint, you should provide the pinpoint information on the short citation. For example:

```
Smith, supra, at 15.
```

Rule 4.2 and Rule 18.8(a) include further details and examples of "supra" short citations. Keep in mind that the examples in these rules include "note X" after "supra." Such an indication is appropriate only when the full citation is in a footnote. According to BP Rule B1.1, for the types of documents that you will write in your legal research and writing course and in practice, your citations should appear directly within the main text of your document, not in footnotes, so you will not include a "note X" indication on a "supra" citation.

2. How to Include the URL in a Full Citation

For an Internet source that is also in print or one that has the characteristics of a print source, you should use the appropriate Bluebook rule for the print source and add the URL at the end of the citation, following a comma and space (see BP Rule B18.1.2 and Rule 18.2.1(b)(ii)). For example, the following is a full citation sentence to an article in a periodical that includes where the article is also located on the Internet:

```
Anna Hemingway et al., Thurgood Marshall: The
Writer, 47 Williamette L. Rev. 211, 215 (2011),
http://www.willamette.edu/wucl/resources/journals
/review/pdf/Volume 47/WLR_47-2 Hemingway.pdf.
```

NAVIGATE

Section C in Chapter 7 covers how to cite material in periodicals.

For an Internet source that does not also exist in print, not only must you include the URL in the full citation, but you must also include other identifying information about the source. Along with the URL, you should include the following information, if available, in a full citation to such an Internet source (see BP Rule B18.1.1 and Rule 18.2.2):

- name(s) of author(s);
- title of specific page of the website;
- title of main page of the website;
- pinpoint information; and
- date and time.

TIP

Many citations to Internet sources will not include pinpoint information because Internet sources often do not include pagination or other such information that you can use to pinpoint the information you are citing. If you have an option for an Internet source that contains such pinpoint information (e.g., a PDF file on the Internet), you should use that option to be able to include pinpoint information in your citation (see BP Rule B18.1.1).

For example, the following is a full citation sentence to a source that does not exist in print and that does not include pagination or other such pinpoint information:

> Ashby Jones, <u>Lindsay (No Last Name Needed), E-Trade, Settle 'Milkaholic' Suit</u>, Wall St. J.: L. Blog (Sept. 21, 2010, 11:35 AM), http://blogs. wsj.com/law/2010/09/21/lindsay-no-last-name-needed-e-trade-settle-milkaholic-suit.

The example above illustrates numerous points regarding citations to Internet sources. First, you should underline the title of the specific page of the website (see BP Rule B18.1.1) and capitalize according to Rule 8 (see Rule 18.2.2(b)(ii)).

TAKE NOTE

Recall that BP Rule B2 allows underlining or italics (i.e., in all instances where this book uses underlining, italics would be appropriate), but this book uses underlining so that you can more easily see when text needs to be underlined or italicized.

Second, for "a [named] blog that has its own content and presence within a larger website," the name of the blog should be included after the title of the main page, following a colon and space—e.g., "Wall Street Journal: Law Blog" (see Rule 18.2.2(b)(iii)).

Third, you should abbreviate the title of the main page (including any sub-name like a blog) according to Table T10 and Table T13—e.g., "Wall Street Journal: Law Blog" becomes "Wall St. J.: L. Blog" (see Rule 18.2.2(b)(i)).

TAKE NOTE

Rule 18.2.2(b)(i) requires that the abbreviation for the main page title be in the LARGE AND SMALL CAPS typeface. BP Rule B2 indicates that such a typeface is not required (it may be used for stylistic purposes) for the documents that the Bluepages cover (e.g., documents you write in your legal research and writing course and in practice). Prior to the 20th edition of the Bluebook (first published in 2015), this typeface was not permitted for these types of documents, so many current lawyers and judges will not be aware that this typeface is permitted for stylistic purposes. This book will not use the LARGE AND SMALL CAPS typeface for such documents.

Fourth, for the date, you should abbreviate the month according to Table T12 (see BP Rule B18.1.1 and Rule 18.2.2(c)).

TAKE NOTE

According to see BP Rule B18.1.1 and Rule 18.2.2(c), if the material cited from the Internet does not have a specific date associated with it, you should list the "last modified" or "last updated" date of the website or, if such a date is not available, the date you "last visited" the website. This date information, with the corresponding description, belongs in a parenthetical after the Internet URL. For example:

```
<URL> (last modified Mar. 27, 2014).
<URL> (last updated Mar. 27, 2014).
<URL> (last visited Mar. 27, 2014).
```

Finally, for websites that are updated frequently (such as blogs) or for a comment to a post on the Internet, you should also include the time listed on the site or comment, when available (see BP Rule B18.1.1 and Rule 18.2.2(c)).

D. Common Rules & Tables

The following table provides the common Bluebook rules and tables for citations to nonprint sources:

Rule or Table	Description
BP Rule B10.1.4	Commercial Electronic Databases: Cases
BP Rule B18.1	Citations to Internet Sources: Full Citations
BP B18.2	Citations to Internet Sources: Short Citations
Rule 8(b)	Capitalization of Internet URLs & Main Page Titles
Rule 10.8.1(a)	Commercial Electronic Databases: Cases
Rule 12.5(a)	Commercial Electronic Databases: Statutes
Rule 18.2.1	General Internet Citation Principles
Rule 18.2.1	Citations to Internet Sources
Rule 18.8	Nonprint Sources: Short Citations
Table T12	Month Abbreviations
Table T13	Periodical Abbreviations (for abbreviations of main page titles)

E. Exercise

Along with using the information in this chapter, you should use your Bluebook when answering these questions (note: do not use any jurisdiction- or court-specific citation rules, which are covered in Section C of Chapter 1 and are set forth in BP Table BT2). Some questions may require you to find and apply rules that were not specifically discussed in this chapter.

For all answers, use only ordinary or <u>underlined</u> typeface. That is, do not use *italics* or LARGE AND SMALL CAPS typeface.

As with some of the examples in this chapter, some of the legal authority used in these questions may be fictional authority designed to test various Bluebook rules.

1. You want to cite <u>Berry v. Thompson</u> (docket number 5:10-HC-2074-FL). The United States District Court for the Eastern District of North Carolina decided the case on February 15, 2011. The case is not published in a reporter. You found the case on WestlawNext with the following database identifier: 2011 WL 677286. Which of the following is the correct full citation sentence to the case (note: the specific information you want to cite is on page 4)?

    A.   <u>Berry v. Thompson</u>, No. 5:10-HC-2074-FL, 2011 WL 677286, at *4 (E.D.N.C. 2011).

    B.   <u>Berry v. Thompson</u>, No. 5:10-HC-2074-FL, 2011 WL 677286, at 4 (E.D.N.C. 2011).

    C.   <u>Berry v. Thompson</u>, No. 5:10-HC-2074-FL, 2011 WL 677286, at *4 (E.D.N.C. Feb. 15, 2011).

    D.   <u>Berry v. Thompson</u>, No. 5:10-HC-2074-FL, 2011 WL 677286, at 4 (E.D.N.C. Feb. 15, 2011).

2. You currently want to cite to page 5 in <u>Berry v. Thompson</u> (docket number 5:10-HC-2074-FL). The United States District Court for the Eastern District of North Carolina decided the case on February 15, 2011. The case is not published in a reporter. You found the case on WestlawNext with the following database identifier: 2011 WL 677286. Previously in the same section/issue of your document, you set forth the full citation to the case with 4 as the pinpoint page. The immediately preceding citation is a citation to a statute, and, therefore, an "<u>id.</u>" short form is not appropriate. Which of the following is the correct current short citation sentence to the case?

A.   <u>Berry</u>, No. 5:10-HC-2074-FL, 2011 WL 677286, at *4.

B.   <u>Berry</u>, No. 5:10-HC-2074-FL, 2011 WL 677286, at 4.

C.   <u>Berry</u>, No. 5:10-HC-2074-FL, at *4.

D.   <u>Berry</u>, No. 5:10-HC-2074-FL, at 4.

E.   <u>Berry</u>, 2011 WL 677286, at *4.

F.   <u>Berry</u>, 2011 WL 677286, at 4.

3. You want to cite a 2013 article in print by Anna P. Hemingway titled "Keeping It Real: Using Facebook Posts to Teach Professional Responsibility and Professionalism." This article starts on page 43 in volume 43 of the New Mexico Law Review. The article is also available on the Internet with the following URL: http://lawschool.unm.edu/nmlr/volumes/43/1/NMX104.pdf. You last visited this website on April 13, 2015. Which of the following is the correct full citation sentence, including the URL, to page 47 of the article?

    A. Anna P. Hemingway, <u>Keeping It Real: Using Facebook Posts to Teach Professional Responsibility and Professionalism</u>, 43 N.M. L. Rev. 43, 47 (2013), http://lawschool.unm.edu/nmlr/volumes/43/1/NMX104.pdf.

    B. Anna P. Hemingway, <u>Keeping It Real: Using Facebook Posts to Teach Professional Responsibility and Professionalism</u>, 43 N.M. L. Rev. 43, 47 (2013), http://lawschool.unm.edu/nmlr/volumes/43/1/NMX104.pdf (last visited Apr. 13, 2015).

4. You previously used a full citation to a 2013 article in print by Anna P. Hemingway titled "Keeping It Real: Using Facebook Posts to Teach Professional Responsibility and Professionalism," including the URL for the Internet source of the article. You last visited the website on April 13, 2015. Which of the following is the correct subsequent short citation sentence to page 48 of the article, assuming that an "<u>id.</u>" short citation is not appropriate?

    A. Hemingway, <u>supra</u>, at 48.

    B. Hemingway, <u>supra</u>, at 48, http://lawschool.unm.edu/nmlr/volumes/43/1/NMX104.pdf.

    C. Hemingway, <u>supra</u>, at 48, http://lawschool.unm.edu/nmlr/volumes/43/1/NMX104.pdf (last visited Apr. 13, 2015).

5.   You want to cite a source that is located only on the Internet. It is located on The Washington Post's blog named Innovations, which has its own content and presence within The Washington Post's website. The blog post you want to cite, dated February 23, 2015, is by Vivek Wadhwa, and its title, as displayed on the website, is "Why I am stepping out of the debate on women in technology." Which of the following is the correct full citation sentence?

A.   Vivek Wadhwa, <u>Why I am stepping out of the debate on women in technology</u>, Wash. Post (Feb. 23, 2015), http://www.washingtonpost. com/blogs/innovations/wp/2015/02/23/why-i-am-stepping-out-of-the-debate-on-women-in-technology.

B.   Vivek Wadhwa, <u>Why I Am Stepping out of the Debate on Women in Technology</u>, Wash. Post (Feb. 23, 2015), http://www.washingtonpost. com/blogs/innovations/wp/2015/02/23/why-i-am-stepping-out-of-the-debate-on-women-in-technology.

C.   Vivek Wadhwa, <u>Why I am stepping out of the debate on women in technology</u>, Wash. Post: Innovations (Feb. 23, 2015), http://www. washingtonpost.com/blogs/innovations/wp/2015/02/23/why-i-am-stepping-out-of-the-debate-on-women-in-technology.

D.   Vivek Wadhwa, <u>Why I Am Stepping out of the Debate on Women in Technology</u>, Wash. Post: Innovations (Feb. 23, 2015), http://www. washingtonpost.com/blogs/innovations/wp/2015/02/23/why-i-am-stepping-out-of-the-debate-on-women-in-technology.

Part IV

Other Bluebook Topics

Chapter 12
Quotations

A. Introduction

At times, you will use a direct quotation from an authority in your writing. When you do so, you need to follow Bluebook rules for (1) formatting the quotation (see Section B) and (2) indicating any omissions (see Section C) or alterations (see Section D) to the quoted language.

WARNING

Although you may use direct quotations in your writing, do not over-rely on them, and do not use many, or any, long quotations. Readers have a tendency to read long quotations very quickly or not at all, so your quotations should focus on key terms or phrases, instead of an entire sentence or sentences from an authority. Too many direct quotations can also cause the reader to think that you did not independently analyze or synthesize the law but rather just compiled quotations from authorities.

This chapter uses the following terminology:

- <u>Quoted language or quoted sentence</u> – This phrase refers to the language/sentence as it appears in the original authority (i.e., it is what you are quoting).

- <u>Quotation</u> – This term refers to the actual quotation in your writing (i.e., your use of the quoted language in your document).

TAKE NOTE

If citations are included with the examples in this chapter, they are typically full citations. Be aware, however, that a full citation is not required after a quotation, and, if a short citation is appropriate, you should use it.

B. Formatting Quotations

1. Quotations with Fifty or More Words

A quotation with fifty or more words should be formatted as a block quotation (see BP Rule B5.2 and Rule 5.1(a)). A block quotation should be put in its own paragraph(s), justified, indented on the left and right, and single-spaced. Likewise, the entire quotation should not be enclosed in quotation marks. The citation for the block quotation should appear on the next line (i.e., not within the block quotation); it should be at the left margin and not indented. For example:

> The class to which DOMA directs its restrictions and restraints are those persons who are joined in same-sex marriages made lawful by the State. DOMA singles out a class of persons deemed by a State entitled to recognition and protection to enhance their own liberty. It imposes a disability on the class by refusing to acknowledge a status the State finds to be dignified and proper.

United States v. Windsor, 133 S. Ct. 2675, 2694 (2013). In Windsor, the Court decided that DOMA violated the Fifth Amendment. Id. at 2696.

If there are any quotation marks within a block quotation (i.e., quotations within quotations), these marks should appear in the block quotation as they do in the original authority.

TAKE NOTE

Notice in the example above that the first line of the block quotation is indented. It is indented only because it is the beginning of a paragraph in the authority being quoted. Rule 5.1(a)(iii) provides details regarding paragraph structure and indentation within block quotations.

---

2. Quotations with Forty-Nine or Fewer Words

A quotation with forty-nine or fewer words should be enclosed in quotation marks and should appear as part of your textual sentence(s); it should not be set off and formatted like a block quotation (see BP Rule B5.1 and Rule 5.1(b)). For example:

> "DOMA singles out a class of persons deemed by a State entitled to recognition and protection to enhance their own liberty." United States v. Windsor, 133 S. Ct. 2675, 2694 (2013). In Windsor, the Court decided that DOMA violated the Fifth Amendment. Id. at 2696.

If there are any quotation marks within a non-block quotation (i.e., quotations within quotations), the first level of such an internal quotation should use single, not double, quotation marks. Other levels of internal quotations should alternate between double and single marks. See BP Rule B5.1, Rule 5.1(b)(i), and Rule 5.2(f)(ii). For example:

Quoted language: This would undermine the clear
dictate of the separation-of-powers principle
that "when an Act of Congress is alleged to
conflict with the Constitution, '[i]t is
emphatically the province and duty of the
judicial department to say what the law is.'"

Quotation: "This would undermine the clear
dictate of the separation-of-powers principle
that 'when an Act of Congress is alleged to
conflict with the Constitution, "[i]t is
emphatically the province and duty of the
judicial department to say what the law is."'"

You should omit internal quotation marks when your entire quotation
consists of only the internal quotation (see Rule 5.2(f)(i)). For example:

Quoted language: As we have recognized before,
patent protection strikes a delicate balance
between creating "incentives that lead to
creation, invention, and discovery" and
"imped[ing] the flow of information that might
permit, indeed spur, invention."

Quotation: The Court considers the "incentives
that lead to creation, invention, and discovery."

TAKE NOTE

Although a period does not appear immediately
after the word "discovery" in the quoted
language above, notice that one does appear in
the quotation because it ends the textual sentence. You should
always put periods and commas inside ending quotation marks,
even if they are not part of the quoted language. Any other
punctuation mark belongs outside the ending quotation mark,
unless it is part of the quoted language. See BP Rule B5.1 and
Rule 5.1(b)(iv).

3. Citations of Quotations within Quotations

If you have a quotation within a quotation, you should generally indicate the authority for the nested quotation in your citation by using a parenthetical (see BP Rule B5.1 and Rule 5.2(e)). For example:

> "The Constitution's guarantee of equality 'must at the very least mean that a bare congressional desire to harm a politically unpopular group cannot' justify disparate treatment of that group." <u>United States v. Windsor</u>, 133 S. Ct. 2675, 2693 (2013) (quoting <u>U.S. Dep't of Agric. v. Moreno</u>, 413 U.S. 528, 534 (1973)).

If you do not indicate the authority for the nested quotation, you should indicate, in a parenthetical, that you have omitted the citation for it. For example, the citation above would be the following:

> <u>United States v. Windsor</u>, 133 S. Ct. 2675, 2693 (2013) (citation omitted).

C. Omissions in Quotations

In certain circumstances, you should indicate the omission of word(s) within a quotation by using an ellipsis (see Rule 5.3). An ellipsis is three periods separated by spaces, including a space before the first period and a space after the last period (note: the caret (^) symbol below represents a space):

> ^.^.^.^

TIP

Because an ellipsis contains spaces between the periods, it can break across lines in your document (i.e., some periods of an ellipsis may be at the end of one line and the rest at the beginning of the next line). To avoid this awkwardly split ellipsis, you can use non-breaking spaces between the periods in an ellipsis.

Your word processor should allow you to add non-breaking spaces. For example, in Microsoft Word, a non-breaking space is a symbol, and you can find it in the "Special Characters" section when choosing to insert a symbol, or you can press Ctrl+Shift+Space (PC) or Option+Space (Mac) to insert a non-breaking space.

In your document, you can use a quotation in two ways — as a phrase or clause within one of your textual sentences or as a full textual sentence(s) in your document. Regardless of how you use a quotation, there are three locations where you may omit words: (1) at the beginning of the quotation, (2) within the quotation (i.e., not at the beginning or the end), and (3) at the end of the quotation.

WARNING

When omitting words from a quotation, be careful not to change the meaning of the original quoted language.

1. Omissions at the Beginning of or Within a Quotation

The following two rules apply to omissions at the beginning of or within a quotation, regardless of whether you use a quotation as a phrase or clause within your textual sentence or as a full textual sentence(s) in your document:

<u>Omission Rule #1</u>: Never indicate an omission at the beginning of your quotation (i.e., do not use an ellipsis at the beginning of your quotation, even if you have omitted words from the beginning of the quoted language) (see Rule 5.3(a) and Rule 5.3(b)(i)).

<u>Omission Rule #2</u>: Always indicate an omission within your quotation (i.e., use an ellipsis in the middle of your quotation if you have omitted words from the quoted language) (see Rule 5.3(a) and Rule 5.3(b)(ii)).

For example:

> <u>Quoted language</u>: It is undisputed that Myriad did not create or alter any of the genetic information encoded in the BRCA1 and BRCA2 genes.

> <u>Quotation #1</u>: The court stated that "Myriad did not create . . . any of the genetic information encoded in the BRCA1 and BRCA2 genes."

> <u>Quotation #2</u>: "Myriad did not create . . . any of the genetic information encoded in the BRCA1 and BRCA2 genes."

The difference between quotation #1 and #2 above is how the quotation is used. Quotation #1 is used as a clause or phrase within the textual sentence, and quotation #2 is used as a full textual sentence. Notice that in both quotations, words from the beginning of the quoted language (i.e., "It is undisputed that") are omitted, but no ellipsis is used to indicate this omission (see Omission Rule #1 above). In addition, in both quotations, words within the quoted language (i.e., "or alter") are omitted, and an ellipsis is used to indicate this omission (see Omission Rule #2 above).

2. Omissions at the End of a Quotation

If the omission occurs at the end of a quotation, whether you need to indicate that omission with an ellipsis depends on how you use the quotation in your document:

Omission Rule #3: If you use the quotation as a phrase or clause within your textual sentence, do not indicate an omission at the end of the quotation (i.e., do not use an ellipsis at the end of the quotation, even if you have omitted words from the end of the quoted sentence) (see Rule 5.3(a)).

Omission Rule #4: If you use the quotation as a full textual sentence, indicate an omission at the end of the quotation (i.e., use an ellipsis at the end of your quotation if you have omitted words from the end of the quoted sentence) (see Rule 5.3(b)(iii)).[1]

For example:

Quoted language: DOMA singles out a class of persons deemed by a State entitled to recognition and protection to enhance their own liberty.

Quotation #1: The court stated that "DOMA singles out a class of persons deemed by a State entitled to recognition and protection."

Quotation #2: "DOMA singles out a class of persons deemed by a State entitled to recognition and protection . . . ."

As with the previous example, the difference between quotation #1 and #2 above is how the quotation is used. Quotation #1 is used as a clause or phrase within the textual sentence, and quotation #2 is used as a full textual sentence. Notice that in both quotations, words from the end of the quoted language (i.e., "to enhance their own liberty") are omitted. In quotation #1, this omission is not indicated (see Omission Rule #3 above). In quotation #2, however, this omission is indicated by an ellipsis (see Omission Rule #4 above).

---

[1] This rule involves using only one sentence of quoted language. See Section C.3 for information regarding omissions involving more than one sentence.

TAKE NOTE

Notice that quotation #2 ends with four periods, separated by spaces. The first three periods are the ellipsis that indicates the omission of words. Recall that an ellipsis is three periods separated by spaces, including a space before the first period and a space after the last period. The fourth period is the period that ends the sentence. See Rule 5.3(b)(iii).

Also, keep in mind that you should not indicate the omission of words that follow the final punctuation of the last quoted sentence. See Rule 5.3(b)(iv). In other words, even if there is another sentence in the original authority after your last quoted sentence, you do not indicate such an omission if you are not quoting from that additional sentence.

3. Omissions When Using More Than One Sentence of Quoted Language

When using more than one sentence of quoted language, you may, at times, omit words *at* the end of one sentence (i.e., before the ending punctuation of that sentence) or *after* the end of that sentence (i.e., at the beginning of the next sentence). You need to indicate such omissions and keep the punctuation at the end of the first sentence by following these rules:

Omission Rule #5: If the omission occurs only *after the end* of the first quoted sentence, keep the punctuation at the end of that sentence and then use an ellipsis before the remainder of the quotation (see Rule 5.3(b)(v)).

Omission Rule #6: If the omission occurs *at the end* and *after the end* of the first quoted sentence, use only one ellipsis before the end of that sentence, follow that ellipsis with the punctuation that ends that sentence (e.g., a period), and continue with the next quoted sentence (see Rule 5.3(b)(vi)).

For example:

> Quoted language: Against this background of
> lawful same-sex marriage in some States, the
> design, purpose, and effect of DOMA should be
> considered as the beginning point in deciding
> whether it is valid under the Constitution. By
> history and tradition the definition and
> regulation of marriage, as will be discussed in
> more detail, has been treated as being within the
> authority and realm of the separate States.

> Quotation #1: Against this background of lawful
> same-sex marriage in some States, the design,
> purpose, and effect of DOMA should be considered
> as the beginning point in deciding whether it is
> valid under the Constitution. . . . [T]he
> definition and regulation of marriage, as will be
> discussed in more detail, has been treated as
> being within the authority and realm of the
> separate States.

> Quotation #2: Against this background of lawful
> same-sex marriage in some States, the design,
> purpose, and effect of DOMA should be considered
> as the beginning point in deciding whether it is
> valid . . . . [T]he definition and regulation of
> marriage, as will be discussed in more detail,
> has been treated as being within the authority
> and realm of the separate States.

Quotation #1 illustrates when the omission occurs only *after the end* of the first quoted sentence. In that instance, the period ending that first sentence comes *before* the ellipsis that indicates the omission of words from the beginning of the next sentence (see Omission Rule #5 above). Notice that there is no space before the period ending the first sentence.

Quotation #2 illustrates when the omission occurs *at the end* and *after the end* of the first quoted sentence. In that instance, the period ending that first sentence comes *after* the ellipsis that indicates the omission of words from the end of that sentence (i.e., the ellipsis indicating the omission comes first, followed by the period ending that sentence). There is not another ellipsis to indicate further omission at the beginning of the second sentence (see Omission Rule #6 above). Notice that there is a space before the first period because it is the first period of an ellipsis and that there is a space before the last of the four periods, which is the period that ends the first sentence, because it follows an ellipsis.

TAKE NOTE

The two example quotations above are not enclosed in quotation marks because they are fifty or more words and would be formatted as block quotations (see Section B.1 above). These examples, however, do not have the indenting and justification that would be required for block quotations.

4. Omissions Necessitating Alterations

Omitting words from a quotation may require you to alter the case of the first letter of the word following the omission (lower to upper case, or vice versa). The previous two example quotations illustrate one situation where such an alteration is required. For information on altering a quotation, see Section D below.

5. Omissions of Citations within Quoted Language

When quoting language that contains footnotes or citations to other authority within it, you can omit the footnotes and citations in your quotation. You should not use an ellipsis to indicate such an omission. Instead, use a parenthetical to indicate the omission—(citation omitted), (citations omitted), (footnote omitted), or (footnotes omitted). See Rule 5.3(c). For example:

Quoted language (from Windsor case): The differentiation demeans the couple, whose moral and sexual choices the Constitution protects, see Lawrence, 539 U.S. 558, and whose relationship the State has sought to dignify.

Quotation & Citation: "The differentiation demeans the couple, whose moral and sexual choices the Constitution protects, and whose relationship the State has sought to dignify." United States v. Windsor, 133 S. Ct. 2675, 2694 (2013) (citation omitted).

D. Alterations in Quotations

At times, you will need or want to alter a quotation to, for example, change letters or words; remove letters; or indicate emphasis added in the quotation, alterations in quoted language, or mistakes in the quoted language.

WARNING

As when omitting words from a quotation, be careful not to change the meaning of the original quoted language when changing or inserting words.

1. Changing Letters or Words & Removing Letters

You may need to change the case of a letter (lower to upper case, or vice versa) in a quotation. More specifically, you may need to make such a change to first letter of the first word of your quotation or the first letter of the first word after an omission within a quotation. In such circumstances, you should determine what the appropriate case should be, given its location in your textual sentence. If that letter in the actual quoted language is not the proper case, put that letter in brackets and change it to the proper case for your quotation (see Rule 5.2(a)). For example:

> Quoted language: Against this background of lawful same-sex marriage in some States, the design, purpose, and effect of DOMA should be considered as the beginning point in deciding whether it is valid under the Constitution.

> Quotation #1: "[T]he design, purpose, and effect of DOMA should be considered as the beginning point in deciding whether it is valid under the Constitution."

> Quotation #2: The Court stated that "[a]gainst this background of lawful same-sex marriage in some States, the design, purpose, and effect of DOMA should be considered as the beginning point in deciding whether it is valid under the Constitution."

Quotation #1 illustrates an instance where a lower case letter from the quoted language needs to be changed to an upper case letter in the quotation because the word is now at the beginning of the sentence. Quotation #2 illustrates an instance where an upper case letter from the quoted language needs to be changed to a lower case letter in the quotation because the word is now not at the beginning of the sentence or in a position that requires an upper case letter.

You may also want to change or insert a word or words within a quotation. To do so, put the changes in brackets (see Rule 5.2(a)). For example:

> Quoted language: It is undisputed that Myriad did not create or alter any of the genetic information encoded in the BRCA1 and BRCA2 genes.

> Quotation: The court stated that "Myriad did not create or alter any of the genetic information encoded in the [breast cancer] genes."

If you need to remove letters from a word, use empty brackets in place of the letters, not an ellipsis (see Rule 5.2(b)). In the example below, "genes" from the quoted language is changed to "gene[]":

> Quoted language: It is undisputed that Myriad did not create or alter any of the genetic information encoded in the BRCA1 and BRCA2 genes.
>
> Quotation: The court stated that "Myriad did not create or alter any of the genetic information encoded in the BRCA1 . . . gene[]."

TAKE NOTE

If you need to remove an entire word or words, do not use brackets; instead, you may need to use an ellipsis (see Section C above).

2. Indicating Emphasis Added & Alterations in Quoted Language

At times, you may want to emphasize language in a quotation by underlining or italicizing it. If you emphasize any language, you must indicate that you have done so by including an "emphasis added" parenthetical to the citation (see Rule 5.2(d)(i)). For example:

> Quoted language: The class to which DOMA directs its restrictions and restraints are those persons who are joined in same-sex marriages made lawful by the State.
>
> Quotation & Citation: "The class to which DOMA directs its restrictions and restraints are those persons who are joined in same-sex marriages <u>made lawful by the State</u>." <u>United States v. Windsor</u>, 133 S. Ct. 2675, 2694 (2013) (emphasis added).

This example demonstrates the added emphasis of the phrase "made lawful by the State" with underlining (i.e., emphasis that is not in the original quoted language).

TAKE NOTE

If the quoted language contains emphasis that you retain in your quotation, do not indicate that emphasis in a parenthetical on your citation (see Rule 5.2(d)(iii)). If, however, you remove emphasis found in the original quoted language, you must indicate such omission on your citation (see Rule 5.2(d)(i)) with the following parenthetical: (emphasis omitted).

If the quoted language contains any alterations that you retain in your quotation (e.g., brackets or ellipses), you should indicate such alterations (see Rule 5.2(d)(i)). For example:

```
Quoted language: As we have recognized before,
patent protection strikes a delicate balance
between creating "incentives that lead to
creation, invention, and discovery" and
"imped[ing] the flow of information that might
permit, indeed spur, invention."
```

```
Quotation & Citation: "As we have recognized
before, patent protection strikes a delicate
balance between creating 'incentives that lead to
creation, invention, and discovery' and
'imped[ing] the flow of information that might
permit, indeed spur, invention.'" Ass'n for
Molecular Pathology v. Myriad Genetics, Inc., 133
S. Ct. 2107, 2116 (2013) (alteration in
original).
```

3. Indicating Mistakes

If you encounter any significant mistakes (e.g., grammar errors) in the quoted language that you do not alter in your quotation, you should put "[sic]" after the mistake in your quotation (see Rule 5.2(c)). For example:

```
In an email to his neighbor, the defendant wrote:
"Your kids has [sic] been harassing me. I'm not
going to take it anymore."
```

E. Common Rules & Tables

The following table provides the common Bluebook rules and tables for quotations.

Rule or Table	Description
BP Rule B5.1	Quotations in General
BP Rule B5.2	Block Quotations
Rule 5.1(a)	Block Quotations
Rule 5.1(b)	Non-Block Quotations
Rule 5.2	Alterations in Quotations
Rule 5.3	Omissions in Quotations

F. Exercise

Along with using the information in this chapter, you should use your Bluebook when answering these questions (note: do not use any jurisdiction- or court-specific citation rules, which are covered in Section C of Chapter 1 and are set forth in BP Table BT2). Some questions may require you to find and apply rules that were not specifically discussed in this chapter.

For all answers, use only ordinary or underlined typeface. That is, do not use *italics* or LARGE AND SMALL CAPS typeface.

As with some of the examples in this chapter, some of the legal authority used in these questions may be fictional authority designed to test various Bluebook rules.

1. Which of the following is the correct way to indicate the omission of a word or words in a quotation?

    A.   ()

    B.   []

    C.   ...

    D.   . . .

    E.   [...]

    F.   [. . .]

2. Which of the following quotations as a full textual sentence is correct?

    A.   `The words `portrait or picture' were
         construed to be broad enough to cover any
         likeness or representation of the plaintiff,
         whether two or three dimensional.'

    B.   `The words "portrait or picture" were
         construed to be broad enough to cover any
         likeness or representation of the plaintiff,
         whether two or three dimensional.'

    C.   "The words `portrait or picture' were
         construed to be broad enough to cover any
         likeness or representation of the plaintiff,
         whether two or three dimensional."

    D.   "The words "portrait or picture" were
         construed to be broad enough to cover any
         likeness or representation of the plaintiff,
         whether two or three dimensional."

3. You wish to quote from the following sentence in an authority:

    Thus far, the legislature has accorded protection only to those aspects of identity embodied in name and face.

    Which of the following quotations as a full textual sentence is correct?

    A.   "the legislature has accorded protection only to those aspects of identity embodied in name and face."

    B.   "[T]he legislature has accorded protection only to those aspects of identity embodied in name and face."

    C.   ". . . the legislature has accorded protection only to those aspects of identity embodied in name and face."

    D.   ". . .the legislature has accorded protection only to those aspects of identity embodied in name and face."

    E.   ". . . [T]he legislature has accorded protection only to those aspects of identity embodied in name and face."

4. You wish to quote from the following sentence in an authority:

    Imitators are free to simulate voice or hair-do, or characteristic clothing or accessories, and writers to comment on and actors to re-enact events.

    Which of the following quotations as a full textual sentence is correct?

    A.   "Imitators are free to simulate voice or hair-do, or characteristic clothing."

    B.   "Imitators are free to simulate voice or hair-do, or characteristic clothing[.]"

    C.   "Imitators are free to simulate voice or hair-do, or characteristic clothing . . . ."

    D.   "Imitators are free to simulate voice or hair-do, or characteristic clothing. . . ."

5.   You wish to quote from the following sentence in an authority:

> Imitators are free to simulate voice or hair-do, or characteristic clothing or accessories, and writers to comment on and actors to re-enact events.

Which of the following quotations as a full textual sentence is correct?

A.   "Imitators are free to simulate voice or hair-do, or characteristic clothing or accessories, and actors to re-enact events."

B.   "Imitators are free to simulate voice or hair-do, or characteristic clothing or accessories, and. . .actors to re-enact events."

C.   "Imitators are free to simulate voice or hair-do, or characteristic clothing or accessories, and . . . actors to re-enact events."

D.   "Imitators are free to simulate voice or hair-do, or characteristic clothing or accessories, and [. . .] actors to re-enact events."

E.   "Imitators are free to simulate voice or hair-do, or characteristic clothing or accessories, and[. . .]actors to re-enact events."

6. You wish to quote from the following sentence in an authority:

> No one is free to trade on another's name or appearance and claim immunity because what he is using is similar to but not identical with the original.

Which of the following quotations within a textual sentence is correct?

A. The court stated that a person is not "free to trade on another's name or appearance and claim immunity because what he is using is similar to but not identical with the original."

B. The court stated that a person is not ". . . free to trade on another's name or appearance and claim immunity because what he is using is similar to but not identical with the original."

C. The court stated that a person is not " . . . free to trade on another's name or appearance and claim immunity because what he is using is similar to but not identical with the original."

D. The court stated that a person is not ". . .free to trade on another's name or appearance and claim immunity because what he is using is similar to but not identical with the original."

E. The court stated that a person is not "[] free to trade on another's name or appearance and claim immunity because what he is using is similar to but not identical with the original."

7. You wish to quote from the following sentence in an authority:

> Imitators are free to simulate voice or hair-do, or characteristic clothing or accessories, and writers to comment on and actors to re-enact events.

Which of the following quotations within a textual sentence is correct?

A.   The court stated that "Imitators are free to simulate voice or hair-do, or characteristic clothing."

B.   The court stated that "[i]mitators are free to simulate voice or hair-do, or characteristic clothing."

C.   The court stated that "Imitators are free to simulate voice or hair-do, or characteristic clothing[.]"

D.   The court stated that "[i]mitators are free to simulate voice or hair-do, or characteristic clothing[.]"

E.   The court stated that "Imitators are free to simulate voice or hair-do, or characteristic clothing . . . ."

F.   The court stated that "[i]mitators are free to simulate voice or hair-do, or characteristic clothing . . . ."

G.   The court stated that "Imitators are free to simulate voice or hair-do, or characteristic clothing. . . ."

H.   The court stated that "[i]mitators are free to simulate voice or hair-do, or characteristic clothing. . . ."

8. Is the following quotation formatted correctly (note: you do not have to verify the accuracy of the words in the quotation):

> The court stated: "Thus far, the legislature has accorded protection only to those aspects of identity embodied in name and face. Imitators are free to simulate voice or hair-do, or characteristic clothing or accessories, and writers to comment on and actors to re-enact events. No one is free to trade on another's name or appearance and claim immunity because what he is using is similar to but not identical with the original."

A. Yes

B. No

Chapter 13
String Citations

A. Introduction

At times, you may need to cite more than one authority for a particular sentence or proposition in your document. To do so, you use what is commonly referred to as a "string citation" (i.e., you string together citations to multiple authorities in one citation sentence or clause).

B. How to String Cite

To create a string citation, you separate the citations for each authority with a semi-colon. If you are using a string citation sentence, you end the entire string citation with a period. If you are using a string citation clause, you end the clause with a comma when it is not at the end of the textual sentence or with a period when it is at the end of the textual sentence. BP Rule B1.1 covers these distinctions with citation sentences and clauses.

For example, if you want a string citation sentence to cite to pinpoint page 453 in <u>Burck</u> first and then to pinpoint page 665 in <u>Lombardo</u>, the string citation sentence would be the following (assuming that neither case had previously been cited, i.e., you need to use a full citation for each case):

> <u>Burck v. Mars, Inc.</u>, 571 F. Supp. 2d 446, 453 (S.D.N.Y. 2008); <u>Lombardo v. Doyle, Dane & Bernbach, Inc.</u>, 396 N.Y.S.2d 661, 665 (App. Div. 1977).

WARNING

Do not put a period after each citation in a string citation. Use a period only at the end of the entire string citation when it ends either the citation sentence or the textual sentence.

Although the example above uses full citations for both cases, full citations are not required in string citations. For each citation in a string, you need to determine whether a full or short citation is appropriate, depending on whether you have already cited the authority, and, if so, where you have done so.

For example, if you want a string citation sentence to cite to pinpoint page 453 in <u>Burck</u> first and then to pinpoint page 665 in <u>Lombardo</u>, the string citation sentence would be the following (assume that <u>Lombardo</u> had previously been cited in the same general discussion, but <u>Burck</u> had not):

```
Burck v. Mars, Inc., 571 F. Supp. 2d 446, 453
(S.D.N.Y. 2008); Lombardo, 396 N.Y.S.2d at 665.
```

TAKE NOTE

The examples in this chapter use citations to cases, but a string citation can contain citations to any type of authority. The following example illustrates a string citation with citations to a statute and one case:

```
N.Y. Civ. Rights Law § 51 (McKinney 2009);
Burck v. Mars, Inc., 571 F. Supp. 2d 446,
453 (S.D.N.Y. 2008).
```

NAVIGATE

For information on short citations for a particular type of authority, see the appropriate chapter for that authority. For example, Chapter 3 covers short citations of cases, and Chapter 4 covers short citations of statutes.

C. Order of Authorities Within a String Citation

BP Rule B1.2 and Rule 1.4 indicate how you should order the authorities within a string citation. More precisely, they indicate the order of authorities within each introductory signal.

NAVIGATE

Chapter 14 covers introductory signals.

When a signal is not used (as is the case in all of the examples in this chapter), BP Rule B1.2 and Rule 1.4 indicate the order of authorities within the entire string citation.

Different types of authorities should be organized in the following order:

1. Constitutions
2. Statutes
3. Treaties and other international agreements
4. Cases
5. Legislative materials
6. Administrative and executive materials
7. Resolutions, decisions, and regulations of intergovernmental organizations

8. Records, briefs, and petitions
9. Secondary materials
10. Cross-references

A string citation may contain multiple authorities of the same type (e.g., multiple cases). If so, Rule 1.4 also dictates the order for each type of authority. For example, Rule 1.4(d) indicates that cases should be organized by "the courts issuing the cited opinions" (i.e., the deciding courts). For cases decided by the same court, the cases should be organized in reverse chronological order.

TAKE NOTE

According to Rule 1.4(d), all United States circuit courts of appeals should be treated as one court when determining the order, and all United States district courts should be treated as one court as well.

Federal cases should come before state cases, and within these groupings, the cases should be ordered according to the rank/hierarchy of the court, with the highest court first (e.g., federal Supreme Court cases, then federal courts of appeals cases, etc.).

Here is an example string citation with multiple cases:

> Johnson v. Harris, 512 F. Supp. 339, 342 (S.D. Ohio 1981); Griffey v. Rajan, 514 N.E.2d 1122, 1125 (Ohio 1987); Colley v. Bazell, 416 N.E.2d 605, 608 (Ohio 1980); Vanest v. Pillsbury Co., 706 N.E.2d 825 (Ohio Ct. App. 1997); Adomeit v. Baltimore, 316 N.E.2d 469 (Ohio Ct. App. 1974).

In this example, the five cases cited involve three deciding courts: (1) the United States District Court for the Southern District of Ohio (the Johnson case), (2) the Supreme Court of Ohio (the Griffey and Colley cases), and (3) the Court of Appeals of Ohio (the Vanest and Adomeit cases). Following the order indicated in Rule 1.4(d), the federal case is listed first, the state cases from Ohio's highest court are listed next, and the state cases from Ohio's intermediate appellate court are listed last.

Within a particular deciding court, notice that the cases are listed in reverse chronological order.

TAKE NOTE

Rule 1.4 contains many more details regarding the order the authorities for each type of authority, so review the applicable portions of the rule in detail when using a string citation.

Regardless of the order specified by Rule 1.4, if one or more authorities "are considerably more helpful or authoritative than the other authorities," you should list those authorities first.

D. String Citations & the Use of Id.

An "id." short form is only appropriate when the immediately preceding citation is to only one authority. Therefore, if the immediately preceding citation is a string citation to multiple authorities, you cannot use an "id." short form for the next citation, even if it is a citation to the last authority cited in the previous string citation. See BP Rule B4 and Rule 4.1.

For example, assume that the immediately preceding citation is the following citation sentence:

> Burck v. Mars, Inc., 571 F. Supp. 2d 446, 453
> (S.D.N.Y. 2008); Onassis, 472 N.Y.S.2d at 261.

If your current citation is to pinpoint page 261 in Onassis, the short citation for it would be the following:

> Onassis, 472 N.Y.S.2d at 261.

Likewise, if your current citation is to pinpoint page 453 in Burck (with the same Burck and Onassis string citation as the immediately preceding citation), the short citation for it would be the following:

> Burck, 571 F. Supp. 2d at 453.

You should use an "id." short form to start a string citation if an "id." short form is otherwise appropriate. For example, assume that the immediately preceding citation is the following:

```
Burck, 571 F. Supp. 2d at 454.
```

If your current citation is a string citation to pinpoint page 454 in Burck first and then to pinpoint page 261 in Onassis second, the string citation sentence would be the following (assume that you have previously cited to Onassis in the same general discussion, i.e., a short form to Onassis is appropriate):

```
Id.; Onassis, 472 N.Y.S.2d at 261.
```

If the pinpoint page to Burck in the same example as the previous example changed to 453, the string citation sentence would change to the following:

```
Id. at 453; Onassis, 472 N.Y.S.2d at 261.
```

E. Common Rules & Tables

The following table provides the common Bluebook rules and tables for string citations.

Rule or Table	Description
BP Rule B1.1	Citation Sentences & Clauses (Use of Semi-Colons)
BP Rule B1.2	Order of Authorities
BP Rule B4	Id.
Rule 1.4	Order of Authorities
Rule 4.1	Id.

F. Exercise

Along with using the information in this chapter, you should use your Bluebook when answering these questions (note: do not use any jurisdiction- or court-specific citation rules, which are covered in Section C of Chapter 1 and are set forth in BP Table BT2). Some questions may require you to find and apply rules that were not specifically discussed in this chapter.

For all answers, use only ordinary or <u>underlined</u> typeface. That is, do not use *italics* or LARGE AND SMALL CAPS typeface.

As with some of the examples in this chapter, some of the legal authority used in these questions may be fictional authority designed to test various Bluebook rules.

1. You currently want to cite to page 723 of <u>Smith v. Cullen</u>, 54 P.3d 715 (Wash. 2011) and page 928 of <u>Hemingway v. Black</u>, 43 P.3d 926 (Wash. Ct. App. 2010). Neither case has previously been cited in this section of your document. Which of the following is the correct citation sentence?

   A. <u>Smith v. Cullen</u>, 54 P.3d 715, 723 (Wash. 2011).; <u>Hemingway v. Black</u>, 43 P.3d 926, 928 (Wash. Ct. App. 2010).

   B. <u>Smith v. Cullen</u>, 54 P.3d 715, 723 (Wash. 2011); <u>Hemingway v. Black</u>, 43 P.3d 926, 928 (Wash. Ct. App. 2010).

   C. <u>Smith v. Cullen</u>, 54 P.3d 715, 723 (Wash. 2011), <u>Hemingway v. Black</u>, 43 P.3d 926, 928 (Wash. Ct. App. 2010).

   D. <u>Smith v. Cullen</u>, 54 P.3d 715, 723 (Wash. 2011). <u>Hemingway v. Black</u>, 43 P.3d 926, 928 (Wash. Ct. App. 2010).

2. You currently want to cite to page 723 of <u>Smith v. Cullen</u>, 54 P.3d
    715 (Wash. 2011) and page 928 of <u>Hemingway v. Black</u>, 43 P.3d 926
    (Wash. Ct. App. 2010). Both cases have previously been cited in full
    in this section of your document. The immediately preceding cita-
    tion to your current citation is the following: <u>Fruth v. Wheeling</u>, 615
    A.2d 352, 359-61 (Pa. 1998). Which of the following is the correct ci-
    tation sentence?

    A.   <u>Smith v. Cullen</u>, 54 P.3d 715, 723 (Wash.
         2011); <u>Hemingway v. Black</u>, 43 P.3d 926, 928
         (Wash. Ct. App. 2010).

    B.   <u>Smith</u>, 54 P.3d at 723; <u>Hemingway v. Black</u>, 43
         P.3d 926, 928 (Wash. Ct. App. 2010).

    C.   <u>Smith v. Cullen</u>, 54 P.3d 715, 723 (Wash.
         2011); <u>Hemingway</u>, 43 P.3d at 928.

    D.   <u>Smith</u>, 54 P.3d at 723; <u>Hemingway</u>, 43 P.3d at
         928.

3. You currently want to cite to page 723 of <u>Smith v. Cullen</u>, 54 P.3d
    715 (Wash. 2011). This case has previously been cited in full in this
    section of your document. The immediately preceding citation to
    your current citation is the following: <u>Hemingway v. Black</u>, 43 P.3d
    926, 928 (Wash. Ct. App. 2010); <u>Smith</u>, 54 P.3d at 723. Which of the
    following is the correct current citation sentence?

    A.   <u>Id.</u>

    B.   <u>Id.</u> at 723.

    C.   <u>Smith</u>, 54 P.3d at 723.

4. You currently want to cite to page 723 of <u>Smith v. Cullen</u>, 54 P.3d 715 (Wash. 2011). The immediately preceding citation to your current citation is the following: <u>Smith v. Cullen</u>, 54 P.3d 715, 723 (Wash. 2011); <u>Hemingway v. Black</u>, 43 P.3d 926, 928 (Wash. Ct. App. 2010). Which of the following is the correct current citation sentence?

   A. <u>Id.</u>

   B. <u>Id.</u> at 723.

   C. <u>Smith</u>, 54 P.3d at 723.

5. You currently want to cite to page 359 of <u>Fruth v. Wheeling</u>, 615 A.2d 352 (Pa. 1998) and page 15 of <u>Avidan v. Dorfmeister</u>, 533 A.2d 10 (Pa. 1992). Both cases have previously been cited in full in this section of your document. The immediately preceding citation to your current citation is the following: <u>Fruth</u>, 615 A.2d at 360. Which of the following is the correct current citation sentence?

   A. <u>Id.</u>; <u>Avidan</u>, 533 A.2d at 15.

   B. <u>Id.</u> at 359; <u>Avidan</u>, 533 A.2d at 15.

   C. <u>Fruth</u>, 615 A.2d at 359; <u>Avidan</u>, 533 A.2d at 15.

6. Which of the following is the correct citation sentence (assuming that no authority is more helpful or authoritative than the others)?

A. United States v. Golson, 743 F.3d 44, 47 (3d Cir. 2014); Commonwealth v. Clark, 28 A.3d 1284, 1286 (Pa. 2011); State v. Hernandez, 704 S.E.2d 55, 58 (N.C. Ct. App. 2010); United States v. McElroy, 587 F.3d 73, 75 (1st Cir. 2009).

B. United States v. Golson, 743 F.3d 44, 47 (3d Cir. 2014); United States v. McElroy, 587 F.3d 73, 75 (1st Cir. 2009); State v. Hernandez, 704 S.E.2d 55, 58 (N.C. Ct. App. 2010); Commonwealth v. Clark, 28 A.3d 1284, 1286 (Pa. 2011).

C. United States v. McElroy, 587 F.3d 73, 75 (1st Cir. 2009); United States v. Golson, 743 F.3d 44, 47 (3d Cir. 2014); State v. Hernandez, 704 S.E.2d 55, 58 (N.C. Ct. App. 2010); Commonwealth v. Clark, 28 A.3d 1284, 1286 (Pa. 2011).

D. United States v. McElroy, 587 F.3d 73, 75 (1st Cir. 2009); United States v. Golson, 743 F.3d 44, 47 (3d Cir. 2014); Commonwealth v. Clark, 28 A.3d 1284, 1286 (Pa. 2011); State v. Hernandez, 704 S.E.2d 55, 58 (N.C. Ct. App. 2010).

Chapter 14
Introductory Signals

A. Signals Basics

A signal before a citation introduces the citation; it indicates the relationship between the proposition stated in the textual sentence and the authority cited for that proposition (see BP Rule B1.2). All of the examples and exercises in the other chapters of this book do not use any signals before the citations, which indicates that (1) the authority cited is the source of a direct quotation in the textual sentence; (2) the authority cited directly states the proposition in the textual sentence; or (3) the authority cited is referred to in the textual sentence (see BP Rule B1.2 and Rule 1.2(a)). For example:

1. The Supreme Court determined that DOMA "imposes a disability on [same-sex married couples] by refusing to acknowledge a status the State finds to be dignified and proper." United States v. Windsor, 133 S. Ct. 2675, 2695-96 (2013).

2. The Supreme Court held that DOMA is invalid. United States v. Windsor, 133 S. Ct. 2675, 2696 (2013).

3. In Windsor, the Supreme Court had to decide the constitutionality of DOMA. United States v. Windsor, 133 S. Ct. 2675 (2013).

In circumstances that do not meet one of the three criteria above, you should use a signal to introduce the citation. A signal precedes the citation, is underlined, and is followed by a space. For example, the following citation uses the signal "e.g." (Section B below outlines the various signals):

E.g., Fruth v. Lear, 688 A.2d 35, 38 (Pa. 1998).

If a signal begins a citation sentence (as it does in the example above), the first letter of the signal should be capitalized. Otherwise (i.e., if a signal begins a citation clause or is in the middle of a string citation), the first letter of the signal should be in lower case. See BP Rule B1.2.

TAKE NOTE

The examples in this chapter use signals with full citations to cases, but a signal can also be used with short citations and with other types of authority (primary or secondary).

TIP

"E.g.," is the only signal that requires a comma at the end of it. According to BP Rule B1.2, this ending comma should not be underlined. The "e.g.," signal can be used in combination with other signals, and, in such circumstances, a comma comes before the "e.g.," (i.e., a comma is within the combined signal). This internal comma should be underlined. For example:

E.g.,	✗ incorrect underlining
See, e.g.,	✗ incorrect underlining
But see, e.g.,	✗ incorrect underlining
E.g.,	✓ correct underlining
See, e.g.,	✓ correct underlining
But see, e.g.,	✓ correct underlining

Recall that BP Rule B2 allows underlining or italics, but this book uses underlining so that you can more easily see when text needs to be underlined or italicized.

B. Categories of Signals

BP Rule B1.2 and Rule 1.2 provide details for each signal that you can use (e.g., when to use a particular signal). Signals are divided into four categories according to the relationship of the authority cited with the proposition stated in the textual sentence:

1. signals indicating support (see Rule 1.2(a));
2. signal suggesting a useful comparison (see Rule 1.2(b));
3. signals indicating contradiction (see Rule 1.2(c)); and
4. signal indicating background material (see Rule 1.2(d)).

Some signals' rules encourage or strongly recommend a parenthetical to explain the relevance of the authority cited to the proposition stated in the textual sentence (see tables below outlining specific signals). Even if an explanatory parenthetical is not encouraged or strongly recommended for a particular signal, you may still have reason to use one.

NAVIGATE

Section D in Chapter 10 covers explanatory parentheticals.

1. Signals Indicating Support

The following signals (including no signal) indicate that the cited authority supports the proposition stated in the textual sentence (see Rule 1.2(a) for details about when to use each of these signals):

Signal	Use of Explanatory Parenthetical with Signal
[no signal]	Not encouraged or strongly recommended
E.g.,	Not encouraged or strongly recommended
Accord	Not encouraged or strongly recommended
See	Not encouraged or strongly recommended
See also	Encouraged
Cf.	Strongly recommended

For the types of documents you will write in your legal research and writing courses, as well as in practice (e.g., a brief, a memo, or an opinion), signals indicating support (including "no signal") are the most commonly used signals.

TIP

Because you will often cite an authority that (1) is the source of a direct quotation in your textual sentence; (2) directly states the proposition in your textual sentence; or (3) is referred to in the textual sentence, you will often not use any particular signal to introduce a citation.

2. Signal Suggesting a Useful Comparison

The following signal suggests that a comparison of the authorities cited supports or illustrates the proposition stated in the textual sentence (see Rule 1.2(b) for details about how to use this signal):

Signal	Use of Explanatory Parenthetical with Signal

Compare . . .
  [and] . . .
  with . . .
  [and] . . .
	Strongly recommended

3. Signals Indicating Contradiction

The following signals indicate that the cited authority contradicts the proposition stated in the textual sentence (see Rule 1.2(c) for details about when to use each of these signals):

Signal	Use of Explanatory Parenthetical with Signal
Contra	Not encouraged or strongly recommended
But see	Not encouraged or strongly recommended
But cf.	Strongly recommended

4. Signal Indicating Background Material

The following signal indicates that the cited authority presents background material for the proposition stated in the textual sentence (see Rule 1.2(d)):

Signal	Use of Explanatory Parenthetical with Signal
See generally	Encouraged

C. Signals & String Citations

At times, you may need to cite more than one authority for a particular sentence or proposition in your document. To do so, you use what is commonly referred to as a "string citation" where the citation for each authority in the string is separated by a semi-colon (see BP Rule B1.1).

NAVIGATE

Chapter 13 covers string citations in general (i.e., without the use of signals).

TAKE NOTE

The cases in the example string citations below use the same deciding court, but a string citation, regardless of whether it uses signals, can include cases decided by different courts.

In addition, none of the examples below use explanatory parentheticals, but such parentheticals are encouraged or strongly recommended for authorities introduced with some signals (e.g., the "cf." signal) (see Rule 1.2).

With a string citation, you can use a signal to introduce the entire string (i.e., the one signal applies to all of the authorities cited in the string), or you can use different signals to introduce different authorities. When using signals with string citations, you must consider how to order and format the following:

1. Multiple authorities within one signal;
2. Different signals within one category; and
3. Signals from Multiple Categories.

TAKE NOTE

Note that Rule 1.2(a) puts "no signal" in the category of signals indicating support. Therefore, all of the rules regarding order and format apply equally if no signal is used as one of the "signals."

1. Order & Format of Multiple Authorities Within One Signal

If you have multiple authorities that you want to introduce with the same signal, you should list the signal only once by putting it before the citation to the first authority introduced by that signal. For example, if you want to introduce the <u>Fruth</u> and <u>Smith</u> cases with an "<u>e.g.</u>," signal, the following would be the string citation sentence (assuming that full citations are appropriate for both cases):

```
E.g., Fruth v. Lear, 688 A.2d 35, 38 (Pa. 1998);
Smith v. Hemingway, 687 A.2d 26, 31 (Pa. 1997).
```

Rule 1.4 indicates how you should order multiple authorities within one particular signal (including "no signal") within a string citation. The example above uses the correct order because cases decided by the same court should be listed in reverse chronological order, unless one or more authorities "are considerably more helpful or authoritative than the other[s]."

NAVIGATE

Section C in Chapter 13 covers, in more detail, the rules for determining how to order multiple authorities within one particular signal.

2. Order & Format of Different Signals from One Category

If you have multiple authorities that you want to introduce with different signals from the same category (e.g., signals indicating support), you should use the signals in the order that they appear in Rule 1.2, which is the order that they are listed in Section B above (see BP Rule B1.2 and Rule 1.3). For example, assume that you want to cite the <u>Raeker</u> and <u>Wingert</u> cases in a string citation. You want to use a "<u>see</u>" signal to introduce <u>Raeker</u> and "<u>cf.</u>" to introduce <u>Wingert</u>. Rule 1.2 lists the "<u>see</u>" signal before the "<u>cf.</u>" signal. The following would be the string citation sentence (assuming that full citations are appropriate for both cases):

```
See Raeker v. Jordan, 691 A.2d 15, 18 (Pa. 2000);
cf. Wingert v. Snyder, 689 A.2d 76, 79 (Pa.
1999).
```

Notice in the example above that the "<u>see</u>" signal is capitalized because it is at the beginning of a citation sentence, but "<u>cf.</u>" is in lower case because it does not begin a citation sentence (see BP Rule B1.2).

TIP

As in the example above, the space between a signal and the authority it introduces should never be underlined.

A string citation with different signals from the same category can also include multiple authorities within a particular signal. In such a circumstance, the order and format rules in Section C.1 above apply. The following is an example string citation sentence:

```
See Raeker v. Jordan, 691 A.2d 15, 18 (Pa.
2000); Fruth v. Lear, 688 A.2d 35, 38 (Pa.
1998); cf. Wingert v. Snyder, 689 A.2d 76, 79
(Pa. 1999); Smith v. Hemingway, 687 A.2d 26,
31 (Pa. 1997).
```

Notice that the string citation above is one string citation sentence even though it includes two different signals. The "<u>see</u>" signal introduces both <u>Raeker</u> and <u>Fruth</u>, and the "<u>cf.</u>" signal introduces both <u>Wingert</u> and <u>Smith</u>.

3. Order & Format of Signals from Different Categories

If you want to introduce multiple authorities with signals from different categories (e.g., signals indicating support and signals indicating contradiction), you should use the signals in the order that they appear in Rule 1.2, which is the order that they are listed in Section B above, (see BP Rule B1.2 and Rule 1.3). The format in such a circumstance depends on whether you use a citation sentence or clause.

NAVIGATE

Section D in Chapter 1 covers the distinction between citation sentences and clauses.

a. Citation Sentence

For citation sentences (see BP Rule B1.1), signals from different categories should be used in different citation sentences (see Rule 1.3). For example:

```
This is the entire textual sentence. See
Raeker v. Jordan, 691 A.2d 15, 18 (Pa. 2000).
But see Rosenthal v. Schrier, 682 A.2d 5, 8
(Pa. 1995); Hayes v. Klion, 680 A.2d 11, 15
(Pa. 1993).
```

Notice that the example above includes two citation sentences, each citation sentence ends with a period, and the signal beginning each citation sentence is capitalized. The first citation sentence cites <u>Raeker</u>, and the case is introduced with a "<u>see</u>" signal, which is in the "signals indicating support" category (see Rule 1.2(a)). The second citation sentence is a string citation and cites to <u>Rosenthal</u> and <u>Hayes</u>, and both cases are introduced with a "<u>but see</u>" signal, which is in the "signals indicating contradiction" category (see Rule 1.2(c)). The order of these two citation sentences is correct because Rule 1.2 lists the "signals indicating support" category (and, therefore, the "<u>see</u>" signal) before the "signals indicating contradiction" category (and, therefore, the "<u>but see</u>" signal).

b. *Citation Clause*

For citation clauses (see BP Rule B1.1), signals from different categories should be used in the same string citation clause (see Rule 1.3). For example:

```
This is the beginning of the textual sentence,
see Raeker v. Jordan, 691 A.2d 15, 18 (Pa. 2000);
but see Rosenthal v. Schrier, 682 A.2d 5, 8 (Pa.
1995); Hayes v. Klion, 680 A.2d 11, 15 (Pa.
1993), and this is the continuation of the
textual sentence after the citation clause
 .  .  .  .
```

Notice that the example above includes a string citation clause in the middle of a textual sentence. In the string citation clause, <u>Raeker</u> is introduced with a "<u>see</u>" signal, and <u>Rosenthal</u> and <u>Hayes</u> are introduced with a "<u>but see</u>" signal (in the order dictated by Rule 1.2 and Rule 1.3). Even though these two signals are from different categories, they are not separated into different sentences with periods because they are used within a citation clause (see Rule 1.3). Because neither signal begins a citation sentence, neither is capitalized (see BP Rule B1.2).

TAKE NOTE

Whether using citation sentences or clauses, a string citation with signals from the different categories can also include different signals from the same category. In such a circumstance, the order and format rules in Section C.2 above apply. The following is an example using citation sentences:

> See Raeker v. Jordan, 691 A.2d 15, 18 (Pa. 2000); Fruth v. Lear, 688 A.2d 35, 38 (Pa. 1998); cf. Wingert v. Snyder, 689 A.2d 76, 79 (Pa. 1999). But see Rosenthal v. Schrier, 682 A.2d 5, 8 (Pa. 1995); Hayes v. Klion, 680 A.2d 11, 15 (Pa. 1993).

D. Common Rules & Tables

The following table provides the common Bluebook rules and tables for introductory signals.

Rule or Table	Description
BP Rule B1.1	Citation Sentences and Clauses
BP Rule B1.2	Introductory Signals, Order of Signals, & Order of Authorities Within Each Signal
Rule 1.2	Introductory Signals
Rule 1.3	Order of Signals
Rule 1.4	Order of Authorities Within Each Signal

E. Exercise

Along with using the information in this chapter, you should use your Bluebook when answering these questions (note: do not use any jurisdiction- or court-specific citation rules, which are covered in Section C of Chapter 1 and are set forth in BP Table BT2). Some questions may require you to find and apply rules that were not specifically discussed in this chapter.

For all answers, use only ordinary or <u>underlined</u> typeface. That is, do not use *italics* or LARGE AND SMALL CAPS typeface.

As with some of the examples in this chapter, some of the legal authority used in these questions may be fictional authority designed to test various Bluebook rules.

1. For the proposition stated in your textual sentence, you want to cite <u>Byrd</u>, which directly states your proposition. Which of the following is the correct citation sentence?

   A.   <u>Byrd v. Holbert</u>, 533 A.2d 145, 150 (Pa. Super. Ct. 1991).

   B.   <u>E.g.</u>, <u>Byrd v. Holbert</u>, 533 A.2d 145, 150 (Pa. Super. Ct. 1991).

   C.   <u>Accord</u> <u>Byrd v. Holbert</u>, 533 A.2d 145, 150 (Pa. Super. Ct. 1991).

   D.   <u>See</u> <u>Byrd v. Holbert</u>, 533 A.2d 145, 150 (Pa. Super. Ct. 1991).

   E.   <u>See also</u> <u>Byrd v. Holbert</u>, 533 A.2d 145, 150 (Pa. Super. Ct. 1991).

   F.   <u>Cf.</u> <u>Byrd v. Holbert</u>, 533 A.2d 145, 150 (Pa. Super. Ct. 1991).

2. For the proposition stated in your textual sentence, you want to cite <u>Cecala</u>, which clearly supports your proposition but does not directly state it. Which of the following is the correct citation sentence?

A. <u>Cecala v. Raymund</u>, 545 A.2d 307, 311 (Pa. 1993).

B. <u>E.g.</u>, <u>Cecala v. Raymund</u>, 545 A.2d 307, 311 (Pa. 1993).

C. <u>Accord</u> <u>Cecala v. Raymund</u>, 545 A.2d 307, 311 (Pa. 1993).

D. <u>See</u> <u>Cecala v. Raymund</u>, 545 A.2d 307, 311 (Pa. 1993).

E. <u>See also</u> <u>Cecala v. Raymund</u>, 545 A.2d 307, 311 (Pa. 1993).

F. <u>Cf.</u> <u>Cecala v. Raymund</u>, 545 A.2d 307, 311 (Pa. 1993).

3. For the proposition stated in your textual sentence, you want to cite two cases—<u>Smith</u> and <u>Hemingway</u>. In your textual sentence, you use a quote from <u>Smith</u>. The proposition in your textual sentence is also stated in <u>Hemingway</u>. Which of the following is the correct citation sentence?

A. <u>Smith v. Cullen</u>, 54 P.3d 715, 723 (Wash. 2011); <u>Hemingway v. Black</u>, 43 P.3d 926, 928 (Wash. Ct. App. 2010).

B. <u>Accord Smith v. Cullen</u>, 54 P.3d 715, 723 (Wash. 2011); <u>Hemingway v. Black</u>, 43 P.3d 926, 928 (Wash. Ct. App. 2010).

C. <u>Smith v. Cullen</u>, 54 P.3d 715, 723 (Wash. 2011); <u>Accord Hemingway v. Black</u>, 43 P.3d 926, 928 (Wash. Ct. App. 2010).

D. <u>Smith v. Cullen</u>, 54 P.3d 715, 723 (Wash. 2011); <u>accord Hemingway v. Black</u>, 43 P.3d 926, 928 (Wash. Ct. App. 2010).

E. <u>See Smith v. Cullen</u>, 54 P.3d 715, 723 (Wash. 2011); <u>Hemingway v. Black</u>, 43 P.3d 926, 928 (Wash. Ct. App. 2010).

F. <u>Smith v. Cullen</u>, 54 P.3d 715, 723 (Wash. 2011); <u>See Hemingway v. Black</u>, 43 P.3d 926, 928 (Wash. Ct. App. 2010).

G. <u>Smith v. Cullen</u>, 54 P.3d 715, 723 (Wash. 2011); <u>see Hemingway v. Black</u>, 43 P.3d 926, 928 (Wash. Ct. App. 2010).

4. You found multiple authorities that support the proposition stated in your textual sentence. You decide to cite only one of these authorities and that citation to the other authorities is unnecessary. What signal should be used to introduce the one authority?

    A.   See, e.g.,

    B.   See e.g.,

    C.   E.g., see

    D.   See

    E.   E.g.,

5. For the proposition stated in your textual sentence, you want to cite Dorfmeister using the "see" signal and to Beidel using the "cf." signal. Which of the following is the correct citation sentence?

    A.   See Dorfmeister v. Avidan, 633 A.2d 15, 18 (Pa. 1992); cf. Beidel v. Heller, 702 A.2d 6, 11 (Pa. 2007).

    B.   Cf. Beidel v. Heller, 702 A.2d 6, 11 (Pa. 2007); see Dorfmeister v. Avidan, 636 A.2d 15, 18 (Pa. 1994).

    C.   A or B is correct depending on which case is more helpful or authoritative.

6. Which of the following is correct when used after an entire textual sentence ends (i.e., after the period ending the textual sentence)?

A.   E.g., _Dorfmeister v. Avidan_, 633 A.2d 15, 18 (Pa. 1992); _Contra_ _Beidel v. Heller_, 702 A.2d 6, 11 (Pa. 2007).

B.   E.g., _Dorfmeister v. Avidan_, 633 A.2d 15, 18 (Pa. 1992); _contra_ _Beidel v. Heller_, 702 A.2d 6, 11 (Pa. 2007).

C.   E.g., _Dorfmeister v. Avidan_, 633 A.2d 15, 18 (Pa. 1992). _Contra_ _Beidel v. Heller_, 702 A.2d 6, 11 (Pa. 2007).

D.   E.g., _Dorfmeister v. Avidan_, 633 A.2d 15, 18 (Pa. 1992). _contra_ _Beidel v. Heller_, 702 A.2d 6, 11 (Pa. 2007).

E.   e.g., _Dorfmeister v. Avidan_, 633 A.2d 15, 18 (Pa. 1992); _contra_ _Beidel v. Heller_, 702 A.2d 6, 11 (Pa. 2007).

7. You want to cite <u>Raeker</u> using the "<u>but see</u>" signal and to <u>Fruth</u> using the "<u>but cf.</u>" signal. Which of the following is correct?

A. <u>But see</u> Raeker v. Jordan, 691 A.2d 15, 18 (Pa. 2000). <u>But cf.</u> Fruth v. Lear, 688 A.2d 35, 38 (Pa. 1998).

B. <u>But see</u> Raeker v. Jordan, 691 A.2d 15, 18 (Pa. 2000); <u>but cf.</u> Fruth v. Lear, 688 A.2d 35, 38 (Pa. 1998).

C. <u>But see</u> Raeker v. Jordan, 691 A.2d 15, 18 (Pa. 2000); <u>But cf.</u> Fruth v. Lear, 688 A.2d 35, 38 (Pa. 1998).

D. <u>But see</u> Raeker v. Jordan, 691 A.2d 15, 18 (Pa. 2000); <u>cf.</u> Fruth v. Lear, 688 A.2d 35, 38 (Pa. 1998).

E. <u>But see</u> Raeker v. Jordan, 691 A.2d 15, 18 (Pa. 2000); <u>Cf.</u> Fruth v. Lear, 688 A.2d 35, 38 (Pa. 1998).

Chapter 15
Pinpoint Information

A. Introduction

When referring to specific information within an authority (e.g., a case), you should provide the specific location of that information in your citation to the authority, regardless of whether it is a full or short citation. This specific location is called the pinpoint information ("pincite"). Providing pinpoint information is very important because it enables the ready to locate the specific information quickly, as some authority may be quite lengthy.

The pinpoint information can be page numbers, sections, paragraphs, and other subdivisions, depending on the type of authority you are citing. This chapter covers the main forms of pinpoint information—pages, sections, and paragraphs. For information on other types of pinpoint information, consult Rule 3.1 (volumes, parts, and supplements) and Rule 3.4 (appended material).

B. Pages in General

When an authority is organized by pages (e.g., a case), you should use page numbers as the primary pinpoint information and then include any other relevant pinpoint information (e.g., footnote or endnote numbers).

1. Page Numbers for Main Text

When citing to information from the main text of a page (compared to other parts of a page such as footnotes or endnotes), you should indicate the page number(s) where the information is located. Often, a pincite will be to only one page, but it can also be to numerous pages. The following rules apply to pincites to multiple pages (see Rule 3.2(a)) for general information about pinpoint pages and BP Rule B10.1.2 for information specific to case citations).

TAKE NOTE

Notice in the following examples that the page numbers are not introduced with any abbreviations (i.e., do not precede pinpoint page numbers of cited authorities with "p." or "pp.") (see Rule 3.2(a)).

When pinciting to non-consecutive pinpoint pages, you should separate them by commas and spaces. For example, if the pincite is to pages 1155, 1157, and 1160, the following would be the correct pinpoint information:

    1155, 1157, 1160

When pinciting to consecutive pinpoint pages, you should include the first and last page of the range, separated with a hyphen or en dash. If the last page number of a range is more than two digits, you can drop any repetitive digits except the last two. For example, if the pincite is to page 1159 through page 1161, the following would be the correct pinpoint information:

    1159-61

If the pincite is to page 114 through page 115, the following would be the correct pinpoint information:

    114-15

You can also have a combination of non-consecutive and consecutive pinpoint pages. For example, if the pincite is to page 1155 and pages 1159 through 1161, the following would be the correct pinpoint information:

    1155, 1159-61

TAKE NOTE

You will often cite an authority that is within a larger source and is not separately paginated from the other authorities in that source (e.g., one case within a case reporter that contains many cases). When you encounter such a situation, you must also include the starting page number on the full citation to the authority. The starting page number precedes the pincite, and the two are separated by a comma and space (see Rule 3.2(a)).

For example, if the case you are citing starts on page 1152 and the specific information is located on page 1155, the following would be correct after the reporter abbreviation in a full citation to the case:

```
1152, 1155
```

If the pincite is the same as the starting page number, you still need to include both on a full citation:

```
1152, 1152
```

2. Footnotes or Endnotes Only

At times, you may cite information located in a footnote or endnote of an authority. When you do so, you need to include the footnote(s) or endnote(s) in the pinpoint information. To inform the reader that you are citing to a footnote or endnote, you should include an "n." (for one footnote or endnote) or "nn." (for multiple footnotes or endnotes) immediately before the footnote or endnote number(s) (i.e., there should not be a space between "n." or "nn." and the number(s)) (see Rule 3.2(b) and Rule 3.2(c)).

Along with the footnote or endnote number(s), you should include the page number. The page number is the page on which the footnote or endnote appears (see BP Rule B10.1.2, Rule 3.2(b), and Rule 3.2(c)). For endnotes, use the page on which the text of the actual endnote appears, not the page on which the call number for the endnote appears (see Rule

3.2(c)). The page number should precede the "n." or "nn." and the footnote or endnote number(s), and it should be separated from them by a space.

For example, if the pincite is to footnote 110 on page 52, the following would be the correct pinpoint information:

    52 n.110

If a footnote or endnote spans multiple pages, use the page on which it starts (see Rule 3.2(b) and Rule 3.2(c)). For example, if the pincite is to footnote 111 that starts on page 52 and continues to page 53, the following would be the correct pinpoint information:

    52 n.111

Citing to consecutive footnotes or endnotes is like citing to consecutive page numbers — use a hyphen or en dash and drop any repetitive digits except the last two. In addition, use "nn." instead of "n." See Rule 3.2(b). For example, if the pincite is to footnotes 112 through 116 on page 53, the following would be the correct pinpoint information:

    53 nn.112-16

Citing to non-consecutive footnotes or endnotes is almost identical to citing to non-consecutive pages. The difference is that an ampersand (&) is used, not of a comma, before the last footnote or endnote number (see Rule 3.2(b)). For example, if the pincite is to footnotes 112, 114, and 116 on page 53, the following would be the correct pinpoint information:

    53 nn.112, 114 & 116

If, however, you are citing to non-consecutive footnotes or endnotes that are on different pages, you need to indicate the pages for the corresponding footnotes or endnotes (see Rule 3.2(b)). For example, if the pincite is to footnote 110 on page 52 and footnotes 112 and 114 on page 53, the following would be the correct pinpoint information:

    52 n.110, 53 nn.112 & 114

TAKE NOTE

Although the examples above involve only footnotes, the rules illustrated apply equally to endnotes.

3. Main Text & Footnotes or Endnotes

When citing to information in a footnote or endnote, you may also want to cite information located in the main text on the page. To do so with information in a footnote, you should use an ampersand (&) between the page number and footnote number (see Rule 3.2(b)). For example, if the pincite is to information on page 52 and in footnote 110 on page 52, the following would be the correct pinpoint information:

```
52 & n.110
```

To cite information in the main text on a page and information in an endnote, you should use an ampersand (&) to separate the main text page number from the page number on which the endnote appears (see Rule 3.2(c)). For example, if the pincite is to information on page 23 and in endnote 78 on page 145, the following would be the correct pinpoint information:

```
23 & 145 n.78
```

If the pincite is to a range of pages and to a footnote within that range, include the page range, a comma, and then the typical footnote information (see Rule 3.2(b)). For example, if the pincite is to pages 50 through 52 and to footnote 110 that is on page 52, the following would be the correct pinpoint information:

```
50-52, 52 n.110
```

C. Pages from Electronic Databases

Even if you find an authority (e.g., a case) in an electronic database such as WestlawNext, Lexis Advance, or Bloomberg Law and the authority is organized in pages, you should give the pinpoint page(s) from the appropriate print source (e.g., a case reporter), if available (i.e., you should not use the page numbers from the printout of an electronic database version). When reviewing the electronic database version of an authority, you will not be able to determine the pinpoint pages as easily as you can when reviewing (and turning) the actual pages from a print source. To enable you to determine the actual page numbers in an authority, electronic databases embed the page numbers within the text of the authority.

Determining page numbers of an electronic database version of a case is often even more difficult because a case is often in multiple reporters, likely with different page numbers. For example, the information that you want to cite in a case may be on page 100 in one reporter (e.g., a state reporter) and on page 234 in another reporter (e.g., a regional reporter). Therefore, to enable you to determine the actual page numbers in each reporter, the electronic databases must embed all of the page numbers from multiple reporters within the text of the case.

TIP

In WestlawNext, you can often get a PDF file of the reporter version of a case. In other words, you can see the actual pagination of the case as if you are turning the pages in the reporter. WestlawNext provides these files for cases in reporters that are published by West.

If your citation uses a reporter published by West, using this PDF file can help you easily determine the pinpoint page(s). If such a file is available for a case, you will see a link to it in the case in WestlawNext.

Electronic databases embed page numbers within the text of an authority using what is often called "star pagination." It is so called because asterisks (i.e., stars) often precede the embedded page numbers. When you find an embedded page number in the text, the next word in the text is the first word on that page in the reporter. For example, assume that you encounter the following text in the electronic database version of a case located in only one reporter:

> If even one claim limitation within the asserted claim ***553** is not found in the accused product, there can be no literal infringement.[1]

The example above includes a "star page" — 553. Given the location of this star page, you can determine that the first words on page 553 of the reporter are "is not found in the accused product," and the last words on the previous page (552) of that reporter are "If even one claim limitation within the asserted claim."

TIP

Keep in mind that star pages are not in the actual reporter; they are only in the version of the case in electronic databases. If you directly quote language that includes a star page, your quotation should not include the star page.

For example, if you quote the language above, the quotation in your document would be the following: "If even one claim limitation within the asserted claim is not found in the accused product, there can be no literal infringement." In your citation for this quotation, you should indicate that the quoted language is on pages 552 through 553 of the reporter (i.e., 552-53).

As another example of star pagination, the following is a printout from WestlawNext of a case located in multiple reporters. Assume that you want to include the following quotation in your document: "Allegedly, the defendant student caused a cabin window to shatter when the infant plaintiff's face was near it." For your citation, you need to determine the pinpoint page(s) where the quoted language is located (the quoted language is highlighted in the printout below).

---

[1] <u>Rhino Assocs., L.P. v. Berg Mfg. & Sales Corp.</u>, 482 F. Supp. 2d 537 (M.D. Pa. 2007).

WARNING

The citations in the case below appear as they are in the original case. They do not comply with Bluebook rules.

This example demonstrates why you should never rely on the citations that you see in other documents. The writers of other documents may not have properly followed Bluebook rules or they may be following other citation rules (e.g., they may be following jurisdiction- or court-specific rules).

Staten v. City of New York, 90 A.D.3d 893 (2011)

935 N.Y.S.2d 80, 274 Ed. Law Rep. 655, 2011 N.Y. Slip Op. 09306

90 A.D.3d 893
Supreme Court, Appellate Division, Second Department, New York.

Marvin STATEN, etc., et al., plaintiffs,
v.
CITY OF NEW YORK, et al., respondents,
Louis Cintron, Sr., et al., defendants,
Camp Chen–A–Wanda, Inc., appellant.

Dec. 20, 2011.

Synopsis

Background: High school student brought suit, seeking damages for injuries sustained at camp when fellow student broke window near plaintiff's face. The Supreme Court, Richmond County, Aliotta, J., denied camp's motion to compel city's department of education (DOE) to disclose disciplinary records of fellow student. Camp appealed.

[Holding:] The Supreme Court, Appellate Division, held that discovery should have been allowed.

Affirmed as modified.

Attorneys and Law Firms

**81 Mound Cotton Wollan & Greengrass, Garden City, N.Y. (Raymond S. Mastrangelo and Rubin, Hay & Gould, P.C. [Rodney E. Gould and Robert C. Mueller] of counsel), for appellant.

Michael A. Cardozo, Corporation Counsel, New York, N.Y. (Stephen McGrath and Victoria Scalzo of counsel; Manisha Padi on the brief), for respondents.

WILLIAM F. MASTRO, A.P.J., ANITA R. FLORIO, PLUMMER E. LOTT, and JEFFREY A. COHEN, JJ.

Opinion

*894 In an action to recover damages for personal injuries, etc., the defendant Camp Chen–A–Wanda, Inc., appeals from an order of the Supreme Court, Richmond County (Aliotta, J.), entered September 13, 2010, which denied its motion pursuant to CPLR 3124 to compel disclosure of certain disciplinary records of the defendant student maintained by the defendant New York City Department of Education.

ORDERED that the order is modified, on the facts and in the exercise of discretion, by deleting the provisions thereof denying those branches of the motion which were to compel disclosure of Exhibit C and so much of Exhibit B as relates to the date of February 14, 2006, and substituting therefor provisions granting those branches of the motion, with the redaction of the name of a nonparty student mentioned in Exhibit B as being involved in the February 14, 2006, incident; as so modified, the order is affirmed, with costs to the appellant.

The infant plaintiff, along with his mother, suing derivatively, commenced this action against, among others, the defendants New York City Department of Education (hereinafter the DOE), City of New York (hereinafter the City), Camp Chen–A–Wanda, Inc. (hereinafter the Camp), and a fellow student who was on the infant plaintiff's high school football team (hereinafter the defendant student). The plaintiffs seek to recover damages for injuries the infant plaintiff allegedly sustained on August 25, 2007, when he was at the Camp with his high school football team. Allegedly, the defendant student caused a cabin window to shatter when the infant plaintiff's face was near it. The plaintiffs allege, inter alia, that the DOE, the City, and the Camp were negligent in failing to ****82** properly supervise the infants in their charge. Prior to joinder of issue, the Camp moved pursuant to CPLR 3124 to compel the DOE to disclose any information it had pertaining to disciplinary or other actions taken by the high school against the defendant student as a result of the incident, as well as any other disciplinary records concerning that student while he was a member of the football team. Following an in-camera review of the material sought to be disclosed, the Supreme Court denied the Camp's motion on the basis that such information was not material or necessary to the prosecution of the action. The Camp appeals. We modify.

[1] "While discovery determinations rest within the sound discretion of the trial court, the Appellate Division is vested with a corresponding power to substitute its own discretion for that of the trial court, even in the absence of abuse" (*Andon v. 302–304 Mott St. Assoc.,* 94 N.Y.2d 740, 745, 709 N.Y.S.2d 873, 731 N.E.2d 589; *see Lewis v. John,* 87 A.D.3d 564, 928 N.Y.S.2d 78).

[2] [3] ***895** Generally, schools are "under a duty to adequately supervise the students in their charge and they will be held liable for foreseeable injuries proximately related to the absence of adequate supervision" (*Mirand v. City of New York,* 84 N.Y.2d 44, 49, 614 N.Y.S.2d 372, 637 N.E.2d 263). In its motion to compel, the Camp contended that it was entitled to discovery of any disciplinary records relating to the defendant student that were in the DOE's possession because such records were relevant to the issue of whether the DOE or the City had prior knowledge of behavioral issues regarding the defendant student, but failed to take reasonable precautions to prevent the incident (*see McLeod v. City of New York,* 32 A.D.3d 907, 822 N.Y.S.2d 562). The Camp argued, in essence, that discovery of such records was relevant to identifying which defendant was at fault for the incident, and thus, was material and necessary to the Camp's defense in this action.

The Supreme Court improvidently exercised its discretion in precluding the disclosure of certain evidence that was relevant to the parties' potential liability. Specifically, disclosure of the document labeled Exhibit C, a letter by the high school's principal regarding any disciplinary action taken by the high school as a result of the incident, should be disclosed, since it is material and necessary to the issue of liability. Further, there were records of prior incidents involving the defendant student's behavior, labeled as Exhibit B. One portion of the disciplinary records of the defendant student contained in Exhibit B is material and necessary to the Camp's defense, that portion being the entry dated February 14, 2006. This portion of Exhibit B is relevant to the issue of whether school officials had actual or constructive notice of prior conduct similar to that which occurred at the Camp and which could constitute a basis for imposing liability (*see Mirand v. City of New York,* 84 N.Y.2d at 49, 614 N.Y.S.2d 372, 637 N.E.2d 263; *Doe v. Department of Educ. of City of N.Y.,* 54 A.D.3d 352, 353, 862 N.Y.S.2d 598; *Culbert v. City of New York,* 254 A.D.2d 385, 388, 679 N.Y.S.2d 148). To the extent that the February 14, 2006, entry contains the name of a nonparty student, that name shall be redacted prior to disclosure.

[4] Lastly, while the material is subject to the Family Educational Rights and Privacy Act of 1974 (20 USC § 1232g) (*see generally United States v. Miami University,* 91 F.Supp.2d 1132, 1134, *affd.* 294 F.3d 797), commonly referred to as the "Buckley Amendment," that statute is not ****83** violated when disclosure is furnished via a judicial order (*see* 20 USC § 1232g[b] [2]).

Parallel Citations
90 A.D.3d 893, 935 N.Y.S.2d 80, 274 Ed. Law Rep. 655, 2011 N.Y. Slip Op. 09306

End of Document
© 2014 Thomson Reuters. No claim to original U.S. Government Works.

The heading in the WestlawNext printout above provides the following information:

> Staten v. City of New York, 90 A.D.3d 893 (2011)
> 935 N.Y.S.2d 80, 274 Ed. Law Rep. 655, 2011 N.Y. Slip Op. 09306

This heading illustrates that the case is located in multiple reporters (note: in electronic versions of a case, this information may be included at the end of the document, as you can see above in the "Parallel Citations" section of the printout above). The two main reporters are the following (note: you can find the relevant reporters in the entry in Table T1.3 for the court that decided the case—the Supreme Court, Appellate Division of New York):

- volume 90 of the Appellate Division Reports, Third Series (A.D.3d), starting on page 893; and
- volume 935 of West's New York Supplement, Second Series (N.Y.S.2d), starting on page 80.

NAVIGATE

Chapter 11 covers how to cite cases that are located in commercial electronic databases but not in reporters.

WestlawNext provides the page numbers for each of these two reporters; the star pages are embedded within the text of the case. For the reporter listed first (90 A.D.3d 893), one asterisk/star (*) precedes each page number for that reporter. For the reporter listed next (935 N.Y.S.2d 80), two asterisks/stars (**) precede the page number for that reporter. If page numbers were embedded for more reporters, the next one would use three asterisks/stars (***), and so on for any remaining reporters.

Given this asterisk/star system for multiple reporters, you can now determine on which page(s) the quotation is located in each reporter.

TIP

When viewing a case online in an electronic database (instead of viewing a printout of the electronic database version), you may not see star pages. Instead, the electronic database may show the page numbers for only one reporter at a time. If you do not see star pages for the reporter you need for your citation, look for an option to change which page numbers are displayed online. For example, the June 2015 version of Lexis Advance has links for each source (e.g., reporter) at the top of the case online, and clicking on the appropriate source's link will display the page numbers for that source in square brackets, without asterisks/stars.

Starting at the beginning of the case above, you can see that the first star page listed is "**81" under the "Attorneys and Law Firms" section towards the beginning of the case. This star page, with two asterisks/stars, indicates that the words immediately after that star page—"Mound Cotton Wollan & Greengrass"—are the first words on page 81 of the reporter listed second (i.e., volume 935 of N.Y.S.2d). Until you encounter the next star page for this reporter—**82—or the end of the case, all of the text after this star page is on page 81. You can see that the quoted language is just a bit before the "**82" star page, indicating that the quoted language is entirely on page 81. Therefore, a citation to this reporter for your quotation should indicate that page 81 is the pinpoint page. Notice that there is only one more star page for this reporter—**83—within the last sentence of the opinion (before the "Parallel Citations" section), indicating that the end of the opinion, starting with the word "violated," is on page 83 of this reporter.

For the other reporter, which was listed first (i.e., volume 90 of A.D.3d), you can see that the first star page is "*894" at the beginning of the text under "Opinion," which is just below the "Attorneys and Law Firms" section. This star page, with one asterisk/star, indicates that the words immediately after that star page—"In an action to recover damages"— are the first words on page 894 of the reporter listed first. Until you encounter the next star page for this reporter—*895—or the end of the case, all of the text after this star page is on page 894. You can see that the quoted language is well before the "*895" star page (which is located at the beginning of the third-to-last paragraph of the opinion), indicating that the quoted language is entirely on page 894. Therefore, a citation to this reporter for your quotation should indicate that page 894 is the pinpoint page. The next star page for this reporter—*895—is the last star page for this reporter, indicating that the end of the opinion, starting with the word "Generally," is on page 895 of this reporter.

NAVIGATE

For your citation, you need to determine which reporter to use or whether you need to use multiple reporters in a parallel citation. Section C.1 in Chapter 2 covers how to determine which reporter to use, and Chapter 9 covers parallel citations.

WARNING

Some electronic databases have a feature where you can copy text from an authority, and when you paste the text into a document, the citation for the authority will also be pasted, including the pinpoint page(s).

Be careful relying solely on such a feature to determine the needed pinpoint page(s) and other citation information. Although the pasted citation may appear to be in Bluebook format, often it is not (even if you chose Bluebook for such pasted citations). Likewise, the pinpoint page(s) are not always correct (e.g., if the copied text spans multiple pages, the pasted citation may include only the last pinpoint page).

D. Sections & Paragraphs

When an authority is organized by sections (e.g., a statute) or paragraphs (e.g., a complaint), you should use these subdivisions as the primary pinpoint information (see Rule 3.3).

For sections, use one section symbol (§) when citing to one section and two section symbols (§§) when citing to multiple sections. The same logic applies to using one (¶) or two (¶¶) paragraph symbols. See Rule 3.3(b)-(c).

TAKE NOTE

If an authority is organized by indented paragraphs that are not introduced by paragraph symbols (e.g., the Declaration of Independence), you should use "para." instead of a paragraph symbol (see Rule 3.3). This situation does not occur often because most of these authorities are primarily organized by pages and, therefore, should be cited by page, not paragraph, numbers.

The word "at" should not precede a section or paragraph symbol (see Rule 3.3). For example:

```
Id. at § 1983.    ✘ incorrect
Id. at ¶ 13.      ✘ incorrect

Id. § 1983.       ✔ correct
Id. ¶ 13.         ✔ correct
```

TIP

As you can see in the examples above and in the remaining examples in this section, you should always use a space between a section (§) or paragraph (¶) symbol and the corresponding number. See Rule 6.2(c).

With this space, a symbol could be at the end of one line in your document and the corresponding number(s) at the beginning of the next line. To avoid this awkward split, you can use a non-breaking space between the symbol and the number(s).

Your word processor should allow you to add non-breaking spaces. For example, in Microsoft Word, a non-breaking space is a symbol, and you can find it in the "Special Characters" section when choosing to insert a symbol, or you can press Ctrl+Shift+Space (PC) or Option+Space (Mac) to insert a non-breaking space.

The remaining discussion and examples in this section cover citations to multiple sections or subsections (see Rule 3.3(b)), but these rules apply equally to paragraphs (see Rule 3.3(c)).

When pinciting to non-consecutive sections, you should separate them by commas and spaces. For example, if the pincite is to sections 135, 138, and 141 the following would be the correct pinpoint information:

§§ 135, 138, 141

When pinciting to consecutive sections, you should include the first and last section of the range, separated with a hyphen or en dash. You should not omit repetitive digits or letters, unless the repetitive digits or letters precede a punctuation mark and their omission would not confuse the reader. For example, if the pincite is to section 135 through section 138, the following would be the correct pinpoint information:

§§ 135–138

Notice in the example above that the beginning "1" from the last section in the range is not omitted because it does not precede a punctuation mark.

In contrast to previous example, if the pincite is to section 23.5.11 through section 23.6.4, the following would be the correct pinpoint information:

```
§§ 23.5.11-.6.4
```

Notice in the example above that the beginning "23" from the last section in the range is omitted because it precedes a punctuation mark and its omission does not confuse the reader.

 TAKE NOTE

The example above cites to entire sections, not subsections within the sections. When a statute uses punctuation to separate subsections from sections, you should retain that punctuation (see Rule 3.3(a)). Commonly, statutes use parentheses to separate subsections from sections. For example:

```
§ 23.5.11(a)
§ 1332(c)(1)
```

Note in the second example above that there is no space between the "(c)" and the "(1)" (you should not use spaces within one section and any of its subsections).

If a statute does not use any punctuation to separate subsections, you should add parentheses to indicate the separations.

The rule for omitting repetitive digits or letters also applies when pinciting to non-consecutive sections. For example, if the pincite is to section 35A:22-3 and section 35A:24-2, the following would be the correct pinpoint information:

```
§§ 35A:22-3, :24-2
```

If using a hyphen or en dash to represent a range of sections would confuse the reader, use the word "to" instead of the hyphen or en dash. For example, assume the pincite is to section 208a-2 through section 208a-4:

§§ 208a-2-4   ✗ incorrect
§§ 208a-2 to -4 ✓ correct

TAKE NOTE

As the previous two examples illustrate, some sections include letters. In other words, these letters are part of the overall section "number"; they are not subsections within an overall section.

In the following example, the pincite is to one entire section:

§ 1396a

In contrast, the following example is a pincite to one subsection of a section:

§ 1332(a)

For sections with letters, do not omit the repetitive digits when citing to multiple sections. For example:

§§ 1396a-1396c

Notice in the example above that two section symbols are used because more than one section is cited.

The consecutive and non-consecutive pincite examples above involve pinciting to different *sections*. If you are merely pinciting to different *subsections* within the same section, you should use only one section symbol. For example, if the pincite is to subsections (a) and (c) of section 1332, the following would be the correct pinpoint information:

§ 1332(a), (c)

If the pincite is to subsections (a) through (c) of section 1332, the following would be the correct pinpoint information:

```
§ 1332(a)–(c)
```

When the information you are citing is located in specific subsection(s), you should cite to the specific subsection(s), not just to the overall section. For example, assume the information you are citing is located in subsection (d) of section 156:

```
§ 156        ✗ incorrect
§ 156(d)     ✓ correct
```

E. Common Rules & Tables

The following table provides the common Bluebook rules and tables for pinpoint information.

Rule or Table	Description
BP Rule B10.1.2	Pinpoint Citations for Cases
Rule 3.2(a)	Pages
Rule 3.2(b)	Footnotes
Rule 3.2(c)	Endnotes
Rule 3.3	Sections & Paragraphs
Rule 6.2(c)	Section (§) & Paragraph (¶) Symbols

F. Exercise

Along with using the information in this chapter, you should use your Bluebook when answering these questions (note: do not use any jurisdiction- or court-specific citation rules, which are covered in Section C of Chapter 1 and are set forth in BP Table BT2). Some questions may require you to find and apply rules that were not specifically discussed in this chapter.

For all answers, use only ordinary or <u>underlined</u> typeface. That is, do not use *italics* or LARGE AND SMALL CAPS typeface.

As with some of the examples in this chapter, some of the legal authority used in these questions may be fictional authority designed to test various Bluebook rules.

This exercise is split into the following categories:

1. Pages
2. Sections & Paragraphs

1. Pages

1. You want to pincite to page 196 through page 198. Which of the following is the correct pinpoint information?

    A.   196 to 198

    B.   196-198

    C.   196-98

    D.   196-8

2. You want to pincite to page 199 through page 201. Which of the following is the correct pinpoint information?

   A. 199 to 201

   B. 199-201

   C. 199-01

   D. 199-1

3. You want to pincite to page 1045 through page 1047. Which of the following is the correct pinpoint information?

   A. 1045 to 1047

   B. 1045-1047

   C. 1045-047

   D. 1045-47

   E. 1045-7

4. You want to pincite to page 1045 and page 1047. Which of the following is the correct pinpoint information?

   A. 1045 and 1047

   B. 1045 & 1047

   C. 1045, 1047

   D. 1045, 047

   E. 1045, 47

   F. 1045, 7

5. You want to pincite to footnote 45, which starts on page 13 and extends onto page 14. Which of the following is the correct pinpoint information?

    A.   `13-14 & n.45`

    B.   `13-14 & n. 45`

    C.   `13 & n.45`

    D.   `13 & n. 45`

    E.   `13 n.45`

    F.   `13 n. 45`

6. You want to pincite to the main text on page 14 and to footnotes 46 through 47 on page 14. Which of the following is the correct pinpoint information?

    A.   `14 & n. 46-47`

    B.   `14 & n.46-47`

    C.   `14 & nn. 46-47`

    D.   `14 & nn.46-47`

    E.   `14 n. 46-47`

    F.   `14 n.46-47`

    G.   `14 nn. 46-47`

    H.   `14 nn.46-47`

7. You are including a quotation in your document from <u>Teris, LLC v. Chandler</u>, decided in 2008 by the Arkansas Supreme Court. It is located in volume 375 of the Arkansas Reports, starting on page 70, and in volume 289 of the South Western Reporter, Third Series, starting on page 63. Your quotation from the case is as follows: "Moreover, this court has recognized that a bifurcated process of certifying a class to resolve preliminary, common issues and then decertifying the class to resolve individual issues, such as damages, is consistent with Rule 23." Look up this case in an electronic database (e.g., WestlawNext, Lexis Advance, or Bloomberg Law). If your citation is to the South Western Reporter, Third Series, version of the case, what is the correct pinpoint information for the quotation?

    A.   16

    B.   17

    C.   16-17

    D.   71

    E.   72

    F.   71-72

    G.   81

    H.   82

    I.   81-82

8. You are including a quotation in your document from <u>Teris, LLC v. Chandler</u>, decided in 2008 by the Arkansas Supreme Court. It is located in volume 375 of the Arkansas Reports, starting on page 70, and in volume 289 of the South Western Reporter, Third Series, starting on page 63. Your quotation from the case is as follows: "Moreover, this court has recognized that a bifurcated process of certifying a class to resolve preliminary, common issues and then decertifying the class to resolve individual issues, such as damages, is consistent with Rule 23." Look up this case in an electronic database (e.g., WestlawNext, Lexis Advance, or Bloomberg Law). If your citation is to the Arkansas Reports version of the case, what is the correct pinpoint information for the quotation?

    A.   16

    B.   17

    C.   16–17

    D.   71

    E.   72

    F.   71–72

    G.   81

    H.   82

    I.   81–82

2. Sections & Paragraphs

9. You want to pincite to section 452 through section 454. Which of the following is the correct pinpoint information?

    A.   § 452 to 454

    B.   § 452-454

    C.   § 452-54

    D.   § 452-4

    E.   §§ 452 to 454

    F.   §§ 452-454

    G.   §§ 452-54

    H.   §§ 452-4

10. You want to pincite to section 766.102 through section 766.103. Which of the following is the correct pinpoint information?

    A.   § 766.102 to 766.103

    B.   § 766.102-766.103

    C.   § 766.102-.103

    D.   § 766.102-103

    E.   §§ 766.102 to 766.103

    F.   §§ 766.102-766.103

    G.   §§ 766.102-.103

    H.   §§ 766.102-103

11. You want to pincite to section 765a through section 765c. Which of the following is the correct pinpoint information?

    A.   § 765a to 765c

    B.   § 765a-765c

    C.   § 765a-c

    D.   § 765(a)-(c)

    E.   §§ 765a to 765c

    F.   §§ 765a-765c

    G.   §§ 765a-c

    H.   §§ 765(a)-(c)

12. You want to pincite to paragraph 7 and paragraph 9. Which of the following is the correct pinpoint information?

    A.   ¶ 7 and ¶ 9

    B.   ¶ 7 & ¶ 9

    C.   ¶ 7, ¶ 9

    D.   ¶ 7, 9

    E.   ¶¶ 7 and 9

    F.   ¶¶ 7 & 9

    G.   ¶¶ 7, 9

13. You want to pincite to subsections (b) through (d) of section 123. Which of the following is the correct pinpoint information?

   A.   § 123(b) to 123(d)

   B.   § 123(b)-123(d)

   C.   § 123(b)-(d)

   D.   §§ 123(b) to 123(d)

   E.   §§ 123(b)-123(d)

   F.   §§ 123(b)-(d)

14. You want to pincite to subsections (b) and (d) of section 123. Which of the following is the correct pinpoint information?

   A.   § 123(b) and 123(d)

   B.   § 123(b) & 123(d)

   C.   § 123(b), 123(d)

   D.   § 123(b), (d)

   E.   §§ 123(b) and 123(d)

   F.   §§ 123(b) & 123(d)

   G.   §§ 123(b), 123(d)

   H.   §§ 123(b), (d)

Chapter 16
Capitalization

A. Capitalization in Textual Sentences

BP Rule B8 and Rule 8(c) cover capitalization in textual sentences (beyond the rule that you always capitalize the first word of a sentence).

NAVIGATE

Section D in Chapter 1 covers the difference between textual sentences and citations.

According to Rule 8(c)(i), you should capitalize "[n]ouns that identify specific persons, officials, groups, government offices, or government bodies." The following textual sentence illustrates such capitalization with "Congress" and "President" (see Rule 8(c)(i) for other examples):

```
The President asked members of Congress to reach
a consensus on the matter.
```

When you use similar terms as other parts of speech (e.g., an adjective), however, you should not capitalize them (e.g., congressional mandate and presidential power).

BP Rule B8 and Rule 8(c)(ii) include further capitalization rules:

- <u>Court</u> – You should capitalize "Court" only in the following three situations: (i) when naming any court in full (e.g., U.S. District Court for the Middle District of Pennsylvania), (ii) when referring to the U.S. Supreme Court, or (iii) when referring to the court that will be receiving your document (see BP Rule B8 and Rule 8(c)(ii)).

TAKE NOTE

The sentence above abbreviates "United States" as "U.S." Rule 6.1 indicates that you may use this abbreviation when using it as an adjective (note: you are not required to use the abbreviation in this circumstance). For example:

✓ In the U.S. Supreme Court, ...

✓ In the United States Supreme Court, ...

✓ The laws of the United States . . . .

✗ The laws of the U.S. . . . .

- <u>Circuit</u> – You should capitalize "Circuit" only when used with a circuit court's name or number—e.g., First Circuit (see Rule 8(c)(ii)).

- <u>Party Designations</u> – You should capitalize party designations (e.g., "Plaintiff," "Defendant," "Appellant," "Appellee," "Petitioner," and "Respondent") only when referring to the parties that are the subject of your document (see BP Rule B8).

TAKE NOTE

When using a party designation (and capitalizing it) to refer to a party that is the subject of your document, do not use an article ("a," "an," or "the") before the party designation. When using a party designation to refer to a party in another case (or when using party designations in general), use an article before the party designation. For example:

> In this case, Plaintiff alleges that
> Defendant fraudulently induced her into
> signing the contract.

> In <u>Lear</u>, the plaintiff proved that the
> defendant wrongfully terminated her.

WARNING

Before using party designations to refer to parties in your case or another case, consider whether another option would be better. For example, referring to your client by name is generally preferable to the party designation. In addition, using relevant descriptions of the parties in other cases (as opposed to names or party designations) will often aid the reader's understanding. For example:

✗ In <u>Lear</u>, the plaintiff proved that the
  defendant wrongfully terminated her.

✓ In <u>Lear</u>, the employee proved that her
  employer wrongfully terminated her.

- <u>Titles of Court Documents</u> – You should capitalize the title of a court document (e.g., Motion for Summary Judgment) only when (i) referring to the actual title of the document, even if in a shortened form, and (ii) the document to which you are referring has already been filed (i.e., submitted) in court (see BP Rule B8).

TAKE NOTE

Although you may shorten the title of a court document, you should not abbreviate any of the words (see BP Rule B8). For example:

✓ `Memorandum of Points and Authorities in Support of Defendant's Motion for Summary Judgment`

✓ `Memorandum in Support of Defendant's Motion for Summary Judgment`

✗ `Mem. of P. & A. in Supp. of Def.'s Mot. for Summ. J.`

✗ `Mem. in Supp. of Def.'s Mot. for Summ. J.`

TIP

Notice in the examples above that not all of the words in the title of the court document are capitalized. Rule 8(a) indicates that you should capitalize the words of a title except articles, conjunctions, and prepositions when they are four or fewer letters, unless such words begin the title or immediately follow a colon.

- <u>Judge / Justice</u> – You should capitalize "Judge" or "Justice" only in the following two situations: (i) when providing the name of a specific judge or justice (e.g., Judge Conner) or (ii) when referring to a Justice of the U.S. Supreme Court (see Rule 8(c)(ii)).

- <u>State / Commonwealth</u> – You should capitalize "State" or "Commonwealth" only in the following three situations:

(i) when providing the full name of the state or commonwealth (e.g., State of Florida and Commonwealth of Pennsylvania), (ii) when referring to the state or commonwealth as a party to a litigation or as a governmental actor, or (iii) when the word it modifies is capitalized (see Rule 8(c)(ii)).

- <u>Constitution</u> – You should capitalize "Constitution" only in the following two situations: (i) when providing the full name of the constitution (e.g., Florida Constitution) or (ii) when referring to the U.S. Constitution. Do not capitalize the adjective "constitutional," even if referring to the U.S. Constitution. See Rule 8(c)(ii).

TAKE NOTE

When referring to specific parts of a constitution, you should capitalize such words only when referring to specific parts of the U.S. Constitution (see Rule 8(c)(ii)). For example:

```
In the Eighth Amendment to the U.S.
Constitution, . . . .

In Article III, Section 1 of the U.S.
Constitution, . . . .

In article I, section 8 of the Pennsylvania
Constitution, . . . .
```

- <u>Act / Code</u> – You should capitalize "Act" or "Code" only when referring to a specific act or code (see Rule 8(c)(ii)). For example:

```
The Act protects individuals from
commercial exploitation.
```

- <u>Federal</u> – You should capitalize "Federal" only when the word it modifies is capitalized (see Rule 8(c)(ii)).

> **TIP**
>
> Keep in mind that the above capitalization rules apply in textual sentences, not citations.
>
> For words in textual sentences that BP Rule B8 and Rule 8(c) do not address, you may refer to another style manual (e.g., Chicago Manual of Style and Government Printing Office Style Manual) to determine whether to capitalize the words.

B. Common Rules & Tables

The following table provides the common Bluebook rules and tables for capitalization in textual sentences.

Rule or Table	Description
BP Rule B8	Capitalization in Textual Sentences
Rule 8(a)	Capitalization in Titles
Rule 8(c)	Capitalization in Textual Sentences

C. Exercise

Along with using the information in this chapter, you should use your Bluebook when answering these questions (note: do not use any jurisdiction- or court-specific citation rules, which are covered in Section C of Chapter 1 and are set forth in BP Table BT2). Some questions may require you to find and apply rules that were not specifically discussed in this chapter.

For all answers, use only ordinary or <u>underlined</u> typeface. That is, do not use *italics* or LARGE AND SMALL CAPS typeface.

As with some of the examples in this chapter, some of the legal authority used in these questions may be fictional authority designed to test various Bluebook rules.

1. The following is a textual sentence in a document that will be submitted in court in the <u>Beidel v. Heller</u> case. It refers to a case decided by the United States District Court for the Middle District of Pennsylvania.

> In <u>Walsh</u>, the ____[1]____ granted the ____[2]____ motion to dismiss.

Which of the following combination of words is correct to fill in the two blanks above?

A. [1] Court - [2] Defendants'

B. [1] Court - [2] defendants'

C. [1] court - [2] Defendants'

D. [1] court - [2] defendants'

2. The following is a textual sentence in a document that will be submitted in court in the <u>Byrd v. State</u> case. It refers to a case decided
   by the U.S. Supreme Court and to the U.S. Constitution.

   In <u>Windsor,</u> the _____[1]_____ determined that DOMA violated
   the ____[2]____ .

   Which of the following combination of words is correct to fill in the
   two blanks above?

   A.   [1] Court - [2] Fifth Amendment

   B.   [1] Court - [2] fifth amendment

   C.   [1] court - [2] Fifth Amendment

   D.   [1] court - [2] fifth amendment

3. The following is a textual sentence that refers to the Environmental
   Protection Agency.

   The _____ set limits for certain contaminants in drinking
   water.

   Which of the following is correct to fill in the blank above?

   A.   Agency

   B.   agency

4. The following is a textual sentence that refers to a case brought by Gary Brown against the Commonwealth of Pennsylvania.

> In <u>Brown</u>, the _____ argued that Mr. Brown's claims were time-barred.

Which of the following is correct to fill in the blank above?

A.   Commonwealth

B.   commonwealth

5. The following is a textual sentence that refers to the State of Florida.

> This Florida statute and subsequent cases demonstrate that the _____ allows the accused to raise an objective and subjective entrapment defenses.

Which of the following is correct to fill in the blank above?

A.   State

B.   state

Part V

Bluebook Rules in Context

Chapter 17

Comprehensive Exercise

A. Instructions

This comprehensive exercise is designed to put Bluebook rules in the context of a legal document with many citations and quotations.

NAVIGATE

Before completing this comprehensive exercise, you should have read and completed any exercises in Chapters 1, 2, 3, 4, 12, and 13 regarding case and statute citations, quotations, and string citations. In addition, you should understand how to determine and set forth pinpoint information, which is covered in some of the chapters referenced above and in Chapter 15.

For this exercise, you will review a portion of a legal document (which is in Section B below). You should correct any Bluebook errors in the citations and quotations.

In determining whether there are Bluebook errors and how to correct any errors, follow these guidelines:

1. Use only Bluebook rules (including tables), not any jurisdiction- or court-specific rules (which are covered in Section C of Chapter 1 and are set forth in BP Table BT2).

2. Use the statute and cases as they appear in the Library in Section C below to verify the citations and quotations in the document (i.e., do not do any independent research into these authorities).

3. Verify the accuracy of direct quotations, and make any needed corrections, but do not verify the accuracy of paraphrased material. If you need to correct a direct quotation, do not add any words to the quotation.

4. Verify the accuracy of pinpoint information only for citations to direct quotations, and make any needed corrections (e.g., if there is a direct quotation from a case, you need to verify that the pinpoint page is where that quotation is located in the case). Do not verify the accuracy of pinpoint information for citations to paraphrased material (i.e., you should assume that the pinpoint information for paraphrased material is correct). For all pinpoint information (to direct quotations or paraphrases), verify that the pinpoint information is formatted correctly.

5. Assume that the entire portion of the legal document that you will review is from the same general discussion of the document and that none of the authorities cited in this portion are previously cited in the document.

6. Use only citation sentences, not citation clauses.

7. Use only ordinary or <u>underlined</u> typeface, not *italics* or LARGE AND SMALL CAPS typeface.

8. Do <u>not</u> do any of the following:

    a. remove any citations;

    b. change the order of citations within a string citation; or

    c. include parallel citations.

9. Assume that there is no relevant prior or subsequent case history for any of the cases cited.

B. Document to Review for Bluebook Errors

By limiting a landowner's liability, the Pennsylvania Recreational Use of Land and Water Act ("RULWA") encourages landowners "to make land and water areas available to the public for recreational purposes . . . ." 68 P.S. § 477-1 (West 2004). The encouragement is specific to "large, private land holdings for outdoor recreational use." Rivera v. Philadelphia Theological Seminary, 507 A. 2d 8 (1986). Under RULWA, a landowner will be immune from liability for injuries sustained by visitors if the land is open to the public for recreational purposes without charge, except in limited circumstances that do not apply in this case. Redinger v. Clapper's Tree Service Inc., 615 A.2d 743, 745 (Pa. Super. 1992).

The issue in this case involves the "land" element. RULWA defines land as ". . . land, roads, water, watercourses, private ways and buildings, structures and machinery or equipment when attached to the realty". §477-2 (2004). Pennsylvania courts have construed this definition to include open unimproved areas. Bashioum v. County of Westmoreland, 747 A.2d 441, 443 (Pa. Cmwlth. 2000). The area cannot be ". . . vastly altered from its natural state . . ." nor highly developed. Mills v. Pa., 534 Pa. 519, 526 (1993). Land may include any improvements or ancillary structures attached to open land. Rivera, at 15, Walsh v. Philadelphia, 585 A.2d 445, 449 (Pa. 1991). Such improvements or ancillary structures qualify as land so long as they do not require "regular maintenance." Id. at 445, 450.

Land under RULWA does not include improved land that requires regular maintenance. Walsh, 585 A.2d at 449-450.; Bashioum v. County of Westmoreland, 747 A.2d 441, 444 (Pa. Cmwlth. 2000). For example, in Walsh, the land was a recreational facility maintained by the city of Philadelphia that

contained basketball courts, boccie courts, and

benches. 585 A.2d 446 & 50. The court held that the

recreational facility did not qualify as land under

RULWA because the improvements to the land required

regular maintenance for safe enjoyment. Id. at 450.

Liability is appropriate when "an improved facility

is allowed to deteriorate and causes a foreseeable

injury. . . ." Id.

Modified land is still unimproved for purposes

of RULWA when the modifications do not require

regular maintenance. Brezinski v. Allegheny, 694

A.2d 388, 390. In Brezinski, the court ruled that a

park that had been sculpted to accommodate a picnic

pavilion qualified as land under RULWA. Id. at 390.

The court determined that "even if the land were

"sculpted," this one-time modification would not

have required regular maintenance[.]" Id..

Therefore, this one-time modification did not strip

the land of its unimproved status. <u>Id.</u>

C. Library of Statute & Cases Used in Document to Review

The Library, which follows this brief introductory material, contains the statute and cases cited and quoted in Section B above. You should use only this Library when reviewing and correcting any Bluebook errors (i.e., do not do any independent research into the authorities because the actual authorities may differ slightly from the versions in this Library).

The Library contains the following authorities (in this order):

1. Recreational Use of Land and Water Act
2. Rivera case (representation of bound reporter version)
3. Redinger case (representation of bound reporter version)
4. Bashioum case (representation of bound reporter version)
5. Mills case (WestlawNext version)
6. Walsh case (representation of bound reporter version)
7. Brezinski case (representation of bound reporter version).

You do not need to read the text of the statute or cases, except to verify direct quotations used in Section B. Language that is quoted is highlighted in the Library so that you do not have to search the text for any quotations.

Not all pages of each case are included in the Library. For the representation of the bound reporter version of a case, only the first page of the case and any page(s) with quotations are included.[1] For the WestlawNext version of a case, all pages of the case are included.

---

[1] These representations are not identical to the actual pages of the bound reporter, but they simulate the actual pages and provide the same information that the actual pages provide with respect to the information needed to cite to the authority in this exercise.

Pennsylvania Consolidated Statutes
Title 68: Real and Personal Property
Chapter 11: Uses of Property

2004 Main Volume[2]

[Note: Portions of this law have been redacted.]

§ 477-1. Purpose; liability

The purpose of this act is to encourage owners of land to make land and water areas available to the public for recreational purposes by limiting their liability.

§ 477-2. Definitions

As used in this act:

(1) "Land" means land, roads, water, watercourses, private ways and buildings, structures and machinery or equipment when attached to the realty.

(2) "Owner" means the possessor of a fee interest, a tenant, lessee, occupant or person in control of the premises.

. . . .

---

[2] You should assume that no amendments to the text of these sections appear in any supplement or pocket part.

Rivera
Case

ATLANTIC
REPORTER

2d Series

507

RIVERA v. PHILADELPHIA THEOLOGICAL SEMINARY   Pa. 1
Cite as 507 A.2d 1 (Pa. 1986)

Concepcion L. RIVERA,
Administratrix of the Estate of
Frederick L. Rivera, Deceased,
Appellant,
v.
The PHILADELPHIA
THEOLOGICAL SEMINARY OF
ST. CHARLES BORROMEO, INC.
a/k/a St. Charles Seminary and Our
Lady of Lourdes Catholic Church,
Appellees.

Concepcion L. RIVERA,
Administratrix of the Estate of
Frederick L. Rivera, Deceased,
Appellee,
v.
The PHILADELPHIA
THEOLOGICAL SEMINARY OF
ST. CHARLES BORROMEO, INC.
a/k/a St. Charles Seminary and Our
Lady of Lourdes Catholic Church.
Appeal of the PHILADELPHIA
THEOLOGICAL SEMINARY OF
ST. CHARLES BORROMEO, INC.
a/k/a St. Charles Seminary.

Supreme Court of Pennsylvania
Argued April 16, 1985
Decided March 14, 1986

Estate of drowning victim brought wrongful death and survival actions against church, seminary, and supervising priest, arising from drowning in seminary's swimming pool. The Court of Common Pleas, Civil Division, Philadelphia County, No. 181 January Term, 1977, McDevitt, J., directed verdict in favor of priest and entered judgment on jury verdict awarding damages to estate and apportioning negligence. Seminary and church appealed, and estate cross-appealed. The Superior Court, Nos. 310, 311, and 476, Philadelphia, 1982, 326 Pa.Super. 509, 474 A.2d 605, reversed and remanded. Appeal and cross appeal were taken. The Supreme Court, Nos. 157, 158 Eastern District Appeal Dockets, 1984, Hutchinson, J., held that: (1) seminary was not immune under the Recreational Use Act; (2) instructions as to duty of seminary to provide lifeguard and as to supervising priest's ability to act as lifeguard were confusing and contradictory; and (3) retrial of seminary's liability did not require retrial of issues of damages or church's liability.

Affirmed as modified.

Nix, C.J., dissented and filed opinion joined by McDermott and Zappala, JJ.

McDermott, J., dissented and filed opinion joined by Nix, C.J., and Zappala, J.

1. Negligence ⚬— 135(7)

Evidence was sufficient to support jury's finding that drowning victim, an altar boy, was five percent negligent in seminary swimming pool.

2. Appeal and Error ⚬— 173(13)

Church waived right to contest judgment in common pleas court as to percentage of church's liability for drowning in seminary pool by failing to preserve that issue before Superior Court, even though church appealed only issue of damages, and even though church appealed only issue of damages done on the theory that it is not reasonable to expect such owners to undergo the risks of liability for injury to persons and property attendant upon the use of their land by strangers from whom the accommodating owner receives no compensation or other favor in return.

The suggested act which follows is designed to encourage availability of private lands by limiting the liability of owners to situations in which they are compensated for the use of their property and to those in which injury results from malicious or willful acts of the owner. In the case of lands leased to states or their political subdivisions for recreational purposes, the legislation expressly provides that the owner will have no remaining liability to recreationists, except as such liability may be incorporated in an agreement, or unless the owner is compensated *15 for the use of the land in addition to consideration for the lease.

The Council of State Governments, Public Recreation on Private Lands: Limitations on Liability, XXIV Suggested State Legislation 150, 150 (1965).

The Recreation Use Act is therefore designed to encourage the opening up of large, private land holdings for outdoor recreational use by the general public by limiting the liability of the landowner. Considering that purpose, we believe the Legislature intended to limit the meaning of the

words "buildings, structures and machinery or equipment when attached to the realty" in Section 2 of the Act, 68 P.S. § 477-2, to ancillary structures attached to open space lands made available for recreation and not to enclosed recreational facilities in urban regions. Grammatically, this construction is indicated by the dual presence of the conjunctive "and" in the list, both before "buildings" as well as after "structures." The position of the limiting clause "when attached to the realty" at the end of the sentence is another such indication. All of these factors make it appropriate to treat the list beginning with the word "buildings" as a restrictive modifer of "land, roads, water, watercourses." *Id.*[17]

The intention of the Legislature to limit the applicability of the Recreation Use Act to outdoor recreation on largely unimproved land is evident not only from the Act's stated purpose but also from the nature of the activities it listed as recreational purposes within the meaning of the statute. Specifically, with the exception of "swimming," which may be either an indoor or outdoor sport, the recreational activities enumerated in the statute are all pursued outdoors.

Moreover, while forty-six states, in addition to Pennsylvania, have enacted recreational use statutes,[18] we have been unable to find a single case in any of those jurisdictions in which an indoor recreational activity was held to fall within the purview of a recreational use act. In fact, most jurisdictions confronted with the question of whether a recreat-

<u>Redinger</u>
Case

ATLANTIC
REPORTER

2d Series

615

REDINGER v. CLAPPER'S TREE SERVICE INC.   Pa.   743

Cite as 615 A.2d 743 (Pa. 1992)

1976, July 9, P.L. 586, No. 142, § 2, effective June 27, 1978.

[4] Instantly, the action of the court of common pleas in reversing the grant of suppression vacated the final order upon which review was premised. The new order is clearly interlocutory as it did not end litigation or dispose of the case, but rather returns appellant to the position he would have been in had the municipal court denied his motion to suppress. The order as it stands at this point is not final. Therefore, this court is without jurisdiction to entertain an appeal as of right. Appellant will have an opportunity to question the validity of the denial of his motion to suppress at the conclusion of trial.

Motion granted; appeal quashed.

John S. REDINGER, and Earline Redinger, His Wife, Appellants

v.

CLAPPER'S TREE SERVICE INC. and Dr. and Mrs. A. L. Garver Memorial Y.M.C.A.-Y.W.C.A. and Pennsylvania Electric Co.

Superior Court of Pennsylvania

Argued April 1, 1992

Filed Oct. 30, 1992

Father who was injured by a falling tree limb while watching his son's baseball game sued the property owner.

The Court of Common Pleas, Blair County, Civil Division, No. 915 CP 1990, Carpenter, J., found that the suit was barred by the Recreation Use of Land and Water Act (RULWA), and appeal was taken. The Superior Court, No. 1344 Pittsburgh 1991, Ford Elliott, J., held that fenced-in baseball field in small community was land used for recreational purpose within meaning of RULWA and, thus, owner of land was not liable where injury did not arise out of any improvement to baseball field.

Affirmed.

1. Theaters and Shows ⚷ 6(10)

Fenced-in baseball field in small community was land used for recreational purpose within meaning of Recreation Use of Land and Water Act (RULWA), and, thus, owner of land was not liable for injury suffered when tree limb fell on father who was observing his son's baseball game; injury did not arise out of any improvement to baseball field but from unimproved section of land. 68 P.S. § 477-1 et seq.

2. Negligence ⚷ 37

Fact that land on which injury to recreational user occurs is partially developed does not preclude land from coming under liability limitation of Recreation Use of Land and Water Act (RULWA). 68 P.S. § 477-1 et seq.

3. Negligence ⚷ 37

Owner of recreational property on which injury occurred was not willful or malicious in dealing with rotting trees on property, for purposes of

<u>Bashioum</u>
Case

ATLANTIC
REPORTER

2d Series

747

BASHIOUM v. COUNTY OF WESTMORELAND   Pa. 441
Cite as 747 A.2d 441 (Pa.Cmwlth. 2000)

soning expressed in the foregoing opinion.

Terry D. BASHIOUM and Michael J. Bashioum, her husband, Appellants

v.

COUNTY OF WESTMORELAND.

Commonwealth Court of
Pennsylvania
Argued Nov. 1, 1999
Decided March 6, 2000

Park visitor, who was injured on giant slide in county park, and her husband brought negligence action against county. The Court of Common Pleas, Westmoreland County, No. 1271 of 1996, Caruso, J., entered summary judgment for county, and park visitor and her husband appealed. The Commonwealth Court, No. 1122 C.D. 1999, Flaherty, J., held that trial court erred in focusing on the entirety of county park which consisted of largely unimproved land, instead of on the giant slide, and concluding as a matter of law that the slide came within the immunity afforded by Recreation Use of Land and Water Act (RULWA) for purposes of negligence action.

Reversed and remanded.

1. Negligence ⚷ 1194

Improvement, such as giant slide, requiring intensive maintenance and inspection did not fall within meaning of "ancillary structure" as contemplated by Rivera, which concluded that legislature intended Recreation Use of Land and Water Act's (RULWA) definition of "land," as including buildings and machinery when attached to realty, to encompass only ancillary structures attached to open space lands made available for recreation and not to encompass enclosed recreational facilities in urban regions which could be maintained. 68 P.S. § 477-2.

See publication Words and Phrases for other judicial constructions and definitions.

2. Negligence ⚷ 1194

Proper focus should be on the specific area where the injury occurred or the specific area which caused the injury to determine whether Recreation Use of Land and Water Act (RULWA) is applicable. 68 P.S. §§ 477-1 to 477-8.

3. Counties ⚷ 143

Trial court erred in focusing on the entirety of county park which consisted of largely unimproved land, instead of on the giant slide, and concluding as a matter of law that the slide came within the immunity afforded by Recreation Use of Land and Water Act (RULWA) for purposes of negligence action brought against county by park visitor who was allegedly injured on slide. 68 P.S. §§ 477-1 to 477-8.

<u>Mills</u> Case from WestlawNext

Mills v. Com., 534 Pa. 519 (1993)

633 A.2d 1115

534 Pa. 519
Supreme Court of Pennsylvania

Ethel MILLS, Appellee,
v.
COMMONWEALTH of Pennsylvania and Penn's Landing
Corporation, Appellees,
v.
CITY OF PHILADELPHIA and Philadelphia Redevelopment
Authority and Penn's Landing Corporation, Appellants.

Argued Jan. 28, 1993 | Decided Nov. 8, 1993

Two pedestrians sued Commonwealth and nonprofit municipal corporation which had leased urban recreational facility, to recover for injuries suffered when they fell while walking along grassy slope and while approaching ticket booth. The Court of Common Pleas, Philadelphia County, No. 6106 June Term 1989, Samuel M. Lehrer, J., entered summary judgment for municipal corporation. Pedestrians appealed. The Commonwealth Court, 145 Pa.Cmwlth. 558, 604 A.2d 755, No. 158 C.D. 1991, Doyle, J., reversed and remanded. Municipal corporation petitioned for allowance of appeal to Supreme Court, which was granted. The Supreme Court, Nos. 0052 and 0056 E.D. Appeal Docket 1992, Cappy, J., held that the Recreation Use of Land and Water Act (RUA), did not apply to municipal corporation.

Affirmed and remanded.

West Headnotes (3)

[1]   **Municipal Corporations**
⊶ Parks and Public Squares and Places

Nonprofit municipal corporation was not entitled to immunity from personal injury actions under Recreation Use of Land and Water Act (RUA), where land which corporation had leased was highly developed recreational area, vastly altered from its natural state, containing attractions for which entry fees were required. 68 P.S. § 477-1 et seq.

23 Cases that cite this headnote

[2]   **Negligence**
⊶ Public Invitees in General

Landowner must bear responsibility of maintaining improvements placed upon land to which general public is permitted access.
Cases that cite this headnote

[3]   **Negligence**
⊶ Recreational Use Doctrine and Statutes

Ordinary users of developed recreation area could reasonably expect area to be maintained in manner safe for their normal recreational pursuits.
16 Cases that cite this headnote

Attorneys and Law Firms

**1116 *520 Alfred W. Putnam, E. Graham Robb, Philadelphia, for Penns Landing Corp.

Peter A. Dunn, Media, for appellants.

T. Jonathan Hankin, Paul C. Quinn, Philadelphia, for Ethel Mills.

Allan E. Ells, Philadelphia, for Commonwealth.

Sharon L. Steingard, Philadelphia, for Anita & Joseph Halber.

Carolann M. Leuthy, Philadelphia, for City of Philadelphia.

Before LARSEN, FLAHERTY, ZAPPALA, PAPADAKOS, CAPPY and MONTEMURO, JJ.

Opinion

*521 *OPINION OF THE COURT*

CAPPY, Justice.

These consolidated cases question the scope of immunity provided by the Recreation Use of Land and Water Act ("RUA"), 68 P.S. § 477-1 et seq., to the owners of a clearly defined 37 acre tract of land containing various improvements. For the reasons that follow we find that the owners of the land in question, Penn's Landing in Philadelphia, are not entitled to immunity pursuant to the RUA.

Penn's Landing is a 37 acre tract of land along the west bank of the Delaware river in the city of Philadelphia where William Penn disembarked and founded the province of Pennsylvania. The land is owned by the Redevelopment Authority of the City of Philadelphia and leased to the O.P.D.C. Penn's Landing Corporation (hereinafter "Penn's Landing"). Penn's Landing is a non-profit municipal corporation. The area itself is open to the public free of charge. However, fees are assessed for entrance to various exhibits, concerts and activities.

Each of the appellees sustained an injury while visiting Penn's Landing. Appellee Mills was injured when she stepped into a hole on a grassy slope while walking towards the concert area where she was to attend a free Melba Moore concert during a July 4th festival. Appellee Halber was injured when she stepped into a drainage hole from which the grate was missing as she was approaching the ticket booth for the U.S.S. Olympia. The U.S.S. Olympia is a museum ship docked at Penn's Landing which the public may tour for a fee.

Appellee Mills filed a complaint in negligence against the Commonwealth of Pennsylvania and Penn's Landing Corporation. Appellee Halber filed a complaint in negligence against the city of Philadelphia, Philadelphia Redevelopment Authority and Penn's Landing. In both cases Penn's Landing filed motions for summary judgment claiming immunity pursuant to the RUA. The trial court involved in each case granted the motions for summary judgment. On appeal to the Commonwealth Court the judgments were reversed, as that Court *522 found the protection of the RUA inapplicable to Penn's Landing. Penn's Landing petitioned for allowance of appeal to this Court. The Petitions were granted and the two cases consolidated for argument and disposition.

A motion for summary judgment should be granted only in those cases where it is clear that no genuine issue as to any material fact exists and the moving party is entitled to judgment as a matter of law. Pa.R.C.P. 1035; *Marks v.*

Tasman, 527 Pa. 132, 589 A.2d 205 (1991). The basis upon which summary judgment was granted in both cases was the determination by the trial courts in each case that Penn's Landing was entitled to immunity under the RUA. The trial court in the Halber case gave no specific reasons beyond citing to the general provisions of the RUA. The trial court in the Mills case stated that "Penn's Landing falls within the parameters **1117 of the [RUA] since the land is made available by the owners free of charge to the public for recreational purposes." (Opinion of the trial court, at No. 6105 June term 1989, p. 3).

The Commonwealth Court reversed the trial court in the Mills case finding that the RUA "protects only owners of unimproved land." 145 Pa.Cmwlth. 558, 560-61, 604 A.2d 755 (1992). The decision of the Commonwealth Court in the Halber case, 146 Pa.Cmwlth. 713, 604 A.2d 1239 (1992), merely referenced its earlier opinion in Mills. Thus, the precise question which must be resolved by this Court is how expansive is the protection afforded by the RUA to land owners who allow public access to their property for recreational purposes without charging a fee.

The pertinent sections of the RUA provide as follows:

§ 471-1. Purpose; liability

The purpose of this act is to encourage owners of land to make land and water areas available to the public for recreational purposes by limiting their liability toward persons entering thereon for such purposes.

§ 477-2. Definitions

As used in this act:

*523 (1) **"Land"** means land, roads, water, watercourses, private ways and buildings, structures and machinery or equipment when attached to the realty.

(2) **"Owner"** means the possessor of a fee interest, a tenant, lessee, occupant or person in control of the premises.

(3) **"Recreational purpose"** includes but is not limited to, any of the following, or any combination thereof: hunting, fishing, swimming, boating, camping, picnicking, hiking, pleasure driving, nature study, water skiing, water sports and viewing or enjoying historical, archeological, scenic, or scientific sites.

(4) **"Charge"** means the admission price or fee asked in return for invitation or permission to enter or go upon the land.

To date this Court has had three opportunities to review the applicability of the RUA to specific claims of liability where the injured party sustained his or her injury while engaged in a recreational activity, on a site commonly used for that purpose, where the landowner charged no fee. In *Rivera v. Philadelphia Theological Seminary,* 510 Pa. 1, 507 A.2d 1 (1986), we found that the RUA was not intended to immunize the owner of an indoor swimming pool who had allowed the plaintiff's decedent to use the pool free of charge. The case of *Commonwealth of Pennsylvania Department of Environmental Resources v. Auresto,* 511 Pa. 73, 511 A.2d 815 (1986), held that the Commonwealth was an "owner" of land entitled to the protection of the RUA where the plaintiff was injured when his snowmobile struck a snow covered tree trunk in a state park. Most recently, in *Walsh v. City of Philadelphia,* 526 Pa. 227, 585 A.2d 445 (1991), this Court held that the protection of the RUA does not extend to a completely improved recreational facility.

None of our previous decisions have addressed the particular question now presented to the Court. However, *Rivera* and *Walsh* are instructive as in each of those cases this Court would not allow a landowner to thwart the basic principles of tort liability by enlarging the scope of protection the legislature ***524** intended to grant under the RUA. As this Court stated in *Rivera:*

> The intention of the Legislature to limit the applicability of the Recreation Use Act to outdoor recreation on largely unimproved land is evident not only from the Act's stated purpose but also from the nature of the activities it listed as recreational purposes within the meaning of the statute. Specifically, with the exception of "swimming," which may be either an indoor or outdoor sport, the recreational activities enumerated in the statute are all pursued outdoors.

510 Pa. at 16, 507 A.2d at 8.

In *Walsh,* this Court focused on the obligation of a landowner regarding "improvements" placed upon an outdoor recreational site.

> When a recreational facility has been designed with improvements that require regular maintenance to be safely used and enjoyed, the owner of the facility has a duty to maintain the improvements. ****1118** When such an improved facility is allowed to deteriorate and that deterioration causes a foreseeable injury to persons for whose use the facility was designed, the owner of the facility is subject to liability. We do not believe that the RUA was intended by the Legislature to circumvent this basic principle of tort law.

526 Pa. at 238, 585 A.2d at 450-51.

Penn's Landing asserts that it is entitled to the protection from liability afforded landowners under the RUA as it is a largely unimproved historic site, open to the general public for recreational purposes, free of charge. That description is not complete. Appellee Mills describes Penn's Landing as "a highly developed inner-city waterfront attraction. It contains restaurants, a museum, historic ships, a marina with slips and a stage with an amphitheater."[1] These specifically enumerated attractions all require a fee for attendance. It is also clear from the record that although Penn's Landing hosts various *525 concerts and festivals free to the public, it is the site of numerous activities for which an admission fee is required.

Further clarification of the nature of Penn's Landing comes from the terms of the lease agreement between the Redevelopment Authority of the city of Philadelphia and OPDC Penn's Landing. That lease, wherein Penn's Landing is referred to as the redeveloper, provides as follows:

> WHEREAS, the Redeveloper is a non-profit corporation organized for the purpose of assisting the City and the Commonwealth of Pennsylvania (the "Commonwealth") and their agencies in the rehabilitation and renewal of the historic site on the bank of the Delaware River at which William Penn disembarked to found the colonial Province of Pennsylvania; aiding in the elimination of blight and deterioration which now exists in this historic area; undertaking the redevelopment of the site, by creating improvements thereon, including museums, public recreation facilities, hotels, residence accommodations, office buildings and appropriate commercial structures and other structures and facilities; and arranging for the proper use of such improvements for the benefit of the City and the Commonwealth and their citizens;

Consolidate Reproduced Record at 72a. Recorded June 30, 1976 in Deed Book DCC No. 1146 at page 531, City of Philadelphia.

[1] Considering the more complete picture of Penn's Landing that emerges from the briefs and record in these two cases, it becomes clear that the area in question has been vastly altered from the natural state in which William Penn discovered it several hundred years ago. In applying the RUA and the case law referred to above to the land as fully described herein, it is apparent that the RUA was not intended to provide immunity to a highly developed recreational area such as Penn's Landing.[2]

*526 We find that the factors relied upon by Penn's Landing, that the area is used for recreational purposes by the general public and that no admission fee is required to enter Penn's Landing, are not dispositive in applying the immunity protections afforded under the RUA. Rather, we believe the intended beneficiaries of the RUA, in addition to the general public, are landowners of large unimproved tracts of land which, without alteration, is amenable to the enumerated **1119 recreational purposes within the act. The purpose of the RUA was to provide immunity to landowners as an incentive to them in exchange for their tolerance of public access to their lands for recreational pursuits. The RUA was not intended to insulate owners of fully developed recreational facilities from the normal duty of maintaining their property in a manner consistent with the property's designated and intended use by the public.

[2] [3] As this Court stated in *Walsh,* a landowner must bear the responsibility of maintaining improvements placed upon the land to which the general public is permitted access. Ordinary users of Penn's Landing may reasonably expect the area to be maintained in a manner safe for their normal recreational pursuits. Although, it could be reasonably argued that the unimproved grassy and wooded areas within Penn's Landing do fall within the ambit of the RUA, such an overly technical application of the RUA would certainly lead to inconsistent results and thwart the intended purpose of the act.

As we conclude that Penn's Landing is not entitled to the protection of the RUA, the granting of summary judgment to Penn's Landing in each of these cases on that basis was *527 improper. Accordingly, we find that the decisions of the Commonwealth Court to reverse the awards of summary judgment in each of the two cases, which have been consolidated for the purposes of this appeal only, are affirmed. The Orders of the Commonwealth Court being affirmed, the cases are hereby remanded to the respective trial courts for further proceedings consistent with this opinion.

NIX, C.J., did not participate in the consideration or decision of this case.

LARSEN, J., did not participate in the decision of this case.

Parallel Citations
633 A.2d 1115

Footnotes

[1]   This description is contained at pp. 5-6 of Appellee Mills' brief and is not contested by appellant in either its original or reply brief to this Court.

[2]   We note that while 46 jurisdictions in addition to Pennsylvania have adopted similar recreational land use statutes, very few states have addressed the issue considered herein. Of those states which have considered the scope of protection to be afforded under their acts the focus has been upon remote unimproved tracts of land in rural or semi-rural areas.

See Keelen v. State, 463 So.2d 1287 (La.1985) (the immunity provisions should apply to owners of large remote undeveloped nonresidential rural or semi-rural lands); *Harrison v. Middlesex Water Company,* 80 N.J. 391, 403 A.2d 910 (1979) (the act should apply only to thinly populated large unimproved tracts of rural or semi-rural lands chiefly associated with hiking, fishing, camping, or hunting); *Tijerina v. Cornelius Christian Church,* 273 Or. 58, 539 P.2d 634 (1975) (application of the act should be limited to land which tended to have recreational value but was not susceptible to adequate policing or correction of dangerous conditions).

End of Document

<u>Walsh</u>
Case

ATLANTIC
REPORTER

2d Series

585

WALSH v. CITY OF PHILADELPHIA   **Pa.   445**
Cite as 585 A.2d 445 (Pa. 1991)

Court at No. 743 Pittsburgh 1986, dated June 15, 1988, reversing the Judgment of Sentence entered on April 28, 1986, 375 Pa.Super. 261, 544 A.2d 462 (1988), and remanding for a new trial in the Court of Common Pleas of Somerset County, Criminal Division, at No. 278 Criminal 1984.

ORDER OF COURT
PER CURIAM.

The Applications for reargument, reconsideration and stays are denied and the mandate of this Court's opinion entered May 10, 1990, 524 Pa. 551, 574 A.2d 584, is amended to read: Accordingly, we reverse the order of the Superior Court, reinstate the judgment of sentence entered by the Court of Common Pleas of Somerset County and remand to Superior Court for disposition of the remaining issues not disposed of by the Superior Court.

Thomas WALSH, Jr., Appellant,
v.
CITY OF PHILADELPHIA,
Appellee.

Supreme Court of Pennsylvania
Argued April 3, 1990
Decided Jan. 9, 1991
Reargument Denied Feb. 11, 1991

Basketball player injured while playing on municipal playground court brought action for damages. The Court of Common Pleas, Philadelphia County,

No. 4457 April Term 1983, Berel Caesar, J., found that city was not immune from liability but that player was not entitled to damages for pain and suffering. On cross appeals, the Commonwealth Court, Nos. 2945 C.D. 1987 and 210 C.D. 1988, 126 Pa.Cmwlth. 27, 558 A.2d 192, Narick, Senior Judge, reversed. Petition for appeal was granted. The Supreme Court, No. 113 E.D.Appeal Docket 1989, Cappy, J., held that: (1) Recreation Use of Land and Water Act, limiting liability for land open for recreational uses, did not apply to inner-city basketball court operated by municipality; (2) player had not sustained a "permanent loss of bodily function" for which compensation could be had under Political Subdivision Tort Claims Act; and (3) player had suffered "permanent disfigurement" compensable under Act.

Reversed and remanded.

Nix, C.J., dissented and filed opinion in which McDermott, J., joined.

McDermott, J., dissented and filed an opinion.

1. Municipal Corporations ☞ 723
Political Subdivision Tort Claims Act imposes liability upon municipality in same circumstances as Sovereign Immunity Act imposes liability upon Commonwealth. 42 Pa.C.S.A. §§ 8522(a), 8542(a).

2. Municipal Corporations ☞ 851
Recreation Use of Land and Water Act, which limits tort liability of owners opening undeveloped land for recreational purposes, did not apply to inner-city basketball court owned and

450 Pa.   585 ATLANTIC REPORTER, 2d SERIES

With these foregoing principles in mind, we now turn to the question of the liability of the City of Philadelphia for the injuries sustained by plaintiff Walsh during a basketball game on a paved inner city playground.

[1, 2] The Political Subdivision Tort Claims Act imposes liability upon the City of Philadelphia in the same circumstances as the Sovereign Immunity Act imposes liability upon the Commonwealth.[8] Thus, there is no doubt that the City of Philadelphia is entitled to the same protection as a private landowner in regard to its ownership of the Guerin Recreational Center. The City charges no fee for the use of the recreational center, allows access to the general public, and developed Guerin Recreational Center for outdoor recreational purposes. The presence of these factors, the defendant argues, places the Gurein Recreation Center within the scope of land as described by the RUA. We do not agree. The physical layout of the Guerin Recreation Center was described by the Commonwealth Court as follows:

The Guerin Recreation Center, owned by the City, is a cement recreational facility, located between Sixteenth, Jackson and Wolf Streets. It is approximately a half city block long and one block wide. It contains two full and two half basketball courts, as well as boccie courts and benches. *Walsh v. City of Philadelphia, supra*, 558 A.2d at 193.

The Guerin Recreation Center is a completely improved recreational facility. To extend the provisions of the RUA to the center-a completely improved recreational facility-would be to ignore the purpose of the Act and to disregard the reasonable expectations of the users of such a facility. By assuming the responsibility of installing the improvements that exist at this facility, the City concomitantly assumed the responsibility for maintaining those improvements. *De Simone, supra*.

In *Rivera*, we stated that the RUA was intended to encourage landowners to allow free access to their property for outdoor recreational purposes. In *Auresto*, we determined that the Commonwealth as an owner of land was entitled to the same protection under the RUA as a private landowner. It would be illogical, however, to extend the RUA to provide blanket immunity to all government owned and operated recreational facilities. Such an extension of the RUA is inconsistent with present public policy trends away from blanket immunity for sovereign authorities. *Mayle v. Pennsylvania Department of Highways*, 479 Pa. 384, 388 A.2d 709 (1978).

When a recreational facility has been designed with improvements that require regular maintenance to be safely used and enjoyed, the owner of the facility has a duty to maintain the improvements. When such an improved facility is allowed to deteriorate and that deterioration causes a foreseeable injury to persons for whose use the facility was designed, the owner of the facility is subject to liability. We do not believe

Brezinski
Case

ATLANTIC
REPORTER

2d Series

694

388 Pa.   694 ATLANTIC REPORTER, 2d SERIES

discretion or an error of law. Searles. This court has held that "[a]ppellate courts cannot properly and efficiently exercise even a limited function of judicial review without the [ZHB's] necessary findings of fact and conclusions of law together with reasons for its decision, even when the record contains complete testimony presented to the [ZHB]." *Upper Saucon Township v. Zoning Hearing Board of Upper Saucon Township*, 136 Pa.Cmwlth. 370, 583 A.2d 45, 48 (1990). *See also Borough of Youngsville v. Zoning Hearing Board of the Borough of Youngsville*, 69 Pa.Cmwlth. 282, 450 A.2d 1086 (1982) (A zoning hearing board must render an opinion delineating sufficient findings to support its conclusion in order to provide for a meaningful judicial review).

Herein, the ZHB did not make specific findings and conclusions of law but merely relied on the minutes of its October 19, 1995 meeting as the basis for its decision to deny Yost's appeal. While the trial court determined that the reasons for the ZHB's decision were clear from the minutes of the ZHB's August 22, 1995 hearing on Yost's appeal, based on our holding in Upper Saucon Township, this is insufficient to enable this court to perform efficient appellate review. Accordingly, the order of the trial court is vacated and this matter is remanded to the trial court for remand to the ZHB for the purpose of properly formulating findings of fact and conclusions of law to support the ZHB's decision to deny Yost's appeal.[6]

ORDER

NOW, this 23rd day of May, 1997, the order of the Court of Common Pleas of Washington County, dated August 26, 1996, at No. 96–1225, is vacated and this case is remanded to the trial court for remand to the Zoning Hearing Board of the Borough of Canonsburg with instructions that the board formulate specific findings of fact and conclusions of law to support its decision.

Jurisdiction relinquished.

JAMES   GARDNER   COLINS, President Judge, dissents.

Jennifer L. BREZINSKI and Jeffrey S. Brezinski, individually and as spouse of Jennifer L. Brezinski,

v.

COUNTY OF ALLEGHENY, Appellant.

Commonwealth Court of Pennsylvania

Argued March 10, 1997

Decided May 27, 1997

Picnic participant and her husband sued county for injuries participant sustained in slip and fall down embankment in county-owned park. The Court of Common Pleas, Allegheny County, No. G.D. 95-9704, McFalls, J., denied county's motion for summary judgment. County filed interlocutory appeal. The Commonwealth Court, No. 2442 C.D. 1996, Jiuliante, Senior Judge, held that county was immune from suit under the

---

390 Pa.   694 ATLANTIC REPORTER, 2d SERIES

68 P.S. § 477-3. A "recreational purpose" for which protected land may be used includes "picnicking." Section 2(3), 68 P.S. § 477-2(3).

[1] The Recreation Use Act applies only to lands that are largely unimproved in character and where no admission fee is charged. *Lory v. City of Philadelphia*, 544 Pa. 38, 674 A.2d 673, *cert. denied*, 519 U.S. 870, 117 S.Ct. 184, 136 L.Ed.2d 123 (1996); *Mills v. Commonwealth*, 534 Pa. 519, 633 A.2d 1115 (1993). The County claims that it should be immune in this case because its park was not improved and because there was no fee charged to Appellee for attending the picnic on the day of Mrs. Brezinski's fall. We agree.

Although "land" is defined in Section 2 of the Recreation Use Act, 68 P.S. § 477-2, to include "buildings, structures and machinery or equipment when attached to the realty," the courts have held that only owners of unimproved land are protected from liability. *See, e.g., Brown v. Tunkhannock Township*, 665 A.2d 1318 (Pa.Cmwlth.1995), petition for allowance of appeal denied, 544 Pa. 636, 675 A.2d 1252 (1996). As the Supreme Court has explained, the Recreation Use Act is designed to encourage the opening up of large, private land holdings for outdoor recreational use by the general public and that "buildings" in the definition of "land" was intended to be limited to ancillary structures attached to open space lands. *Rivera v. Philadelphia Theological Seminary*, 510 Pa. 1, 507 A.2d 1 (1986). In further describing what constitutes unimproved recreat-

ional land, the Supreme Court has stated:

> When a recreational facility has been designed with improvements that require regular maintenance to be safely used and enjoyed, the owner of the facility has a duty to maintain the improvements. When such an improved facility is allowed to deteriorate and that deterioration causes a foreseeable injury to persons for whose use the facility was designed, the owner of the facility is subject to liability.

Walsh v. City of Philadelphia, 526 Pa. 227, 238, 585 A.2d 445, 450 (1991).

[2] The trial court in the case at bar denied summary judgment concluding that there were material issues of fact regarding the County's characterization of the park as "unimproved" and whether or not the County charged a fee for use of the park. Our review of the record satisfies us that there were sufficient facts before the trial court to decide, as a matter of law, that the park was unimproved for purposes of the Recreation Use Act. Appellees referred to the hillside where Mrs. Brezinski fell as "unimproved" in their complaint (R.R. at 5), and the only suggestion otherwise is their argument that the land in the park had been "sculpted" for the picnic pavilion. Even if the land were "sculpted," this one-time modification would not have required regular maintenance as in *Walsh*. Regardless, such a picnic shelter is a building within the definition of land in Section 2, and certainly not more than an ancillary structure as in *Rivera*. Moreover, inasmuch as picnicking is specifically

Appendix
Differences in Rules for Scholarly Writing

The preceding chapters and exercises in this book cover Bluebook rules for "non-academic legal documents," which are the types of documents that one would write in a legal research and writing class and in practice (e.g., a brief, a memo, or an opinion). For such documents, the Bluepages rules add to, and sometimes change, the standard Bluebook rules in the Whitepages.

When writing or editing "academic legal documents" (i.e., scholarly writing such as law review and journal articles), you do not follow the additions and changes in the Bluepages rules; you follow only the rules in the Whitepages. Likewise, you use only the tables after the rules in the Whitepages, not the Bluepages tables.

This appendix covers the main differences in citations in scholarly writing. It does not cover all of the differences; consult the applicable Whitepages rules for more detail. The main differences fall into three categories:

    A. location of citations;
    B. typefaces in citations and text; and
    C. short citations.

A. Location of Citations

Citations in scholarly writing belong in footnotes, not within the main text of your document (see Rule 1.1). In other words, the main text of your document will consist of only textual sentences with references to footnotes that contain the citations. The following example represents a

page of a document with the citations in footnotes (note: you can com-
pare this example to the example in Section D of Chapter 1, which includes the citations within the main text):

    Under Pennsylvania's right-of-publicity
statute, a person's "name or likeness" cannot
be "used for any commercial or advertising
purposes" without that person's written
consent if that person's "name or likeness
has commercial value."[11] A well-known chef's
name may have commercial value,[12] but a well-
known intellectual property attorney could
not prove that his name did.[13]

    [The remaining text of this
example page has been omitted.]

---

[11] 42 PA. CONS. STAT. § 8316 (2007).
[12] Lewis v. Marriott Int'l, Inc., 527 F. Supp.
2d 422, 428 (E.D. Pa. 2007).
[13] Tillery v. Leonard & Sciolla, LLP, 437 F.
Supp. 2d 312, 318, 329 (E.D. Pa. 2006).

TAKE NOTE

Footnote text is generally in a smaller font size
than the main text. The footnote examples in this
appendix use the same font size as the main text
for ease of reading.

A footnote may contain more than one citation (e.g., a string citation). In
addition, a footnote may contain a textual sentence(s). If information

within such a textual sentence requires a citation, the citation should appear immediately after the material cited in either a citation sentence or a citation clause (see Rule 1.1(b)). For example:

```
         The class to which DOMA directs its
    restrictions and restraints are those
    persons  who  are  joined  in  same-sex
    marriages  made  lawful  by  the  State.
    DOMA  singles  out  a  class  of  persons
    deemed   by   a   State   entitled   to
    recognition and protection to enhance
    their   own   liberty.   It   imposes   a
    disability  on  the  class  by  refusing
    to   acknowledge   a   status   the   State
    finds  to  be  dignified  and  proper.25


         [The  remaining  text  of  this
    example  page  has  been  omitted.]




    ─────────────────────
    25 United  States  v.  Windsor,  133  S.  Ct.  2675,
    2694  (2013).  In  Windsor,  the  Court  decided
    that  DOMA  violated  the  Fifth  Amendment.  Id.
    at  2696.
```

The footnote above contains (1) a citation to the authority — *Windsor* — for the block quotation in the main text, (2) a textual sentence providing the Court's decision, and (3) a citation sentence — *Id.* at 2696 — to the authority supporting the assertion in the entire preceding textual sentence in the footnote. A citation sentence is appropriate for the last citation in the footnote because it supports the assertion in the entire textual sentence (see Rule 1.1(b)(i)). If an authority supports an assertion in only part of the textual sentence, you should use a citation clause (see Rule 1.1(b)(ii)).

B. Typefaces

"Typeface" refers to the style of the text in a document. As you learned in the chapters of this book, non-academic legal documents use primarily two typefaces: (1) ordinary (plain text) and (2) <u>underline</u> or *italics* (see BP Rule B2).

TAKE NOTE

BP Rule B2 allows the LARGE AND SMALL CAPS typeface in certain circumstances for stylistic purposes.

Scholarly writing uses three typefaces: (1) ordinary (plain text), (2) *italics*, and (3) LARGE AND SMALL CAPS (see Rule 2). The appropriate typeface to use in scholarly writing differs in citations versus textual sentences.

1. Typefaces in Citations

In citation sentences or citation clauses, you should use the ordinary (plain text) typeface unless Bluebook rules require one of the other two typefaces.

The following list includes the most common required uses of *italics* in both full and short citations, unless noted otherwise:

- case names in short citations only (note: case names in full citations should be in ordinary (plain text) typeface, except for any procedural phrases such as *ex rel.*) (see Rule 2.1(a));

- titles of articles in periodicals (see Rule 2.1(c));

- introductory signals in citation sentences and clauses (see Rule 2.1(d));

- explanatory phrases such as those used with prior and subsequent case history (see Rule 2.1(e));

- *id.* (note: the period is also italicized) (see Rule 4.1); and

- *supra* (see Rule 4.2).

The following list includes the most common required uses of LARGE AND SMALL CAPS in both full and short citations:

- authors and titles of books (see Rule 2.1(b));

- names of periodicals (see Rule 2.1(c));

- names of statutory codes (see examples in Rule 12 and Table T1);

- jurisdiction abbreviation and the word "CONST." in a citation to a constitution (see examples in Rule 11); and

- titles of rules (see examples in Rule 12.9.3).

TIP

In your word processor, the LARGE AND SMALL CAPS typeface is a formatting option for whatever font type you are using. In some word processors (e.g., Microsoft Word), this formatting option is called "Small Caps."

The following are example citations illustrating the typeface rules above (note: to help you see italicized text, such text is also in bold, but keep in mind that Bluebook rules do not permit bold text in citations):

---

[1] 42 PA. CONS. STAT. § 8316 (2007).

[2] Lewis v. Marriott Int'l, Inc., 527 F. Supp. 2d 422, 428 (E.D. Pa. 2007); ***see also*** Tillery v. Leonard & Sciolla, LLP, 437 F. Supp. 2d 312, 318, 329 (E.D. Pa. 2006).

[3] Anna P. Hemingway, ***Making Effective Use of Practitioners' Briefs in the Law School Curriculum***, 22 ST. THOMAS L. REV. 417, 421-24 (2010).

[4] RONALD D. ROTUNDA, LEGAL ETHICS IN A NUTSHELL 13-15 (4th ed. 2012).

5 Hemingway, **supra** note 3, at 422.

6 *Lewis*, 527 F. Supp. 2d at 427.

7 *Id.* at 428.

8 Bowers v. Hardwick, 478 U.S. 186, 194 (1986), **overruled by** Lawrence v. Texas, 539 U.S. 558 (2005).

9 PA. CONST. art. I, § 8.

10 FED. R. CIV. P. 15(a).

2. Typefaces in Textual Sentences

Recall from Section A above that the main text of a scholarly document (i.e., all of the text that is not in footnotes) will consist entirely of textual sentences. Textual sentences may also appear in footnotes along with citation sentences and citation clauses.

In textual sentences in the main text, you should use ordinary (plain text) except in the following circumstances, when you should use *italics* (see Rule 2.2(a)):

- case names (full or short);

- titles of publications (e.g., books and periodicals), articles, and speeches;

- words you want to emphasize or that are emphasized in quoted material.

For textual sentences within footnotes, Rule 2.2(b) includes detailed rules for the appropriate typeface to use for case names, all other types of authorities, explanatory parentheticals, and punctuation. For example, Rule 2.2(b)(i) indicates that you should italicize a case name when the name is grammatically part of the textual sentence. If the case name is merely part of a citation clause within a textual sentence, you should follow the rules for typefaces of case names in citations in Section B.1 above. Consult Rule 2.2(b) for more details regarding typefaces in textual sentences within footnotes.

C. Short Citations

A short citation to an authority can be either an *"id."* short form or an abbreviated version of a full citation to the authority (if the authority has an abbreviated version). According to Rule 4.1, you should use an *"id."* short form when citing to the immediately preceding cited authority (1) within the same footnote or (2) within the immediately preceding footnote if that footnote cites to only one authority.

If an *"id."* short form is not appropriate, the rules for each type of authority indicate when you can use a short citation with that authority's abbreviated version of a full citation. For example, according to Rule 10.9(a), you should use such a short citation for a case citation when that case is previously cited (1) in the same footnote or (2) in full or short form (including an *"id."* short form) in one of the previous five footnotes. Other types of authorities have the same or substantially similar rules for when to use such a short citation—e.g., statutes (see Rule 12.10(b)) and administrative regulations (see Rule 14.5(c)).

For authorities that use *"supra"* as part of the abbreviated version (see Rule 4.2(a)), such a short citation is appropriate when you have previously provided the full citation to the authority—e.g., books (see Rule 15.10) and periodicals (see Rule 16.9); no restriction exists regarding how far away (in footnotes) the full citation is from the *"supra"* short form.

In scholarly writing, the abbreviated version of a full citation to an authority is the same as in non-academic legal documents, except for some differences in typefaces as outlined in Section B.1 above. In addition, a *"supra"* short form differs slightly from such forms in non-academic legal writing; it includes a reference to the number of the footnote that contains the full citation to the cited authority (see Rule 4.2(a)).

For example, assume that footnote 12 of a document contains a full citation to an article by Kathy-Ann Marlin. The following would be a subsequent citation sentence to page 34 of that article, assuming an *"id."* short form is not appropriate:

[165] Marlin, *supra* note 12, at 34.

TIP

When using "*supra*" short forms with references to footnote numbers, be aware that you will need to update many, if not all, of the references when you add or delete footnotes. For this reason, you should avoid manually typing in the footnote numbers. Instead, you should use your word processor's cross-reference feature, which links the numbers to the actual footnotes. If any footnotes are added or deleted, you can then easily update these cross-references automatically (i.e., you will not have to check, and possibly change, each one individually). Consult your word processor's help feature to learn how to insert and update cross-references.

Index

This index includes the pages in this book where you can find references to specific Bluebook rules and tables. It lists Bluepages (BP) rules and tables before Whitepages rules and tables. To find a particular topic in this book, use the detailed Contents pages at the beginning of the book (starting on page iii).

BP Rule B11 (Constitutions)

BP Rule B12 (Statutes)

BP Rule B14 (Administrative Regulations)

BP Rule B15 (Books)

BP Rule B16 (Periodicals)

BP Rule B17 (Court & Litigation Documents)

BP Rule B18 (Nonprint Sources)

Rule 6 (Abbreviations, Numerals, & Symbols)

Rule 8 (Capitalization)

Rule 9 (Titles)

Rule 10 (Cases)

Rule 11 (Constitutions)

Rule 12 (Statutes)

Rule 14 (Administrative Regulations)

Rule 15 (Books)

Rule 16 (Periodicals)

Rule 18 (Nonprint Sources)

Table T1 (U.S. Jurisdictions)

Table T6 (Cases Names & Institutional Authors in Citations)

Table T7 (Court Names)

Table T8 (Explanatory Phrases)

Table T10 (Geographical Terms)

Table T12 (Months)

Table T13 (Periodicals)

Table T16 (Subdivisions)